Fortress Island
Malta

To Dad, one of many who helped save Malta during the Second World War

Fortress Island Malta

Defence and Re-Supply During the Siege

Peter Jacobs

Pen & Sword
AVIATION

First published in Great Britain in 2016 by
Pen & Sword Aviation
an imprint of
Pen & Sword Books Ltd
47 Church Street
Barnsley
South Yorkshire
S70 2AS

ISBN 978 1 78346 332 9

A CIP catalogue record for this book is available from the British
Library

Typeset in Ehrhardt by
Mac Style Ltd, Bridlington, East Yorkshire
Printed and bound in the UK by CPI Group (UK) Ltd,
Croydon, CRO 4YY

Pen & Sword Books Ltd incorporates the imprints of Pen & Sword
Archaeology, Atlas, Aviation, Battleground, Discovery, Family
History, History, Maritime, Military, Naval, Politics, Railways, Select,
Transport, True Crime, and Fiction, Frontline Books, Leo Cooper,
Praetorian Press, Seaforth Publishing and Wharncliffe.

For a complete list of Pen & Sword titles please contact
PEN & SWORD BOOKS LIMITED
47 Church Street, Barnsley, South Yorkshire, S70 2AS, England
E-mail: enquiries@pen-and-sword.co.uk
Website: www.pen-and-sword.co.uk

Contents

Acknowledgements

A book such as this would not have been possible without the help of so many people. First and foremost, I must thank those who helped enrich me with their stories of Malta. Three in particular took part in the Malta campaign, albeit in different capacities, but it was by talking to them that I became aware of the island's long siege during the Second World War.

One of the three was my father, who served in the destroyer HMS *Wishart* on convoy duties from Gibraltar throughout the siege. Through his diary and photographs, I am able to share some of his experiences of what it was like to take part in the critical convoys, particularly Harpoon and Pedestal. The second of the three was Tony Spooner, who led the Air to Surface Vessel (ASV)-equipped Wellingtons of the Special Duties Flight at Luqa. Tony and I first met more than twenty-five years ago, after which we met and talked a number of times. At that stage we were years apart in age and experience but we had so much in common. Tony was then an experienced aviator, with forty years of flying behind him, and had become an accomplished author while I was still in my early years of flying in the RAF and had just started out in my other interest of military history by writing a few articles for aviation magazines. But Tony was kind enough to share his experiences with me, both as an aviator and as an author, and to provide me with his personal accounts and photographs, some of which are included in this book. The third of the 'special three' is Pat Wells. One of 'The Few' from the Battle of Britain, Pat was a Hurricane pilot with 249 Squadron at the time and flew off the aircraft carrier HMS *Ark Royal* in May 1941. Like my father and Tony, Pat was keen to share his stories with me and provided me with a copy of his log book as well as numerous accounts and photographs during the many years I knew him; again, some of these you see here today. Through Pat, I was also privileged to meet some of his 249 colleagues from the Second World War, including Ginger Neil and Tommy Thompson, both of whom served in the air defence of Malta and were only too keen to share their experiences.

Unfortunately, I am unable to thank any of these three very special men – my father, Tony Spooner or Pat Wells – in person. All have long left us but I know they would have loved to have read the book. But I do want to publicly record my love, great memories and gratitude to them all; they all inspired me in different ways.

However interesting the stories of three men would be, they would not tell the complete story of Malta's siege during the Second World War. It was, therefore, necessary to turn to public records and other sources, published or otherwise, to piece the story together. As far as public records go, my first port of call is always The National Archives at Kew. Books like this could not be written without the help and support given by the staff at this marvellous facility; it really is a national treasure and so I must thank them for their help and assistance over so many years. Similarly, I would like to offer my collective thanks to the staff at the Imperial War Museum and the Air Historical Branch at RAF Northolt. Both have provided much help over the years with access to files and other material as well as many images, some of which you will see in this book.

In addition to these formal institutions and establishments, there are more and more online websites and forums available. Run by enthusiasts, they provide a wealth of knowledge and so I must thank everyone who contributes to these, in whatever capacity, to help keep the memories alive. From their contributions, I continue to learn so much.

I must also acknowledge some of the excellent books written about Malta during the Second World War and thank the authors for keeping this story alive. Among them is *Fortress Malta: An Island Under Siege, 1940–1943*, by James Holland. Captured under one cover, the remarkable personal accounts and experiences of those who were there makes this book the best in class when it comes to understanding what it was like to have been on the island at the time, and provides us with a lasting memory of Malta under siege. *Malta Convoys* by Richard Woodman is another work that provides a definitive and extraordinary account of the numerous convoys sent to the besieged island; some successful, some not. It really is a 'must-read' for anyone trying to find out more about a specific convoy or a specific ship and I congratulate Richard on his work; it must have taken years to complete. As for the air war over Malta, there are no better works than *Malta: The Hurricane Years, 1940–41*, and *Malta: The Spitfire Year, 1942* by Christopher Shores and Brian Cull with Nicola Malizia. As someone who has probably spent too many hours, days and weeks at a time working my way through countless public records and personal accounts, these two books tell the story of the air war over Malta on a day-to-day basis; again, they must have taken years to write.

Among many other wonderful and detailed books on the subject of Malta in the Second World War are Tony Spooner's *Supreme Gallantry*, Shankland and Hunter's *Malta Convoy*, and a number of specialist works including: *Pedestal* by Peter C Smith; *249 at War* by Brian Cull, which details the part played by one of Malta's fighter squadrons; *Warburton's War*, also by Tony Spooner; and other personal accounts such as *Malta Spitfire* by George Beurling and Leslie Roberts, and Denis Barnham's *Malta Spitfire Pilot*. And so the list goes on. Whatever the reader's interest, there is almost certainly a book written about it. A comprehensive bibliography at the end of this book will help guide the reader to specific areas of interest.

I must also thank the George Cross Island Association. The GCIA was founded in 1987 to honour the people of Malta and those who fought to defend and supply the island during the siege. The Association held its first annual reunion in Malta with more than 300 veterans present, and within three years had more than 2,000 members from across the world. It has ensured that those who fell during the siege will always be remembered by erecting a 10-tonne bronze Siege Bell Memorial at Valletta, overlooking Grand Harbour, which was inaugurated by Queen Elizabeth II and the President of Malta in 1992. I suspect that had the GCIA not formed then many families, my own included, would never have learned so much about Malta and its wonderful people, and what happened there during the Second World War. Without the GCIA, this book, for one, would never have been written.

Finally, I wish to pay a personal tribute to the men and women who bravely played their part in keeping the fortress island of Malta afloat during the long siege. Without their courage there would be no stories to be told. My thanks also go to the management and staff at Pen and Sword, particularly Laura Hirst for all her work behind the scenes, to enable this story to be told.

Introduction

The introduction of Italy into the Second World War on 10 June 1940 signalled the start of the siege of Malta, the longest in British history, and for the next two and a half years the Axis powers did all they could to batter the small island into submission.

Malta's defences were initially verging on non-existent, stemming from a pre-war lack of priority in Britain's defence budget, based on the conclusion that the island was indefensible; but the British Prime Minister, Winston Churchill, could not give up on Malta. The island was too important strategically and was the key to the door for the war being fought in the desert of North Africa. Malta lay at the crossroads of the Mediterranean where the main north-south supply route between Italy and the Axis armies in Libya crossed the west-east Allied sea route between Gibraltar and Alexandria, almost exactly at its mid-point.

If Malta could be held then it would allow British forces – aircraft, ships and submarines – to maintain an offensive capability in the Mediterranean and prevent Axis supplies from reaching North Africa. But everything needed to fight a campaign – people, food, fuel, ammunition, medical stores, aircraft and spares – would have to be delivered to Malta in sufficient numbers and on a regular basis. It would take a monumental maritime effort just to survive, let alone hit back, and to manage both would require those in command to carefully balance Malta's precious and limited resources.

And so began the heroic defence and re-supply of Malta. Who knows what the outcome of the Second World War would have been had the island fallen. Its loss would surely have led to defeat for the Allies in North Africa, after which Egypt would almost certainly have fallen and then the Suez Canal. And then what?

I have been fortunate to write many books during the past twenty years, but none have been more personal than this. My father served in the

Mediterranean during the siege of Malta as a naval seaman in HMS *Wishart*, a modified W-class destroyer. The ship took its name from James Wishart, a British admiral who, rather appropriately, was present at the capture of Gibraltar in 1704 during the War of the Spanish Succession. And it was from Gibraltar during the Second World War that HMS *Wishart* helped provide the Malta convoys with protection in the western Mediterranean.

And so my interest in Malta began. During my long career in the Royal Air Force I was fortunate to visit the island on three occasions. Twice, during the late 1990s, I spent a few days on the island when I took a Tornado F3 to the annual air show at Luqa. On my return I talked to my father about Malta and this, for him, triggered further memories and the sharing of many stories. The third time I went to Malta, during a staff tour, was ten years after my first visit. My father had died seven years before and so my visit to the island took on a whole different meaning.

It seems hard these days to imagine what those great naval convoys must have looked like at sea. Operation Pedestal, for example, the largest and most famous convoy of them all, involved more than sixty ships, with many more in support. It was the last attempt to save Malta, which, in August 1942, was on the brink of surrender. Fourteen merchant vessels were allocated to the convoy, and its protection, which included four aircraft carriers, was the most powerful ever provided by the Royal Navy.

More than fifty years later, I remember flying over the western Mediterranean having taken off from Gibraltar bound for Malta. Following the route once taken by the convoys, I enjoyed a commanding view from above 20,000 feet; the same view that Italian and German pilots, who were out to prevent the ships from getting through, would have once enjoyed. I could appreciate just how exposed the convoys would have been. There was nowhere for the ships to hide and on a clear day like that, as it was for most of the summer of 1942, there was no way a convoy could have slipped through the Med unnoticed. Then, when approaching Malta, it was the same feeling. From altitude the island looked small, with Grand Harbour and the airfield at Luqa easy to see. Again, for those defending the island, there would have been nowhere to hide. Equally, though, I did not like the idea of being in an Axis dive-bomber and having to penetrate a frightening barrage of determined defensive anti-aircraft fire, either from the ships or Malta's defences. The war was fought equally hard on both sides.

With the siege of Malta lasting for two and a half years, and with the campaign having been fought in so many dimensions – in the air, at sea (both on the surface and beneath the waves) and on the island itself – it is difficult to tell the whole story under one cover. Deciding what to include and what to leave out was hard. But I wanted to blend Malta's defence and re-supply with the island's ability to hit back at the enemy, to show how Malta's survival led to a strategic British victory in the Mediterranean. Only space prevents me from writing more. Enjoy the book!

Peter Jacobs

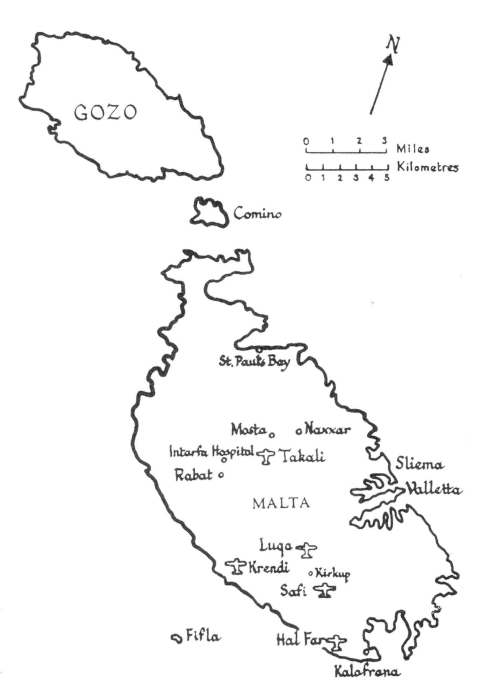

Map of Malta during the Second World War showing position of airfields, seaplane base at Kalafrana and two main harbours at Valletta. (*via Tony Spooner*)

Chapter One

A Strategic Island Left in a Hopeless Situation

Today, Malta is a popular tourist destination with thousands of visitors every year. The archipelago of seven islands in the Mediterranean Sea provides those who flock there with a wonderful blend of sunshine and sea, as well as an opportunity to sample the culinary delights of the local restaurants and to learn something of the island's history spanning 7,000 years. With its unique temples, some of the oldest stone buildings in the world, Roman catacombs and the extraordinary architectural legacy of the Knights of St John, Malta has, perhaps, a greater density of historic sights than any other country.

The main island of Malta measures just 11 miles (17km) by 9 miles (14km), making the island just a bit smaller than the Isle of Wight. The majority of Malta's population, now more than 400,000 (but about 250,000 in 1939), lives in and around its capital, Valletta, Grand Harbour and the so-called 'Three Cities' (a collective description of the three fortified cities of Cospicua, Vittoriosa and Senglea), making Malta one of the most densely populated areas in the world.

Malta's position – 50 miles (80km) to the south of Sicily, 200 miles (320km) north of Libya and 175 miles (280km) east of Tunisia – has always given it great strategic importance as a naval base for a succession of powers, including the Phoenicians, Romans, Normans, Knights of St John, French and British. With its extensive docks and wharves, Grand Harbour, otherwise known as the Port of Valletta, on the eastern side of the island, has provided a natural harbour for thousands of years.

In relatively recent times, Britain had gained a foothold in the Mediterranean after capturing Gibraltar in the early eighteenth century. Then, after the defeat of Napoleon, the Royal Navy turned Malta into its main base for the Mediterranean Fleet to provide Britain with the vital link with its empire overseas, particularly as a staging post to Egypt and the Suez

Canal, which, in turn, provided the route to India and the Far East. But the changing political situation in Europe during the late 1930s, leading to the signing of the Berlin-Rome 'Axis' Pact of Steel between Adolf Hitler's Nazi Germany and Benito Mussolini's Fascist Italy in May 1939, saw the Royal Navy move the headquarters of its Mediterranean Fleet away from Malta's capital, Valletta, to the relative safety of the Egyptian port of Alexandria.

The British government and admiralty publicly maintained to the Maltese that the island could be defended just as well from Alexandria as it could be from Grand Harbour, but in reality, this would prove to be quite different; Alexandria, being at the far eastern end of the Med, would soon become rather remote from the main Mediterranean action.

The decision to move the headquarters was made as the new commander-in-chief, Admiral Sir Andrew Browne Cunningham, known to his men as 'ABC', was taking command of the Mediterranean Fleet from Sir Dudley Pound, after Pound's elevation to First Sea Lord.

Aged 57 and a veteran of the Second Boer War and the First World War, during which he had been awarded the Distinguished Service Order (DSO) three times, Cunningham's rise in rank had been rapid since graduating from the Britannia Royal Naval College aged just 15. He knew the Mediterranean well, having held a number of senior posts there during the 1930s, and would later describe his appointment as 'the finest command the Royal Navy had to offer' and that he 'probably knew the Mediterranean better than any naval officer of his generation.'[1]

Considering Malta was the only British base between Gibraltar and Alexandria, and known to be of such strategic importance, its defences at the outbreak of the Second World War were poor, verging on non-existent, stemming from a pre-war lack of priority in Britain's defence budget based on the conclusion that the island was indefensible. Pre-war promises of fighter squadrons, barrage balloons, searchlights and anti-aircraft guns had failed to come to fruition. The RAF's fighters were needed elsewhere and so Malta was left with just a dozen or so coastal guns and just thirty-four heavy

1. Simpson, *Life of Admiral of the Fleet Andrew Cunningham: A Twentieth Century Naval Leader*, p.42.

anti-aircraft guns to protect an island with three airfields and a vital harbour complex. There were cities in northern England better protected.[2]

The quiet and inactivity of the Mediterranean backwater during the early months of the war meant that a number of Cunningham's ships, including the huge 33,000-tonne Queen Elizabeth-class battleships HMS *Warspite* and HMS *Barham*, were recalled to the Home Fleet following the loss of the *Royal Oak* at Scapa Flow in October 1939. Also recalled so that ships could be assigned to the campaign in Norway were Cunningham's heavy cruisers of the 1st Cruiser Squadron, the light cruisers of the 3rd Cruiser Squadron, the aircraft carrier HMS *Glorious* and many destroyers.

Cunningham's great command had quickly become decimated, leaving him just one major battleship, HMS *Malaya*, in the Mediterranean and not much more than a handful of Malta-based submarines, most of which were outdated, and some motor torpedo boats left to defend the island from the sea.

To say Malta was lightly defended during the opening months of the war is an understatement. Air Commodore 'Sammy' Maynard arrived in January 1940 as air officer commanding Malta to muster whatever defences he could. Aged 46, Maynard was also a veteran of the First World War and had run up a string of victories on the Western Front, but he arrived in Malta to find he had nothing to command except for a handful of Fairey Swordfish biplanes, used for target-towing duties for the island's anti-aircraft gunners, and a few Tiger Moths, Fairey Gordons and Miles Magisters.

If that was not bad enough, none of Malta' three airfields – Hal Far, Luqa and Takali – were fully operational. Hal Far, at the southern end of the island, was Malta's first permanent airfield when it opened in the late 1920s as HMS *Falcon* for the Royal Navy. Although the airfield had some hangars and other domestic and technical buildings, there was no runway as such to operate large aircraft. Luqa, now the island's international airport, is more central on the island and just a couple of miles to the north of Hal Far. With two runways, it was much the biggest of the three airfields at the time, but was still undergoing construction in early 1940. The third airfield, Takali

---

2. Holland, *Fortress Malta: An Island Under Siege 1940–43*, p.22.

(also spelt 'Ta Kali', 'Ta Qali' or 'Taqali'), to the north-west of Luqa, had been constructed just before the war but had no facilities. Its grassy surface, like Hal Far, deteriorated quickly in bad weather and often made it unusable. There was also a seaplane base at Kalafrana, on the southernmost tip of the island on the edge of Marsaxlokk bay, and, later on, an emergency landing strip known as Safi Strip, connected to Luqa by a narrow track, but more akin to a roller coaster than a taxiway.

It was a grim overall situation for Maynard, but there were positives as well. Having three airfields would be a massive plus when it came to fighting a defensive air campaign as it would provide him and his pilots with options whenever an airfield suffered damage. Malta also had Radio Direction Finding (RDF), otherwise known as radar, situated high on the cliffs at Dingli on the west coast; at about 830 feet above sea level (253m), it is the highest point on the islands and would provide Malta with warning of attack.

Although having three airfields and radar was all well and good, the lack of fighters was the biggest concern, and so it must have come as something of a small relief when Maynard learned of a number of crated Gloster Sea Gladiator biplanes that had been left at Kalafrana.

It appears there had been eighteen aircraft belonging to 802 Naval Air Squadron left at Kalafrana in crates for some time, for a few months at least, after they had been offloaded from the aircraft carrier HMS *Glorious* to be held in reserve. By April 1940, twelve were still there, after three had been shipped off, still in their crates, to Egypt, and three others had embarked on *Glorious* as she left the Mediterranean for Norway.

The twelve Gladiators at Kalafrana were destined for the aircraft carrier HMS *Eagle*, soon due to arrive in the Mediterranean from the Indian Ocean, and it was these airframes that Maynard had learned about. Having approached Cunningham, the C-in-C agreed to Maynard's request to use these aircraft for Malta's defence.

After some administrative wrangling between the Royal Navy and the RAF, and a number of farcical orders and counter-orders that ended up with aircraft being assembled and then put back into crates again, the twelve Gladiators were finally transferred to Hal Far to form the Malta Fighter Flight. This was also known as the Hal Far Fighter Flight, and was made up of a mix of RAF and Royal Navy personnel. And so it would be left to a number of outdated and effectively obsolete Gladiator biplanes to provide Malta's air defence.

The Gladiator was the last British biplane fighter to be built. Armed with four machine guns, its radial engine gave the aircraft a maximum speed of about 250mph (400km/h), but its design had been totally eclipsed by the newer generation of monoplane fighters, the Supermarine Spitfire and the Hawker Hurricane, and would be no match for the latest generation of fighters that had appeared across Europe during the late 1930s. The harsh reality was the Gladiator was outdated, there was a distinct lack of spares and the pilots who would fly them lacked any operational experience.

With no current fighter pilots in Malta at all, volunteers had to be found. A handful emerged from the various RAF ranks on the island, including Sammy Maynard's personal assistant, 24-year-old Flight Lieutenant George Burges, a fit and hearty man from Sheffield and a former flying boat captain at Kalafrana who would lead the flight. Others to volunteer included two from the Station Flight: Flight Lieutenant Peter Keeble and a 27-year-old Irishman, Flying Officer William 'Timber' Woods. There were also Flying Officer John Waters and Pilot Officer Peter Hartley, both Swordfish pilots serving with the target-towing Army Co-Operation Unit, Squadron Leader Alan 'Jock' Martin, the commanding officer at Luqa, and another soon to join the flight was Pilot Officer Peter Alexander who had been operating radio-controlled Queen Bee target drones.

Six of the twelve crated Gladiators were soon assembled so that two could provide continuous stand-by during the hours of daylight, with the remaining airframes intended to be cannibalized as spares. The few Swordfish target-towing aircraft were also to be put to better use for air-sea rescue but Cunningham and Maynard lacked air and maritime intelligence, and the best they could hope for would come from the efforts of a few flying boats in the region.

As far as Malta's limited ground defences were concerned, there were still only five infantry battalions on the island, totalling fewer than 5,000 men: 1st Dorsets; 2nd Devons; 2nd Royal Irish Fusiliers; 2nd Queen's Own Royal West Kents; and 8th Manchesters. There was also the locally based territorials, the King's Own Malta Regiment (KOMR), the latest in a series of locally raised militia units, and the Malta Volunteer Defence Force. Their task was to man the pill-boxes along the coastline and beaches and to mount regular patrols to foil any enemy raids or landings.

Malta's countryside, with its patchwork of fields and stone walls, would make a large-scale invasion of the island difficult. The island's army units had already set about building anti-invasion defences across Malta, making full use of natural defences, such as steep cliffs and the rocky southern coastline, and had made best use of the steep natural escarpment running across the island that would prevent enemy vehicles from moving inland should they ever land on the northern beaches.

The seemingly desperate situation in Malta intensified when the governor of Malta, General Sir Charles Bonham-Carter, fell ill and had to return to England. Finding a temporary replacement at such a time was not easy. Given the strategic position of Malta and with Italy's entry into the war imminent, the British government needed someone who could hold the people together and fight for Malta's cause in the vital months ahead.

The man chosen was 40-year-old William Dobbie, a Scot and an engineer by background and formerly the general officer commanding Malaya. With the acting rank of lieutenant general, Dobbie took up the appointment of governor and commander-in-chief of Malta at the end of April.[3] With his engineering expertise, Dobbie immediately set about organizing civil defence of the island and training those limited resources he had available.

Ancient catacombs were enlarged and more shelters were built by tunnelling into the rock. The island's male population were drafted to work while the number of dependants on the island was reduced as much as possible; they were simply put on board a civilian ship bound for England. Dobbie was ably supported by the flag officer Malta, Vice Admiral Wilbraham Ford, who had been in post for more than three years and knew the island well. From his headquarters in Fort Saint Angelo, a large and ancient fortification at Birgu in the centre of Grand Harbour, Ford had specific responsibility for Malta's vital dockyard and port facilities.

---

3. Dobbie's appointment was officially confirmed on 19 May 1940.

Mussolini's invasion of Abyssinia in 1935 and then Albania in 1939, combined with his signing of the Pact of Steel with Hitler, had signalled Italy's intent in the region. Mussolini had always considered Malta part of Italy's overseas expansion in the Mediterranean and now had an estimated 250,000 troops in Libya and anything up to 350,000 more in East Africa.[4] There had even been suggestions that Mussolini might consider discussions with the British over the future of Malta as some sort of concession to any future peace, and to meet Mussolini's personal desire to expand Italy's control in the Mediterranean and Africa; regions, at that time, dominated by the British and French.

But as far as Britain's new Prime Minister, Winston Churchill, was concerned, no concessions would be made. Churchill already had enough on his plate with Britain facing a potential invasion by Hitler's forces. And so Malta would have to remain on the back-burner until Britain's own future was safe; for the time being at least.

The German invasion of France and the Low Countries in May 1940 left a dire situation in Europe. If there had been any previous doubt among the Maltese about the severity of the situation they were about to find themselves in, it quickly disappeared. Malta was now preparing for war, the outcome of which could be one of two things: a rapid invasion by the enemy or a long siege.

Mussolini's declaration of war against Britain on 10 June 1940 signalled Italy's all-out offensive in the Mediterranean and the start of what was to become the siege of Malta; the second in the island's history after the Great Siege of Malta in 1565 when the Ottoman Empire invaded the island, then held by the Knights Hospitaller, which saw the Knights and Maltese people win one of the most celebrated events in sixteenth century Europe.

On the day Italy declared war, Dobbie issued a statement to Malta's garrison:

'The decision of His Majesty's government to fight until our enemies are defeated will be heard with the greatest satisfaction by all ranks of the

---

4. Although there is a general acceptance that there were about 250,000 Italian troops in Libya, the figure for Eritrea varies between 200,000 and 350,000 according to source.

Garrison of Malta. It may be that hard times lie ahead of us, but I know that however hard they may be, the courage and determination of all ranks will not falter, and that with God's help we will maintain the security of this fortress. I call on all officers and other ranks humbly to seek God's help, and then in reliance on Him to do their duty unflinchingly.[5]

With France's surrender imminent, and knowing that Britain would still be licking her wounds from the failed defence of France and the Low Countries, conditions were more than favourable for Mussolini to mount an assault against Malta as a prelude to an offensive in Egypt. Everything seemed to be in favour of the Italian dictator who dreamed of a new 'Mediterranean Empire' and had longed to hit Britain hard, and who seemingly wanted to get in on the act before Germany's victory was complete.

Mussolini knew the conquest of Malta was essential to his ambitions in the Mediterranean. He already had a plan for an invasion of the island and, assuming it would be successful, it would give him naval and air control in the central Mediterranean. This would make it difficult, if not impossible, for the British to maintain a supply route to its forces in Egypt through its port in Alexandria. But as long as there were British forces in Malta, they posed a real threat to Italy's conquest of the Mediterranean. Large numbers of Italian ships and aircraft would need to be held back to deal with Malta, which, in turn, would weaken Mussolini's forces in Africa.

The size, disposition and operational readiness of the Italian Navy, the Regia Marina, posed a significant threat to Cunningham's Mediterranean Fleet. But although the Italians had many warships to challenge the Royal Navy for control of the region, Italy had invested little in the way of modern technology, such as radar and sonar. This would severely limit Italy's capability of operating at night or in bad weather, and would limit their range-finding when engaging with surface units.

Italy also lacked an equivalent to the Royal Navy's Fleet Air Arm, although this lack of capability was nullified to an extent by the disposition of Italian airfields in the central Mediterranean. It was never imagined that the Italian

5. Royal Engineers Museum (taken from a detailed biography).

fleet would operate too far from a friendly airfield and so resources had been channelled elsewhere. Its fleet would also suffer from a lack of fuel reserves as Italy suffered from a shortage of natural resources to fight a war. Roughly a quarter of her coal and anthracite was imported, more than three-quarters of her crude oil, two-thirds of her scrap steel, almost all her nickel and other rare materials were brought in by sea. Furthermore, much of Italy's imports came from sources either within the British Empire or from countries allied or associated with it, and the rest had to be transported through sea routes relatively simple for the British to block, such as the Suez Canal, the Dardanelles or the Straits of Gibraltar.[6]

Nonetheless, the Regia Marina would have available six main battleships (although two of these were undergoing a refit at the outbreak of the war and two more were yet to be completed); nearly twenty cruisers, of which seven were powerfully-armed heavy cruisers; more than sixty high-speed destroyers and a similar number of torpedo boats as well as more than a hundred submarines. In addition to this impressive armada, the Italians had corvettes, auxiliaries, minesweepers, minelayers and attack craft. There was also the Italian merchant fleet comprising nearly 800 ships with a gross tonnage exceeding 500 tonnes, and another 200 ships between 100 and 500 tonnes. But when Italy declared war, as many as 200 of these merchant ships were stranded outside of the Mediterranean, and almost all of these would subsequently be captured or sunk.

Numerically, the Regia Marina was a formidable force and was well dispersed at a number of bases: in Italy, Sicily and Sardinia, at bases in the North African ports of Tripoli and Tobruk, as well as in Dalmatian ports, the Dodecanese, Albania and Rhodes. With so many ports available to him, it is easy to understand why Mussolini had described the Mediterranean as *Mare Nostrum* (Our Sea).

Mussolini's naval forces were to support the Axis forces in North Africa while obstructing the British supply route to Alexandria and cut off supplies to Malta. The Royal Navy's major effort, meanwhile, would be to maintain the supply routes to British forces in the Mediterranean, including Malta,

---

6. Woodman, *Malta Convoys*, p.15.

as well as interdicting enemy shipments to North Africa. And so the Royal Navy and Regia Marina were about to engage in a struggle for control of the Mediterranean that would last for two and a half years.

With Malta being so close to Italy and Sicily, air attacks against the island were more than a strong possibility. The Italian air force, the Regia Aeronautica, was the smallest of the Axis air forces with only about 2,000 of its 3,000-plus aircraft on strength ever fit for operations. Among these was the biplane fighter, the Fiat CR.42, of which about 300 were known to be in service at the time, which gave hope that Malta's Gladiators would enjoy some success. But the CR.42 was a more modern design and its development had been based on combat experience gained during the Spanish Civil War when Mussolini's forces had flown alongside Hitler's. With a top speed of more than 270mph (440km/h), it was faster than the Gladiator and its different wing design, where the upper wing was larger than its lower wing, meant the CR.42 was highly manoeuvrable due to its very low wing loading.

Although the CR.42 would later struggle against the RAF's newer fighters, it was a match for the Gladiator in terms of its firepower and was a better aircraft overall, on paper at least, given its performance and manoeuvrability. Besides, the Italians already had a better fighter in service, the Macchi MC.200. With a top speed of more than 310mph (500km/h), the MC.200 boasted excellent manoeuvrability and handling characteristics, and its strong all-metal construction made the aircraft ideal for ground-attack. It would fly more operational sorties than any other Italian aircraft during the war but would also struggle against better Allied opponents, when the MC.200 proved to be under-powered and under-armed for a fighter of its generation.

Malta's Gladiator pilots faced a formidable force. Even the Italian's principal bomber, the three-engine Savoia-Marchetti SM.79, known colloquially to its crews as '*Gobbo Maledetto*' ('damned hunchback') because of its distinctive fuselage dorsal 'hump', was faster than the Gladiator. The SM.79 had been designed as a fast passenger aircraft, setting many records during the late 1930s, and had already seen action in the Spanish Civil War. It was the fastest medium bomber in the world at the time and an outstanding aircraft of its day, although its maximum bomb load of 1,250kg (2,750lb) and bomb bay design prevented any large bombs from being carried. With the Regia Aeronautica having more than a thousand aircraft based in Italy and Sicily, and with nearly 300 more in North Africa, command of the air seemed, for Mussolini, assured.

Until 10 June 1940, Malta had been fortunate to enjoy a quiet war, but the French collapse, just days later, simply added to Malta's plight. The truth was that Malta was unprepared for war, especially a war without French support. The balance of naval power in the Mediterranean had altered dramatically and with many responsibilities elsewhere, only a small portion of the large British fleet could be spared to take care of the Italian threat. Furthermore, there was only enough food on the island to feed its population for about six weeks.

Cunningham knew only too well the strategic importance of Malta. The island lay at the crossroads of the Mediterranean where the main north-south supply route between Italy and the Axis armies in Libya crossed the west-east Allied sea route between Gibraltar and Alexandria, almost exactly at its mid-point. He also knew that the battle for Malta would significantly affect the outcome of the war in North Africa. Greece was also threatened, which, in turn, would threaten Britain's interest in the rest of the Middle East. And so it went on.

Only by holding Malta would it allow British forces to maintain an offensive capability in the Mediterranean, but the only way this could be achieved was through continuous replenishment of the island. This did not just mean the re-supply of military equipment and personnel but also bringing in food and other basic necessities. It presented a huge logistical challenge. Everything needed to fight a campaign – people, food, fuel, ammunition, medical stores, aircraft and spares – would have to arrive on a regular basis if Malta was to survive, let alone hit back. It would take a monumental maritime effort, with merchant shipping protected by Royal Navy escorts, to get the supplies through and to keep Malta in British hands.

Cunningham's main concern would be for the safety of the convoys heading from Gibraltar to Malta and Egypt and so even before Italy's entry into the war he had brought his fleet to a heightened state of readiness. There would also need to be a decisive air war fought in support of the huge maritime campaign if Malta was to survive. Fighters were needed to fend off the enemy's marauding bombers and reconnaissance aircraft to provide the long-range eyes of the defenders, all provided from British bases in Malta, Egypt and Gibraltar, and from the Mediterranean Fleet. Unless all this could be achieved, Malta would be starved and bombed into impotence.

And so the scene was set for one of the greatest sieges in twentieth century history. Britain was about to enter a war in the Mediterranean at a key point in the Second World War. Her intervention in the Nazi occupation of Norway had collapsed and the remnants of the British Expeditionary Force had been clutched from the jaws of defeat at Dunkirk as France fell. Hitler's forces were now just across the Channel and posing a serious threat to Britain's very existence.

Britain now stood alone. Malta could hardly have been in a worse position but the island did have its indomitable people and a quite remarkable sense of fortitude. If Malta could be turned into an unsinkable aircraft carrier then survival could, after all, be possible.

Chapter Two

First Day of Siege – 11 June 1940

T he midnight chimes sounding from Malta's many churches marked the beginning of a new day. It was now 11 June 1940, a Tuesday, and the chimes announced Malta's second siege in the history of the fortress island.

Daylight broke to signal the start of another beautiful sunny morning in Malta. Until that moment in time, the early risers had been quietly going about their business: in the town, at the harbour and in their homes. They could only wonder how their lives would change now that Italy had declared war, but they would not have to wonder for long. War for the Maltese was now just minutes away.

It was just before 7.00 am when the air raid sirens wailed over Valletta. From nearly 20,000 feet above the Mediterranean at that time of the morning, the SM.79 bomber crews of the Regia Aeronautica's 2^a Squadra Aerea (2nd Air Region) would have enjoyed a commanding view of the island ahead. Thirty bombers of 34° Stormo Bombardamento Terrestre (34th Terrestrial Bombing Wing) from Catania-Fontanarossa were heading for the airfield at Hal Far, fifteen more from 11° Stormo at Comiso were to attack the dockyards at Valletta, and ten from 41° Stormo at Gela were heading for the seaplane base at Kalafrana. Escorting them were eighteen MC.200s from 6° Gruppo Autonomo Caccia Terrestre from Comiso; their task to provide fighter protection for the bombers.[1]

It had been a particularly early start for the raiders. Although Malta was just over fifty miles from their bases in southern Sicily, it had been dark when the crews had climbed out of their beds to attend briefing. They had been in Sicily for the past week, waiting and preparing for this moment, and were now to announce Italy's arrival in the Mediterranean war.

---

1. Shores and Cull with Malizia, *Malta: The Hurricane Years 1940–41*, pp.1–4.

The clear and sunny morning made conditions ideal for a raid. As the Italian crews approached Malta it would have been easy for them to make out their targets in the distance. Grand Harbour was easy. Its mouth faces north-east and is bounded to the north by Saint Elmo Point and to the south by Ricasoli Point. Its north-west shore is largely covered by the city of Valletta and its peninsula divides Grand Harbour from the second and parallel natural Marsamxett Harbour; its south-eastern shore forms a number of inlets and headlands. No one could miss that, and from such obvious features the dockyards at Valletta could easily be found. The coastal seaplane base at Kalafrana would have stood out equally as well, although it would have been harder to pick out the airfield at Hal Far.

With Malta being such a small island, there was nowhere for anything or anyone to hide. Those at Hal Far had been standing by since first daylight for a possible attack and the air raid sirens signalled detection of the first enemy radar plots high out over the sea. With the sirens still wailing, the Gladiators, just three aircraft – flown by George Burges, Jock Martin and Timber Woods – roared off down the runway but they were still struggling to gain height when the first Italian bombers arrived over the island.

Descending to 14,000 feet for their attack, the first group of Italian raiders approached Malta from the south-west to attack Kalafrana. Flying at medium altitude over the island in clear weather conditions, and with the element of relative surprise, the Italian crews could not fail to cause terror and devastation.

On the ground, as more and more realized they were coming under attack, people rushed to take cover anywhere they could. Aerial bombing in 1940 was not much of a science and so the bombs could land almost anywhere. Sure enough, the bombs came to earth in a series of devastating explosions. Thirty bombs fell in the area of the seaplane base and its neighbouring coastal village of Birzebugga.

The first air raid was over in just minutes but then the next waves of bombers were overhead. Sixteen bombs fell on Hal Far, although damage was limited to searchlights and vehicles, and those bombers arriving over Grand Harbour found it to be all but empty; all the Royal Navy had left behind was the ageing Royal Navy Erebus-class monitor, HMS *Terror*, and two Insect-class gun boats, *Aphis* and *Ladybird*, moored in Marsamxett Harbour.

The naval ships now opened up against the attackers: *Terror* with her two 3-inch (76mm) anti-aircraft guns and the gun boats with machine guns. Those living close to the 2-pounder pom-pom at Senglea and the 40mm Bofors guns around the dockyard were shaken as they also opened up; their windows and doors rattling as each gun threw up all it could in defence. Many took cover wherever they could while others looked up to see puffs of black smoke from the anti-aircraft guns as they made out the first black dots of enemy aircraft high above them against the bright blue sky.

The Gladiator pilots, still struggling to gain height, saw Hal Far under a cloud of smoke and then explosions around Grand Harbour. They saw so many enemy aircraft and had soon become split up. Burges noticed a number of bombers turning to the south of the island and about to start their journey northwards back to their base in Sicily. What he was looking at was probably a rear section from the wave of aircraft that had already hit the airfield of Hal Far. Cutting across to head them off, Burges gave chase but the SM.79 that he was so desperately trying to close down was simply too quick. He fired anyway but was hopelessly out of range. Besides, he had never been given any formal air-to-air gunnery training and so had never shot at an aircraft before, and so it would have been all too easy for him to misjudge the distance.[2]

For nearly an hour the air raid sirens wailed and nearly 150 bombs were dropped on the three main targets during the morning raid. The vast majority were 100kg (220lb) bombs but at least thirty were the heavier 250kg (550lb) type. Damage to the dockyard was slight but one bomber carried out a low attack against the historic fifteenth century Fort Saint Elmo, standing on the seaward shore of the Sciberras Peninsula and dividing Marsamxett Harbour from Grand Harbour, and commanding the entrance to both. Half a dozen bombs fell in a line across the fort, causing Malta's first military casualties of the siege – six members of the Royal Malta Artillery.[3] Their job had been to keep a lookout for any attempted enemy landing by sea but in a

---

2. Interview by George Burges for National War Museum Association Malta.
3. The six casualties were: Bombardier Joseph Galea; and Gunners Michael Saliba, Richard Micallef, Carmel Cordina, Paul Debono, and a 16-year-old boy soldier, Philip Busuttil.

futile attempt to deter the raiders they were reportedly last seen firing at the Italian bomber with their rifles.[4]

Bombs had also fallen at Corradino and at Portes des Bombes, where two bombs fell on the water and electricity department, killing two Maltese workmen, and at Pieta Creek, Sa Maison and Msida, where a house was destroyed and killing two more civilians, and a bomb also hit St Luke's Hospital. Bombs had also fallen near Fort Campbell, the last of the British ports built on the island, and there were near misses at St Georges and Tigne Point near Sliema.

In the aftermath of the morning raids, civilians living in and around the main target areas, particularly those living near Grand Harbour and the dockyard, fled for safety. The pre-war carefully considered plans for such a situation went out of the window as families fled before the raiders returned. Although they had been warned, many times, that an attack such as this was likely to happen, it took the sight of bombs falling and houses being demolished for the reality to be hammered home. Clearly, many had not expected to be attacked so soon. Chaos followed.

For the Maltese, it was now clear what lay ahead and during the following few days it is estimated that about 100,000 civilians – 40 per cent of Malta's population – had taken to the roads. They took as much as they could carry to seek shelter in the outlying towns and villages, or, for that matter, anywhere that could offer them protection as far away from the bombing as possible. Some took refuge in the old disused railway tunnel beneath Valletta, taking blankets, pillows and clothing to make themselves as comfortable as possible.

The air raid sirens sounded a number of times throughout that first morning and into the afternoon, although no more bombs fell for the time being. A single SM.79 passed over the island to carry out a post-raid assessment of the earlier raids and was chased by two Gladiators, but the reconnaissance aircraft merely turned safely away.

Throughout the day, announcements were broadcast on radio stations and in public places, ordering all military personnel to go to their place of duty. Not that it was really needed. It was obvious what was happening, although

---

4. *Times of Malta*, 11 June 2014.

those on the unaffected parts of the island had yet to realize to what extent, even though they would have heard the raids taking place to the south.

The Italians seemed intent on neutralizing Malta as quickly as possible and the bombers returned twice more on that first day. An attack just before 5.30 pm involved ten aircraft, in two formations of five, without fighter escort. The raiders crossed the island at about 15,000 feet; their targets included the two other airfields of Luqa and Takali.

There was then a much heavier raid, the worst of the day, lasting about half an hour, involving twenty-five bombers. It occurred at about 7.30 pm. The Gladiators had again been scrambled and having climbed to about 15,000 feet Timber Woods spotted five Italian bombers approaching Valletta at a similar height. Chasing one of them down as best he could, Woods opened fire from a range he estimated to be 200 yards. He was now out to sea and so turned back towards the island when he spotted another section of five aircraft. Again, he got into a position to open fire on an aircraft from the stern before he found himself involved in the first aerial engagement of the campaign, which took place to the south of Valletta. Woods was caught up with an escorting MC.200 and later recalled:

> 'I suddenly heard machine-gun fire from behind me. I immediately went into a steep left-hand turn and saw a single-engine fighter diving and firing at me. For quite three minutes I circled as tightly as possible and got the enemy in my sight. I got in a good burst, full deflection shot, and he went down in a steep dive with black smoke pouring from his tail. I could not follow him down, but he appeared to go into the sea.'[5]

The defenders of Malta had claimed the first enemy fighter but Woods' claim would remain unconfirmed;[6] in fact, it later turned out that the Macchi made it safely back to Sicily. Nonetheless, word would have soon got around the Italian pilots that the Gladiators were far from an easy prey.

---

5. Air Battle of Malta; Official Account RAF 1940–2.
6. Shores and Williams, *Aces High*, p.646.

The main target during the evening raid had been the dockyards but many bombs fell elsewhere, mostly on the fortified Cospicua, the largest of the Three Cities. Fortunately, most buildings were made of stout stone blocks, with virtually no wood at all to burn, and the ground was mainly soft limestone, and so each falling bomb only made a small crater. But these last two raids of the day had seen a further 200-plus bombs dropped on the island, causing widespread damage and more civilian casualties.

Late in the day, a single SM.79 flew over the island to carry out a post-raid reconnaissance sortie. Two Gladiators were scrambled with one pilot, Flying Officer John Waters, claiming to have shot the enemy aircraft down; the first of his five claims made while flying over Malta.

By the end of the first day of the siege, during which the air raid sirens had sounded eight times, the morale of Malta's inhabitants had taken a significant hit. Although Malta's defences may have surprised the Italian raiders, they failed to impede them.

As the sun set at the end of that first day of hostilities, the Maltese could never have imagined that it was only the start of a siege that was to last for nearly two and a half years. Some 200 houses lay in ruins around Grand Harbour and more than twenty civilians were dead, including six killed in one heavy bombing raid on the town of Gzira on the northern side of Marsamxett Harbour, in addition to the six men of the Royal Malta Artillery who had been killed at Fort Saint Elmo during the first attack of the day. Among the civilian deaths were two children, aged 6 and 7, and a baby of just 5 months.[7] War had, indeed, come to Malta.

---

7. Malta War Diary, 11 June 1940.

Chapter Three

Reinforcements

The first day of the siege had been a hard one for the people of Malta. Morale had been shaken, homes destroyed and lives lost. Darkness on that first evening of 11 June 1940 could not have come soon enough.

Those who woke the following morning fearing more of the same were relieved and, no doubt, surprised to find there would be no further raids that day. Cloud over the island meant that just a lone Italian reconnaissance aircraft was spotted above the island while carrying out a post-raid assessment from the evening before. The Gladiators again scrambled to intercept it and George Burges claimed to have struck the SM.79 between Hal Far and Valletta, but only slight damage was caused.

At Hal Far, the Gladiator pilots discussed the first couple of days. Although Malta's radar situated high on Dingli cliffs had detected the incoming raids, the small amount of warning time and the performance of the Gladiator meant they had been unable to gain enough height to take on the raiders before they bombed their targets. They felt they would have to do much better in the future and so decided to mount periods of readiness with the pilots already in the cockpit. All that would then be required is for the ground crews to leap to the starter batteries and soon after the touch of a button the fighters could be tearing down the runway and airborne within seconds rather than minutes.

This, the pilots felt, would buy them some valuable time in order to engage the bombers before they hit their targets. But the reality was that maintaining cockpit readiness throughout the heat of the day, for up to four hours at a time, in a cramped cockpit and wearing full flying clothing, was physically tiring and so the pilots' routine would change during the days ahead. This meant that only a couple of Gladiators could be on stand-by at any one time and the reality was they would make little difference to the overall result of any bombing raid. But the sight of the Gladiators climbing into the air to bravely take on the raiders, combined with the sound of the anti-aircraft guns, would do much to help maintain the morale of the Maltese people at this vital time. It made the islanders feel that Malta at least had a chance.

It was also during these early days of the siege that three of the Gladiators acquired their now legendary names of '*Faith, Hope* and *Charity*', named after a group of Christian martyred saints. How these names came about has attracted post-war speculation but one explanation is given in James Holland's book *Fortress Malta*, where it is suggested the names were first used by an RAF corporal, after which they seemed to stick.[1]

With Italy's introduction into the war, Cunningham's Mediterranean Fleet was soon reinforced with three battleships: HMS *Warspite* returned to the Mediterranean after being in action off Norway; HMS *Valiant*, another Queen Elizabeth-class, was now assigned to Cunningham from Gibraltar; and the third battleship was the 28,000-tonne HMS *Royal Sovereign*, a Revenge-class battleship, although she had not been modernized during the inter-war period and so would always struggle for speed.

Cunningham could also once again call on the elderly C-class light cruisers of the 3rd Cruiser Squadron: *Caledon, Calypso, Capetown* and *Delhi*.[2] These light cruisers were augmented by other ships to form the 7th Cruiser Squadron: the Leander-class light cruisers *Orion* and *Neptune*; two new Town-class light cruisers *Gloucester* and *Liverpool*; and the Australian warship HMAS *Sydney*, a modified Leander-class. Other ships arriving to reinforce the Mediterranean Fleet included the aircraft carrier *Eagle*, the Revenge-class battleship *Ramillies* and another C-class cruiser *Carlisle*, as well as ten submarines and a number of other vessels. The build-up was so quick that Cunningham's deputy, Rear Admiral John Tovey, who commanded the Mediterranean Fleet's cruisers, destroyers and other light forces, soon commanded nine cruisers and more than twenty destroyers from his flagship *Orion*.

---

1. Holland, op. cit., p.43 (The RAF Corporal is named as Harry Kirk and quoted by Roy Nash in '*The Unknown Air Ace*', *Daily Star*, March 1958).
2. Woodman, op. cit., p.34.

Cunningham now ordered his 2nd Destroyer Flotilla to set sail from Alexandria and push out into the Mediterranean. This would prevent any Italian surface vessels or submarines from laying hazardous minefields close to Alexandria. Also sailing was *Eagle* and *Malaya*, the 7th Cruiser Squadron under Tovey and two of the elderly cruisers, *Caledon* and *Calypso*, of the 3rd Squadron, all protected by nine destroyers.

Flying his flag in *Warspite*, Cunningham was keen to engage the Italian fleet at the earliest opportunity. His plan was to push no further west than Malta and if they could not engage the Italian fleet head on then they would at least try to disrupt the Italian merchant supply line to North Africa. As things were to turn out, nothing was seen.[3] The ships did not even come under attack from the air, as they would have expected. They did, however, encounter an Italian submarine about fifty miles to the south of Crete when *Calypso* was sunk to become the first Royal Navy vessel to be lost to the Regia Marina in the war. She was struck by a torpedo from the *Alpino Attilio Bagnolini* during the early hours of 12 June; one officer and thirty-eight ratings were killed, although the rest of her complement of nearly 350 were picked up by the destroyer HMS *Dainty* and taken back to Alexandria.

Meanwhile, six Malta-based submarines had also gone on the offensive, seeking any enemy shipping in and around the Italian ports. Of the six, three were soon to be lost in action. HMS *Odin*, an O-class submarine commanded by Lieutenant Commander Ken Woods, was located in the Gulf of Taranto and sunk by two Italian destroyers on 14 June. Then, sometime after 16 June, *Grampus*, a Porpoise-class sub commanded by Lieutenant Commander Charles Rowe, went missing while on patrol off Syracuse. *Grampus* had sailed from Malta on the night of the Italian declaration of war to patrol to the east of Sicily before laying a minefield off Augusta. The exact circumstances behind her loss is unknown but one suggestion is that she was sunk by two patrol boats. The third loss during what turned out to be an awful week for the Malta-based submarines was *Orpheus*, another O-class, commanded by Lieutenant Commander James Wise. She had also left Malta on the night of

---

3. Cunningham, *A Sailor's Odyssey: The Autobiography of Admiral of the Fleet Viscount Cunningham of Hyndhope*, p.235.

10 June for a patrol off Syracuse but was declared overdue on 27 June. She is believed to have been sunk by an Italian destroyer about twenty-five miles north of Tobruk.

On the island of Malta there had been something of a respite for the islanders during the days following the initial onslaught. The weather had turned, leaving Malta hidden from the air by low cloud. There was a raid on 13 June, but with minimal damage, and the Italians lost their first aircraft of the campaign, an SM.79, during an attempt at first light on 14 June to mount a further raid. The loss was not due to Malta's defending fighters or anti-aircraft guns but due to misfortune and misjudgement by the Italian crew. The bombers had encountered bad weather soon after take-off and two were forced to abort their mission; one crashed while coming into land at its base at Catania, and with a full bomb load on board the aircraft blew up and killed all the crew.[4]

For the next two days there was minimal air activity over Malta, with the Italian bombers only appearing in small numbers and achieving little success. These half-hearted raids by the Italians were, in reality, having little impact on Malta. Mussolini was not solely focused on the island; far from it. He could see France was collapsing and so felt that now was the time to pursue his dream of Italian expansion in Africa by having a go at French-held Tunisia.

The decision to launch one initial onslaught on Malta and then back off not only shows the lack of any real Italian strategy over this period in the Mediterranean war but also suggests that despite Italy's lengthy build-up to the Second World War, the country was not particularly well prepared to fight a major conflict on more than one front.

Nonetheless, Malta could expect more air raids. Two more crated Gladiators were released to the Malta Fighter Flight and both aircraft were immediately assembled. But, just a few days later, one aircraft crashed during take-off and another struck an object on landing. In both incidents the pilots were fine but the aircraft were not, although from the two damaged aircraft one airworthy Gladiator would emerge.

---

4. Shores and Cull with Malizia, op. cit., p.8.

In addition to the Gladiators, Malta soon gained twelve torpedo-carrying Swordfish. These aircraft had originally been used by two Royal Navy training squadrons in France but with the French on the verge of surrender, they had hastily flown to Hal Far via Algeria to form 830 Naval Air Squadron under the command of Lieutenant Commander Frankie Howie.

Malta now had a limited strike capability. There was a further boost, too. William Dobbie's request to the War Office for modern fighters, made in the aftermath of the first air raids against Malta, and stating that the Gladiators were too slow, had received support. Dobbie knew that five Hurricanes were currently in Tunisia on their way to Egypt and strongly supported a request by Sammy Maynard to the Air Ministry for them to be diverted to Malta.

Three Hurricanes and a Lockheed Hudson arrived at Luqa the following day, but they all soon departed to continue their journey to Egypt. Although approval had not been received in time to retain these first three Hurricanes to have landed in Malta, there was still hope. They had been part of an original formation of six Hurricanes and two Hudsons that had set off from southern England a week before. With the Hurricanes fitted with underwing external fuel tanks, and escorted by the Hudsons, the long transit to Egypt took the formation across France, then still in the war. The aircraft had landed three times in France to refuel, before they arrived at El Aouina in Tunisia, after which their route would take them to the British airfield at Mersa Matruh in Egypt via Malta.

With two of the three remaining Hurricanes and the other Hudson still in Tunisia (the third Hurricane had crash-landed in France), Maynard and Dobbie's request was granted. Hurricane spares and equipment that were in Gibraltar at the time and on their way to Egypt were instead loaded on a cargo vessel destined for Malta. Then, on 21 June, the two Hurricanes and the Hudson flew from Tunisia to Luqa. Having arrived in Malta, the two Hurricane ferry pilots, Flying Officer Fred Taylor, known as 'Eric', and Pilot Officer Tom Balmforth, were then told they were to remain on the island, much to their surprise.

There followed something of a rush to get more aircraft on the way to Malta before France fell. Early the following afternoon, the day when France signed an armistice with Germany, three Bristol Blenheims and two more Hurricanes arrived at Luqa, after a journey lasting four days. Two more Hurricanes arrived later that afternoon and then two more just as darkness fell.

Malta briefly had eight Hurricanes on the island, five more than the three now at Alexandria. But Egypt's needs were still considered a higher priority than Malta's and to address this imbalance, three Hurricanes and the Blenheims departed for Mersa Matruh two days later, leaving five Hurricanes and three extra pilots at Luqa – Pilot Officers Barber, McAdam and Sugden – in addition to Taylor and Balmforth, as well as the Hudson and its two pilots.[5]

It was on that same day, 22 June, that George Burges claimed his first confirmed success over Malta. Having been scrambled from Hal Far with Timber Woods during the late afternoon, they spotted an unescorted SM.79 at medium altitude and heading south-eastwards across the island, presumably on a reconnaissance mission. Woods was the first to attack, followed by Burges who scored hits on the port engine. The aircraft then caught fire and crashed in the sea off Kalafrana. It was a rare occasion when the Gladiator pilots had found everything to be in their favour: position, height and surprise. Burges' first success of the war had been witnessed by many watching from the ground and provided another morale-boosting moment for the Maltese.

The fact that France was now out of the war caused the British concerns in the Mediterranean for a number of reasons. Even before the French had signed the armistice, British merchant ships had stopped passing through the Mediterranean because of the obvious risk posed, and there was also the fact that the Royal Navy would have a reduced number of ports available for its Mediterranean Fleet. But there was a more immediate problem facing the Royal Navy: what was to happen to the French fleet? Even before the signing of the armistice there had been discussions among senior British naval officers about how to persuade the French to hand over their ships to the Royal Navy, but the terms of the armistice stipulated that the French Navy was to be disarmed under French or Italian control.

---

5. Ibid, p.24.

It was crucial that the French fleet, the fourth largest at the time, should not fall into the hands of the Germans. The thought of the Royal Navy having to take on French ships in addition to the might of the Axis navies was simply too much. For the British, denying the French ships passage through the Strait of Gibraltar would be a start but there would also come a time when the French Navy would need to be neutralized in its home bases and overseas ports.

There was a further problem, too, and that was because the earlier Anglo-French Alliance had seen the Mediterranean divided in half. The French Navy was responsible for the western Mediterranean, using its main naval bases at Toulon in Southern France and the Algerian port of Mers-el-Kebir, and the Royal Navy would control the east from its main base at Alexandria. With France now out of the war, it was unlikely that Cunningham could control the whole Mediterranean with the resources he had. Furthermore, should Spain be persuaded to enter the war on the side of the Axis, the problem would be even greater.

Although there was talk of the Royal Navy withdrawing from the eastern Mediterranean, particularly given that Cunningham was potentially facing overwhelming odds and now found himself at the end of a lengthy supply line that extended round the South African cape, nothing came of the idea. How close the Royal Navy came to withdrawing from the eastern Mediterranean is only known by those involved in the discussions at the time, but clearly Churchill was against the idea. Besides, any such withdrawal would surely have ended in a catastrophic outcome for Malta, and, in turn, the entire Mediterranean and North African campaigns. The idea simply disappeared but the major outcome from these discussions was the decision to form a powerful naval squadron, called Force H, to replace the loss of French naval power in the western Mediterranean. It was to be ready for action by the end of June.

Force H was put together in lightning speed. It was based at Gibraltar but as an organization sat oddly in the Royal Navy's chain of command. There was already flag officer commanding North Atlantic, Admiral Sir Dudley North, based at Gibraltar, but the new commander of Force H, Vice Admiral Sir James Somerville, would not have to report through North but was given a direct reporting line to the first sea lord, Sir Dudley Pound, instead.

Somerville, a former fleet wireless officer in his late fifties and veteran of the First World War's Gallipoli campaign, was a tough and blunt-spoken senior naval officer. He would fly his flag in the battlecruiser HMS *Hood* and his force was a powerful one: the aircraft carrier HMS *Ark Royal*; two battleships, *Resolution* and *Valiant*; two light-cruisers, *Arethusa* and *Enterprise*; and four destroyers.[6]

Ark Royal and *Hood*, escorted by four destroyers, arrived at Gibraltar on 23 June having sailed from Scapa Flow. The 22,000-tonne *Ark Royal*, commanded by Captain Cedric Holland, was the pride of Force H. She was still a new ship, having been completed less than a year before the outbreak of the Second World War, and was the second purpose-built aircraft carrier for the Royal Navy. Designed to carry a large number of aircraft – a mix of Fairey Swordfish, Blackburn Skuas and Fairey Fulmars – her design differed from other carriers. She was the first ship on which the flight deck and hangars were an integral part of the hull, instead of being an add-on, and had two hangar deck levels. She was also designed with anti-aircraft warfare in mind, as she could expect to come under air attack, whereas any threat from surface ships or submarines would be dealt with by use of her speed of up to 31 knots. The mighty *Hood*, at 47,000 tonnes, was also fast. She was capable of 30 knots and was one of the Royal Navy's four Admiral-class battlecruisers. She was significantly larger than her predecessors of the *Renown* and *Courageous* classes and with four gun turrets, each boasting two powerful 15-inch guns, she was a formidable weapon.

Discussions about the French fleet continued until Churchill gave Somerville the unenviable task that if all other options were to fail, then Force H was to neutralize the main element of the French battle fleet – including four battleships and half a dozen destroyers – in the French Algerian port of Mers-el-Kebir. Whatever Somerville's private thoughts were, he knew the French ships would pose a serious threat if they were allowed to set sail under Axis control. It would certainly tip the balance in the Mediterranean and so Force H sailed for Mers-el-Kebir as part of Operation Catapult to neutralize the French fleet.

---

6. Woodman, op. cit., p.37.

As far as the British were concerned, various options were on offer. The French naval commander, Admiral Marcel-Bruno Gensoul, was to be given the opportunity to join the British fleet or sail to a British port and then have his crews repatriated to the unoccupied part of France. Alternatively, his fleet could sail to a neutral country, such as the United States or Martinique, where his ships would be decommissioned, or he could even scuttle his fleet where they were already anchored.[7]

Cunningham and Somerville both knew that the destruction of the French fleet could result in a serious backlash and fuel anti-British feeling among otherwise friendly allies. But the situation came to a head at the beginning of July 1940, by which time Force H had arrived off Mers-el-Kebir in the Bay of Oran.

The ultimatum was to be delivered to Gensoul aboard his flagship *Dunkerque* by Cedric Holland, a French speaker and Francophile with experience from his time as naval attaché in Paris. Holland was taken into port on board the destroyer HMS *Foxhound* early on 2 July to negotiate with the French.[8] But Gensoul, affronted that negotiations were not being conducted by a senior Royal Navy officer, sent his own lieutenant to meet with Holland, which only led to delay and confusion. Written notes were exchanged but as negotiations dragged on, it became clear that neither side was likely to give way.

Exactly what Gensoul reported to his own higher authorities has been the subject of much post-war speculation. Whether he was anti-British is uncertain. Some suggest that Gensoul considered himself pro-British. It may well be that, for whatever reason, Gensoul chose not to report all the options that were on offer from the British. There also appears to be mistrust between the two nations at this most crucial time. Churchill had earlier been assured that the French fleet would not fall into Nazi hands but the English translation of some of the wording of the French armistice with Germany was interpreted as the French fleet would be controlled by the Axis powers

---

7. Kappes, *Mers-el-Kebir: A Battle Between Friends*, (taken from MilitaryHistoryOnline. com).

8. Rossiter, *Ark Royal: The Life, Death and Rediscovery of the Legendary Second World War Aircraft Carrier*, pp.132–3.

and, therefore, could be used against the British. Whatever the truth, the outcome was that Gensoul was ordered to fight rather than allow a foreign power to attempt to seize the ships under his command.

In the end the British Admiralty pressed for a solution to negotiations. Holland was instructed to break off discussions and he was taken back to his ship. Back in London, Churchill, concerned that French reinforcements might be on their way, gave Somerville the order for Force H to resolve the impasse and to settle matters quickly if none of the British proposals were met. It was now just before 5.30 pm on 3 July and both sides had boxed themselves into a corner.

With the French refusing to comply with British conditions, Force H attacked the French ships at Mers-el-Kebir just before 6.00 pm. Although there were comparisons in strength between the two forces, the British had the advantage. The French ships were anchored in a narrow harbour and were not fully prepared for battle. The main armament of the two modern battleships, *Dunkerque* and *Strasbourg*, were on their bows and so could not immediately be brought to bear.

The *Hood*'s 15-inch shells first struck the *Dunkerque*, setting her on fire and putting the ship out of action within minutes. The French ships could offer only a token resistance compared to the onslaught from *Hood*, *Valiant* and *Resolution*. The bombardment was brief but devastating. The elderly battleship *Bretagne* was hit and blew up. She sank with the loss of more than a thousand French sailors. The *Provence*, another elderly battleship, was also hit and badly damaged, and there were damaging hits on *Strasbourg* and *Dunkerque*, although *Strasbourg* picked its way through the burning wrecks and escaped with four destroyers. As they did so they came under attack from *Ark Royal*'s Swordfish. The French responded with anti-aircraft fire and shot down two of them, although both crews were picked up. Although two of Somerville's cruisers gave chase, he eventually called them off, feeling that his ships were not well placed for a night engagement. The *Strasbourg* and her escort arrived at Toulon the following day.

Columns of black smoke marked the Algerian port. Nearly 1,300 French sailors were killed or missing and several hundred more wounded. The British had not suffered a single casualty but the damage to British-French relations was incalculable. It was one of the great naval tragedies of the Second World War.

Whether Hitler would have utilized the French ships in some way is unknown. Winning the battle of the Atlantic with his U–boats, and starving Britain into defeat, was his greater priority and, in truth, he would probably have struggled to provide the manpower required to take many of these ships to war against the British. Hitler may have simply decided to intern the ships in French ports under Axis supervision or to scuttle them. Either way, it made no difference now.

After carrying out the most unpleasant task of Operation Catapult, Force H would settle down to more normal operations in the western basin of the Mediterranean, which, for Malta, would be vital for the island's survival.

Chapter Four

An Opportunity Missed

Apart from the initial aerial onslaught against Malta on Italy's entry into the war, the lack of urgency shown by the Italian fleet to engage the Royal Navy would not only have come as a relief to the British commanders but it would have also brought into question Italy's ability to fight a major conflict in the Mediterranean.

However, the French signing of the armistice with Germany saw the Italians turn their attention to Malta once more. By the end of June the number of air raids against the island had risen to more than fifty, including the first night raid on 20 June when six SM.79s dropped about forty bombs on the island, although they caused little damage.

There was little the defenders could do against night raids, but the last day of June marked a notable event in Malta's air war when Swordfish of 830 Squadron attacked an oil refinery at Augusta on the island of Sicily. Although it achieved no great success, the raid signalled the start of Malta's fight back against the Italians.

With the matter of the French fleet now resolved, Cunningham could turn his attention to Malta. The support given to the island by Churchill came as welcome news to both him and Dobbie. It was now a case of deciding how to best provide naval protection for the convoys that were needed to carry vital supplies to Malta.

There was a further consideration, too, for Cunningham. An engagement between Tovey's 7th Cruiser Squadron and three Italian destroyers, which took place off the south-west of Cape Matapan at the end of June, resulted in just one enemy ship sunk. Although the pursuit and engagement might normally have been considered worthwhile, the amount of weapons expended by five of his ships to sink what was just one small vessel could not be sustained or justified. The British were facing a lengthy conflict in the Mediterranean and were at the end of a flimsy supply line.

Cunningham, fully aware of Malta's plight, prepared to bring some aid to the island but it was first necessary to retrieve a number of merchant vessels that had been stranded there by war. With the Italian siege of Malta taking hold, the decision was also made to evacuate to Egypt as many British non-combatants as possible in addition to essential naval supplies from the dockyards. This would be done by two convoys, one faster than the other. The faster convoy, carrying the evacuees, would consist of three ships. Given the designation MF1, it included a passenger liner that had become stranded in Malta while transiting between France and Egypt before the outbreak of hostilities. The second convoy, designated MS1, was made up of five slower cargo vessels; these would be loaded with naval stores desperately needed in Alexandria.[1]

On the evening of 7 July, the Mediterranean Fleet left Alexandria. Cunningham divided his fleet into four groups. Tovey's 7th Cruiser Squadron made up Force A, and Cunningham, in *Warspite*, led Force B with five destroyers. Force C, led by the new commander of the 1st Battle Squadron, Vice Admiral Henry Pridham-Wippell in *Royal Sovereign*, consisted of *Eagle*, *Malaya* and *Gloucester*, screened by ten destroyers. Force D, consisting of four destroyers, was to act as escorts for the two convoys from Malta. They were to join three more destroyers already at Malta – HMS *Jervis*, HMS *Diamond* and HMAS *Vendetta* – and were now awaiting the order to sail.

The following morning, Cunningham received word that the Italian fleet, consisting of two battleships, fourteen cruisers and twenty-four destroyers, had been spotted about 200 miles to the east of Malta and heading south. Guessing the Italian warships were escorting an Axis convoy heading for Libya, Cunningham gave the order to intercept.

That same morning, 8 July, Somerville sailed from Gibraltar with Force H and headed east. His force were to act as a diversion but it was not long before they were spotted by an Italian reconnaissance aircraft. For three hours during the afternoon, Force H endured several air attacks. However, wary of the anti-aircraft defences of the Royal Navy ships, the Italian bombers were

---

1. Woodman, op. cit., p.43.

attacking from heights above 10,000 feet and so bombing proved inaccurate. Nonetheless, it was enough for Somerville to decide that it was not worth putting ships such as *Ark Royal*, plus her complement of aircraft, at risk just to continue what was only a minor operation. That evening he ordered his ships to return to Gibraltar at full speed, although one destroyer was hit by an Italian submarine and later sank.

To the east, Cunningham's fleet had also been spotted and had come under air attack. During the course of the day there were a dozen air raids against the fleet but the attackers were also bombing from too high and so no ships were lost; only one, *Gloucester*, was hit. Further to the west, the Italian ships turned north back towards Italy and so Cunningham ordered a change of heading to intercept them somewhere off the Calabrian coast of south-east Italy.

By mid-afternoon on 9 July, his ships, although outgunned and outnumbered, had closed to about thirteen miles and were now at the maximum range to open fire. The Italian ships disappeared behind a trail of smoke as the Regia Aeronautica launched countless air attacks against the pursuing ships of the Royal Navy. All of Cunningham's ships came under repeated attack from the air but they pressed on, now only twenty-five miles from the coast of Italy and in danger of falling into a submarine trap.

Cunningham eventually called off the chase as darkness set in. His ships had, he felt, been lucky to survive intact. It was a surface action later to be given the name Battle of Calabria with the Royal Navy having damaged one Italian battleship and one cruiser. With the chase over, Cunningham ordered his ships southwards to join up with the convoy.

Meanwhile, from his headquarters at Fort Saint Angelo, Wilbraham Ford had decided to ignore the instructions to hold the merchant ships at Malta. As soon as he knew the outcome of the action off Calabria he ordered MF1, the faster of the two convoys, to set sail for Alexandria under the cover of darkness.

Cunningham was needed back in Egypt and so *Warspite* set course for Alexandria, and Pridham-Wippell was given responsibility of protecting the slower convoy, MS1. Tovey's force was now split; some ships were to catch up with and provide cover for MF1, which was proceeding at no more than 10 knots, and the others would join *Warspite* for the journey home.

But for Cunningham the action was far from over. Having decided to follow a more southerly course back to Alexandria along the North African coast, *Warspite* and her escorting destroyers came under air attack once again, this time from Italian aircraft based in Libya. The air raids continued over the next couple of days but the ships came through unscathed. Cunningham's lead group arrived back at Alexandria during the early morning of 13 July, followed three hours later by the safe arrival of MF1. Meanwhile, MS1, having been joined by her escort, and having somehow survived intact, sailed into Alexandria two days later.

It was a marvellous achievement but it would be convoys and supplies *to* Malta that would be needed in the coming weeks and months, and not convoys *from* Malta. Nonetheless, Cunningham was delighted with his fleet's ability to get merchant ships safely to their destination and had also been encouraged by their engagement with the Regia Marina. It was true there were deficiencies in the performance of one or two of his ships, such as the maximum speed and range of armament of ships such as *Malaya* and *Royal Sovereign*, but when confronted head-on, the Italian ships had made off towards home rather than fight on equal terms. Although this suggested to Cunningham that Malta could be used more freely, the number of air raids against the island gave cause for concern.

The Regia Aeronautica was clearly capable of mounting large raids against Malta and this did not bode well for the island's future. Cunningham, Maynard and Dobbie all knew that with more British fighters and more anti-aircraft guns, the Axis powers would find Malta a difficult nut to crack. Fortunately, back in London, Churchill agreed. He was even growing impatient, and stressed, yet again, the urgent need to build up Malta's anti-aircraft defences.[2]

Malta's newly arrived Hurricanes entered the combat arena in early July, coinciding with the Regia Aeronautica sending CR.42s to Sicily to provide fighter escort for the Italian bombers. The two recent arrivals clashed for the first time on 3 July to the south of Malta. Nine CR.42s were escorting

---

2. The National Archives, CAB 120/624, Note from Churchill to the First Sea Lord dated 15 July 1940.

two SM.79s carrying out a reconnaissance of the island when the two recce aircraft were attacked by Flying Officer John Waters in a Hurricane. It would have come as something of a surprise to the crews of the SM.79s, with the speed and firepower of the Hurricane unlike anything the Italian crews had encountered before. One SM.79 plunged into the sea off Kalafrana.

Waters had been involved in many of the early interceptions and had claimed two Italian bombers on the opening two days of the campaign while flying the Gladiator, although neither had been confirmed, but now he had gained his first confirmed victory of the war.[3] But as Waters returned to land he was set upon by CR.42s and his aircraft repeatedly hit, forcing him to crash-land and writing off the Hurricane; Waters survived unhurt. This was the Regia Aeronautica's first confirmed success over Malta, although, interestingly, the Italian pilots reported the victim to have been a Spitfire.[4]

The following morning the CR.42s were back over Malta, this time causing havoc at Hal Far when they strafed the airfield at low level and claimed several aircraft destroyed on the ground. Over the next few days Italian raids continued against Valletta and the dockyards, as well as the airfields at Hal Far and Takali. Meanwhile, Frankie Howie's 830 Squadron continued to hit back. Led by Howie, a raid by nine Swordfish against the Italian airfield at Catania on 5 July proved particularly successful: a number of enemy aircraft were either destroyed or badly damaged on the ground.

Following the first success of John Waters, Timber Woods scored his first victory flying a Hurricane on 7 July when he shot down a SM.79 over Valletta attacking the main dockyard. Two days later, George Burges scored his first success in a Hurricane. He had been scrambled against the day's only air raid with Flying Officer Roger 'Jock' Barber. They were vectored onto a single SM.79 carrying out what had become a routine daily reconnaissance of the island, escorted by four CR.42s. While Barber held the marauding Italian fighters at bay, Burges attacked the lone SM.79 and watched it plummeting towards the sea before he was attacked by three of the CR.42s and had to

3. Shores and Williams, op. cit., p.618.
4. Shores and Cull with Malizia, op. cit., p.26.

break away.[5] Then, the following day, Eric Taylor shot down an SM.79 over Grand Harbour; it was Taylor's turn to score his first success of the war.

By the second week of July, a month into the siege, the total number of air raids against the island had risen to more than seventy, with sometimes as many as five raids a day. With the death toll mounting, people fled the heavily targeted areas. Since the opening day of the siege, the civilian population around the normally densely populated areas of Valletta and Sliema had dropped by an estimated 90 per cent. Only those who needed to be there seemed to have stayed but for those who did remain in Valletta, business stood still. Many shops closed and when the air raids came, the Maltese took to whatever shelter they could; in the slit trenches or the additional shelters erected by the defenders, or in the caves that had been dug many hundreds of years ago into the fortifications of the bastions of Valletta and the Three Cities.

As the air fighting intensified, Malta suffered its first pilot killed. On the morning of 16 July, Flight Lieutenant Peter Keeble, flying a Hurricane, was scrambled alongside George Burges in a Gladiator to intercept a dozen CR.42s carrying out an armed reconnaissance of the island. Keeble was seen to attack one CR.42 but was then attacked by two more. After a long chase Keeble's aircraft was hit and it dived towards the ground. It appeared to flatten out as if to attempt some sort of crash landing but then dived into the ground near radio masts at Rinella.[6] Keeble is buried in Malta's Capuccini Naval Cemetery.

By the end of July, Malta's air defenders had claimed twelve enemy aircraft destroyed and George Burges became the first pilot of the Fighter Flight to be decorated for his courage when he received the Distinguished Flying Cross (DFC); the citation crediting him with three confirmed victories and three more as probably destroyed.

---

5. Burges was credited with the SM.79 as his third confirmed victory of the war but the Italian bomber, with the pilot dead and one gunner mortally wounded, made an emergency landing at Comiso. See Shores and Cull with Malizia, pp.29–30.

6. Shores and Cull with Malizia, op. cit., pp.37–8. (Account given by Wing Commander Carter Jonas, the officer commanding Luqa, who, from the ground, had witnessed Keeble's final moments.)

But the number of sorties being flown, and the lack of spares, was taking its toll. For example, on 31 July only three Gladiators – flown by Peter Hartley, Eric Taylor and Timber Woods – were available to intercept a lone reconnaissance SM.79 escorted by nine CR.42s. The SM.79 turned away but a dogfight between the fighters soon raged over Hal Far. Woods shot down the Italian lead aircraft, which came down into the sea off Grand Harbour, his fifth claim over Malta, but Hartley was also shot down. His aircraft had been hit in the fuel tank, causing it to explode. Although Hartley baled out into the sea, he suffered severe burns and would spend many months in Imtarfa Hospital before returning to England.[7]

By early August the Fighter Flight appeared to be on its last legs, although, fortuitously, this period of high unserviceability coincided with an irregular period of enemy air raids. Furthermore, after more than a month of aerial bombardment, the troops in Malta were running low on ammunition, and some doubt was expressed whether Malta was worth the supplies it required.[8]

But help was on its way, although getting new fighters to Malta would not be easy. Aircraft could no longer transit through France and with Spain being neutral, the only way of getting more fighters to Malta was from an aircraft carrier in the western Mediterranean, supported by Somerville's Force H from Gibraltar. The only alternative, otherwise, was to sail round the Cape of Good Hope but this would cause significant delay. Besides, the delivery carrier and the fighters would still have to run through the eastern Med from Alexandria to Malta, which, if anything, was considered more risky than the Gibraltar option.

Although flying Hurricanes off a carrier in the western Med was the preferred option, there were two main problems. Firstly, fighters would have to be released by the RAF at a most critical time back in Britain. The second problem was the presence of Italian submarines in the western Mediterranean. There would, in fact, become a third problem too. The carrier would look to release the fighters as soon as it came within range of

---

7. Ibid, p.41.
8. Shankland and Hunter, *Malta Convoy*, p.92.

Malta, to minimize the risk to itself and its escort, and this would mean a long transit for the fighters, leaving them without the fuel to engage in any air combat should the need arise.

Nonetheless, the decision was made to go ahead and re-supply Malta as quickly as possible. Under the codename Operation Hurry, the plan was to ferry twelve Hurricanes to Malta on board the ageing aircraft carrier, HMS *Argus*. The carrier sailed from Greenock on 23 July and arrived in Gibraltar with her four escort destroyers a week later. On board were the Hurricanes and two Fleet Air Arm Skuas, as well as personnel and supplies bound for Malta.

The following morning, Somerville's Force H plus *Argus* and her escort sailed from Gibraltar. It was a sizeable and powerful force: two aircraft carriers: *Ark Royal* and *Argus*; three battleships: *Hood*, *Valiant* and *Resolution*; two cruisers: *Arethusa* and *Enterprise*; and six destroyers in addition to *Argus*' flotilla of four. Ahead of them were anti-submarine patrols provided by Gibraltar-based aircraft as well as those flown off the *Ark*.

The ships were spotted later that day and although the Italians launched an attack from airfields in Sardinia, the ships escaped damage and Force H-plus pressed on eastwards at 17 knots. The combination of air patrols flown by the *Ark*'s Skuas, some accurate anti-aircraft fire during an air attack on the second day, some deceptive radio messages transmitted from one of the ships and some clever manoeuvring to deceive the enemy, meant the ships proceeded unscathed.

By the early hours of 2 August the ships were little more than a hundred miles from the enemy coast and *Ark Royal* was in a position to launch her Swordfish to carry out a diversionary raid against the Italian air base of Cagliari on the island of Sardinia. Then, as daylight was breaking, *Argus* had reached a position from where its aircraft could fly off, even though they were still about 350 miles away from Malta.

Flying in the wake of the Skuas to provide the navigation, the Hurricanes all landed safely at Luqa just over two hours after setting off from the carrier. Two days later, Somerville's ships arrived back at Gibraltar. Operation Hurry had been a success.

Somerville would briefly return to England on the ill-fated *Hood*, sailing with *Argus*, *Valiant* and several destroyers. During his stopover he met with Sir Dudley Pound at the Admiralty to discuss future operations in the Mediterranean, and specifically a planned operation to reinforce Cunningham in the eastern Mediterranean, before Somerville returned to Gibraltar later that month aboard his new flagship, the modernized battlecruiser HMS *Renown*.

It would take a few days for the newly arrived Hurricanes to be ready for operations as spares and other key equipment had yet to arrive in Malta; they would soon arrive using all available means, such as on board flying boats or by submarine. As for the newly arrived pilots, they soon discovered that their life was to be very different from what they had been used to back home. For a start, they had not been told when they left England that they would be staying in Malta. They had been told they were required to ferry the Hurricanes to an unknown destination and had assumed they would be returning to England once their job was done. With very few clothes or possessions between them, they were, understandably, not very happy.[9]

Although it might not have been a good start for the new pilots, Sammy Maynard now had fifteen Hurricanes and eighteen pilots, enough to form a squadron. The Malta Fighter Flight moved to Luqa to join up with the newly arrived Hurricanes to become 261 Squadron; Malta's first fighter squadron. There was further reason to be optimistic as the number of air raids had declined since the opening onslaught in June. The Italians had missed the opportunity to press home their initial advantage.

9. Holland, op. cit., p.54.

Chapter Five

A Period of Optimism

With the remaining aircraft of the Fighter Flight incorporated into the new 261 Squadron, an initial squadron composition was put together under the command of Squadron Leader Jock Martin. It was based on a three-flight system with six pilots allocated to each flight, although this would soon be changed to a two-flight system, of nine pilots each, with newly promoted Squadron Leader Duncan Balden replacing Jock Martin.

There was also a night fighter section formed to counter the increasing number of night raids. The first night engagement took place on 13 August when a number of raids, carried out by single attacking bombers, took place late in the evening over a period lasting nearly two hours. Flying Officer Jock Barber was flying one of two Hurricanes scrambled to intercept the raids and spotted an SM.79 'coned' by searchlights to the south of the island. He was then able to make out the aircraft against the moonlight and pulled up underneath it, firing into its belly until it fell away.

The radar plot promptly disappeared but Barber was only credited with a probable victory at the time because no one had witnessed its demise. However, it later became known that the bomber did not make it back to its base and fell into the sea short of the Sicilian coast, and so Barber's success was later acknowledged to be the first aircraft shot down by a night fighter outside of Europe during the Second World War.[1]

With more aircraft than before, the squadron was usually scrambled using four fighters at a time, and sometimes six, to meet the daily air raids. Although this does not seem many, it was more than previously. Furthermore, the

---

1. Shores and Cull with Malizia, op. cit., p.52.

Hurricane was a far more capable fighter than the Italians had come up against before.

In response, the Italians also received reinforcements, including German-built Junkers Ju87 'Stuka' dive-bombers, which, with wailing sirens and devastating accuracy, brought a new fear to those in Malta. The Stukas operated with 96° Gruppo at Comiso and first appeared over Malta on 4 September when five aircraft arrived over Grand Harbour looking for merchant ships to attack. When none were seen they attacked Fort Delimara instead.

To counter the increasing number of raids, an early warning system, based on the RAF's success back home during the height of the Battle of Britain, was set up in Malta. Details of suspect radar plots detected high up on Dingli Cliffs were passed to Malta's War Headquarters at Lascaris beneath the Upper Barrakka Gardens in Valletta. From this underground complex of tunnels and chambers, built into the bastions overlooking Grand Harbour, the defence of Malta was co-ordinated and conducted. Down among the passageways and tunnels there were rooms for each of the fighting services, and from the RAF Operations Room a fighter controller would then ring down to the airfield to scramble the fighters. It was primitive compared to Fighter Command's set-up back home but it worked.

As far as the naval campaign was progressing, Somerville's return to Gibraltar towards the end of August was timed to prepare for another operation – Operation Hats. This had several objectives. Firstly, it would reinforce Cunningham's Mediterranean Fleet with more ships: the new radar-equipped aircraft carrier HMS *Illustrious*; the modernized radar-equipped battleship HMS *Valiant*; two anti-aircraft cruisers, *Coventry* and *Calcutta*; and four destroyers. These ships were designated Force F. Secondly, the operation would provide Malta with much needed supplies and, thirdly, the ships were to attack a variety of Italian targets along the way.

The operation began on the morning of 30 August with Somerville's Force H escorting Force F eastwards into the Med. It was the largest British fleet to enter the Mediterranean since the start of the war. The plan was for Force H to escort Force F as far as the Sicilian Narrows, after which ships of Force H would carry out a raid on Cagliari.

Meanwhile, at the opposite end of the Mediterranean, Cunningham's fleet had already sailed from Alexandria the evening before. Under its wings were four destroyers – *Jervis*, *Juno*, *Dainty* and *Diamond* – tasked with escorting the convoy going into Malta, designated MF2 and consisting of the Royal Fleet Auxiliary *Plumleaf*, carrying fuel, and two cargo steamship merchantmen, *Volo* and the much larger *Cornwall*, a cargo liner of 10,000 tonnes carrying anti-aircraft ammunition.

The passage to Malta was anything but straightforward. *Cornwall* suffered considerable damage during an air raid on the second day to the south of Crete when three bombs struck her, setting the ship on fire and killing the young second radio officer, 19-year-old Peter Chamberlain, and wounding several more of the crew. The explosions also caused major structural damage to the ship and flooded the engine room, causing her to heel to port. Those observing from the other ships could only watch and pray as *Cornwall* was on fire and listing.

On board the stricken *Cornwall* the crew bravely fought the fires to keep her afloat. As *Cornwall* dropped back, *Juno* dropped back with her in support but it looked like the merchantman was lost. But she was then seen to get underway once more, and after a couple of erratic circles she lurched after the convoy in an attempt to catch up.[2] It was a remarkable piece of seamanship by the skipper, Captain Pretty, and his crew. As *Cornwall* limped forward at less than 10 knots, the surrounding ships took station and nearly five hours after she had first been hit, the last of the fires were put out.

MF2 was still heading for Malta, albeit at a reduced speed, and during the morning of 2 September, *Volo* and *Plumleaf* sailed into Valletta under the escort of *Dainty* and *Diamond*. But the crippled *Cornwall*, now accompanied by *Jervis* as well as *Juno*, was lagging well behind. Her speed had dropped again as the merchantman limped towards port. Once within sight of Malta, two dockyard tugs hurried out to her assistance and the heavily listing *Cornwall* was towed into Grand Harbour; just two hours behind her consorts. Crowds had gathered along the dockside to welcome the ships into harbour, but it would not be the last time they would see a crippled merchant ship limping into Grand Harbour. It was merely a sign of things to come.

---

2. Woodman, op. cit., pp.67–9.

Soon after the arrival of *Cornwall* and her escorts, the ships of Force F approached from the west. Their transit had gone much as planned. Swordfish from *Ark Royal* had carried out an attack against Cagliari during the early morning of 1 September as planned and, with its aircraft back on board, the *Ark* then took up a course for the Sicilian Narrows. Later that evening the ships were halfway between the south-eastern tip of Sardinia and the western tip of Sicily when Somerville split his force into two. Force H turned north to prepare for a second attack on Cagliari before returning to Gibraltar, arriving safely two days later, and Force F continued south-eastwards towards Malta and to rendezvous with Cunningham's Mediterranean Fleet.

The two forces came together during the early morning of 2 September. Three naval ships – *Valiant*, *Coventry* and *Calcutta* – were all carrying supplies for Malta and sailed into Grand Harbour with four escorting destroyers in the aftermath of an air raid, while the rest of the Mediterranean Fleet waited to the south of the island.

In addition to offloading army and RAF personnel, the ships unloaded anti-aircraft guns with height-finders, replacement gun barrels, and thousands of rounds of ammunition for the island's Bofors and Bren guns. While the ships were unloading they came under air attack as the Italians tried desperately to destroy the warships and their stores, but all three survived intact and by early evening all had left Malta.

Cunningham now split his fleet. Tovey took the cruiser squadron northwards into the Gulf of Nauplia, Pridham-Wippell in *Malaya* took *Eagle*, *Coventry* and eight destroyers towards Alexandria via the south of Crete, and Cunningham, in *Warspite*, took *Illustrious*, *Valiant*, *Calcutta* and seven destroyers back to Alexandria via the north of Crete. All the ships returned safely to Alexandria on 5 September.

Operation Hats had been a success. One of its biggest bonuses was the courage shown by the civilian merchant sailors, particularly on *Cornwall*, who had withstood the hardships of running convoys in the Mediterranean; something that would be so important in the coming months if Malta was to survive.

Back in London, the success of Hats was welcome news for Churchill at a time when Britain was struggling to survive. Nonetheless, more aircraft were made available for Malta and were soon on their way to the island. A reconnaissance flight of three American-designed twin-engine Martin Marylands, led by an Australian, Flight Lieutenant 'Titch' Whiteley, arrived in Malta on 6 September. They had taken the extremely risky route of flying across enemy territory at night and had then flown over Sardinia to take some pictures of the island before landing in Malta to form 431 Flight at Luqa.

With a crew of three, the Maryland had been designed as a light-bomber and so it was well armed. Its top speed in excess of 300mph, combined with its manoeuvrability, made it an ideal reconnaissance aircraft. Among the newly arrived crews was a rather troublesome young pilot, 22-year-old Pilot Officer Adrian Warburton. Known as 'Warby', he was no stranger to Malta. The son of a naval officer, he had been christened on board a yacht in Grand Harbour and had been commissioned into the pre-war RAF. But Warburton had always attracted trouble, and so he had been sent on a navigational course before his transfer to Malta as an observer, and not as a pilot. Warburton would soon regain his pilot status when two of the Maryland pilots went down with the dreaded Malta Dog, a form of dysentery, and the flight was soon conducting photographic and maritime reconnaissance sorties from the island.

Things were coming together in Malta but the lack of submarines concerned Cunningham. The Axis were shipping large quantities of weapons and supplies to North Africa from Italian ports, and with Malta laying perfectly between the two, the island was an ideal location from where a submarine flotilla could inflict considerable losses on the enemy. Cunningham wrote to Sir Dudley Pound to express his concern about the whole submarine situation. He not only needed submarines but also needed an experienced submariner to run the submarine base at Manoel Island, a small island within Marsamxett Harbour.

The man chosen by the Admiralty was 39-year-old Commander George Simpson, known as 'Shrimp' due to his small and stocky stature, and then second-in-command of the Third Submarine Flotilla at Harwich. His new appointment would be Captain (S) Tenth Submarine Flotilla and so Simpson was briefed to make his way to Malta and to be ready to take over the base and a flotilla of the new Unity-class submarines at the turn of the year.

At a little over 500 tonnes, and with a surface speed of just 11 knots, the U-class was neither big nor fast compared to the Axis submarines. But since long-range patrols would not be necessary, a flotilla of these smaller submarines based in Malta would be ideal to disrupt the Axis supply lines to North Africa.[3]

Pending the arrival of the new U-class subs in the New Year, four of the larger T-class submarines were sent on ahead to Malta under the command of Lieutenant Commander Ron Mills, commander of HMS *Tetrarch*. *Tetrarch* would arrive in Malta during October, having completed her first Mediterranean patrol from Gibraltar. By the end of the year several T-class subs would be operating from Malta with some success, although they were often too large and unwieldy for the waters around the island and three of Malta's T-class subs were lost within weeks of their arrival.

With Malta having been under siege for fourth months, life on the island seemed to have settled down. The Italians were no longer bombing Malta with any great intensity and those on the island accepted the war with bravery and pragmatism. The Maltese had settled into something of a routine way of life where new laws and initiatives had been introduced, particularly regarding the use of oil, the most important commodity. For example, transportation was reduced to a minimum and so people moved back into the towns and cities once more, although there were still curfews enforced. For the military personnel there were even short periods of leave introduced so they could get away from their normal surroundings, even if it was for just one night.[4]

Living in such harsh conditions meant that diseases – such as Sandfly fever, scabies and Malta Dog – were always a problem and became a part of everyday life. It was already obvious that Malta was in for a lengthy siege but the people were coping well and the arrival of reinforcements provided the Maltese with a welcome reminder that they had not been forgotten.

Malta was getting stronger. Two cruisers of the Mediterranean Fleet, *Liverpool* and *Gloucester*, safely arrived in Grand Harbour to offload more

3. Spooner, *Supreme Gallantry: Malta's Role in the Allied Victory 1939–1945*, p.17.
4. Holland, op. cit., p.68.

troops and supplies before quickly putting to sea once more. Then, the turn of weather and heavy thunderstorms enabled a further convoy to reach Malta intact on 11 October. This was MF3 from Alexandria, which consisted of four merchantmen, including two Clan Line steamships, *Clan Macualay* and *Clan Ferguson*, as well as the *Lanarkshire* and Blue Funnel liner *Memnon*. They left the following day with the discharged vessels, *Plumleaf* and *Volo*, from the earlier convoy.

The Italian air raids continued into October but the fighters of 261 Squadron were always there to meet them and successes mounted. Malta's fighter pilots had now recorded more than seventy interceptions, including two by night, and had claimed a total of twenty-two Italian aircraft destroyed, with nearly as many again either probably destroyed or at least damaged. To add to these figures, Malta's anti-aircraft defences had claimed a further three enemy aircraft shot down with up to five more claimed as probably destroyed or damaged.[5]

Then, on 28 October 1940, came a sudden and dramatic change to the war in the eastern Mediterranean when Mussolini's forces invaded Greece. Britain was committed to protecting Greece and during the months ahead this would change the character of the war in the Med as British commanders competed for limited resources to support their military operations. But Churchill was still supporting the re-supply of Malta, stating that every time ships were passing through the Mediterranean then supplies and reinforcements should be dropped off at Malta. He had even gone as far as saying that Malta should be the first priority.[6]

With Churchill's unwavering support for Malta, more aircraft arrived on the island at the end of October. This time the new arrivals were twelve Wellington bombers. With the fighters of 261 Squadron migrating across to Takali, which was now operating as a full RAF station, the Wellingtons moved into Luqa where the airfield's proper runways and facilities were more suited for operating heavier aircraft.

---

5. Shores and Cull with Malizia, op. cit., pp.73–4.
6. Woodman, op. cit., p.83.

Malta now had a small bomber unit, initially called the Wellington Flight but soon to become 148 Squadron, as well as fighters and reconnaissance aircraft, but it would take some time for the Wellington ground crew and spares to catch up by sea. And so the manpower already on the island, at Hal Far, Luqa and at Kalafrana, where Sunderland flying boats of 228 Squadron had also been established, was spilt among all the various units.

There was a great feeling at Luqa on the night of 31 October when the Wellingtons took off for their first bombing raid; their target was Naples. It was such a momentous occasion that even Dobbie and Maynard turned up to witness the departure of Malta's first heavy bomber raid, although the laden Wellingtons struggled to get into the air.

But the joy of watching the Wellingtons depart for their first mission soon turned to tragedy three nights later when, on 3 November, two of the four over-laden bombers crashed just after take-off. The first, flown by 25-year-old Sergeant Raymond Lewin, sank shortly after getting airborne and crashed into open ground at Tal-Handaq and burst into flames. Lewin extricated himself from the wreckage and saw three of his crew climbing out of the escape hatch. Ordering them to run clear, Lewin then ran round the blazing wing, in which full petrol tanks were burning, and crawled under it to rescue his injured co-pilot. Despite his own injuries, Lewin dragged and carried his colleague some forty yards to take cover, with Lewin lying over his co-pilot to provide him with extra protection, just as the bombs exploded. This superbly gallant deed, for which Lewin was awarded the George Cross, was performed in the dark under most difficult conditions and in the certain knowledge that the bombs and petrol tanks would explode.[7]

The second Wellington crashed into houses on the outskirts of Qormi, killing a married couple, before the wrecked aircraft came to rest in a quarry, killing all the crew with the exception of one. The rescue workers were quickly on the scene and could hear moaning from inside the wreckage. In a desperate attempt to save the life of the one surviving crew member, a Maltese policeman, Carmel Camilleri, tied a rope around himself and was lowered into the inferno to lift the sole survivor out, disregarding the risk

---

7. *London Gazette*, 7 March 1941.

of exploding bombs. Camilleri bravely hauled the crew member to safety for which he was later awarded the George Medal; he was the only Maltese police officer to be so recognized.[8]

These losses were a severe setback to Malta's operations but the arrival of the Marylands had meant that it was now possible to further explore one of many ideas that had been under consideration for a while. With the senior Italian naval commanders showing little appetite to engage in a surface battle with the Royal Navy, it was becoming increasingly important to carry out a strike against the Italian fleet before the Germans decided to enter the Mediterranean war. Churchill, in particular, seemed to be growing impatient and had been prodding away at Cunningham to do more against the Italian fleet.[9]

During the early days of November, Adrian Warburton carried out a couple of long-range reconnaissance flights over the Italian naval bases at Taranto and Brindisi in southern Italy. These were dangerous missions as flying so close to the Italian mainland and over a main naval base attracted obvious attention from marauding fighters. During the first sortie, Warburton's aircraft had been intercepted by three CR.42s and during the attack his aircraft was hit. A round had grazed his chest, resulting in an initial loss of consciousness as he fell forward over the control column, and so his observer, Sergeant Frank Bastard, took over temporary control until Warburton had recovered enough to regain control. Bastard subsequently assisted Warburton, whose left arm was useless, by manipulating the throttle when landing back at base; it was an act that saw Bastard awarded the Distinguished Flying Medal.[10]

Warburton made a speedy recovery and five days later, on 7 November, he undertook another seven-hour reconnaissance flight over Taranto and Brindisi. Again, the Italian fighters were airborne to intercept but the Maryland had a fast turn of speed and escaped. Safely back at Luqa, Warburton reported that he had spotted five battleships with several cruisers and destroyers in the harbour at Taranto. Armed with this vital intelligence,

8. *Times of Malta*, 8 July 2012.
9. Woodman, op. cit., p.74.
10 *London Gazette*, 11 February 1941.

the Royal Navy commenced its next, and rather complex operation, and continued planning for a daring raid that was now just days away.

The complex naval operation was Operation MB8, made up of various forces and convoys to deceive the Italians into thinking that normal convoying was underway. It was made up of six forces – a total of two aircraft carriers, five battleships, ten cruisers and thirty destroyers, to protect four distinct supply convoys – and consisted of six distinct phases.

For Malta, the first phase, called Operation Coat, which left Gibraltar on 7 November, was a reinforcement convoy carrying troops and anti-aircraft guns for the island. It was made up of the battleship HMS *Barham*, two cruisers, *Berwick* and *Glasgow*, and three escorting destroyers, with more than 2,000 men from an infantry battalion, two field batteries, a light tank troop, and one light and two heavy anti-aircraft batteries; their heavy equipment would follow later on board a number of merchant ships. Protecting the convoy were the main ships from Force H: the carrier *Ark Royal*, the light cruiser *Sheffield* and three more destroyers that, as usual, would go as far as the mid-Mediterranean. During the transit to Malta, the *Ark*'s Swordfish were to carry out another part of the overall operation, called Operation Crack, an attack against Cagliari.

With the convoy underway, another convoy of three merchant ships, MW3, had already set sail for Malta from Alexandria on 4 November. The plan once the ships arrived in Grand Harbour was for convoy ME3 to make the return trip to Alexandria, and other merchantmen of convoy AN6 would head for Greece and Crete. All the ships bound for Malta, from both ends of the Med, arrived safely in Grand Harbour during the 9 November and 10 November, and by noon on 10 November Cunningham had received his reinforcements from the west.

The sixth piece of the MB8 jigsaw was Operation Judgement, an attack against the Italian fleet at Taranto. In his final reconnaissance of Taranto during the late afternoon of 11 November, which had been carried out at extremely low level in appalling weather conditions, and timed to coincide when HMS *Illustrious* was 170 miles from the Italian port, Warburton had spotted that a sixth battleship had arrived in harbour. This brought the reported number of Italian warships at Taranto to fifty or more, including the six battleships, fourteen cruisers and twenty-seven destroyers.[11]

That evening Cunningham gave the order to attack and during the night of 11/12 November 1940, twenty-one Swordfish of the Fleet Air Arm took off in two waves from the carrier *Illustrious* to attack the Italian fleet at Taranto. The now legendary attack has been well documented elsewhere, and is still celebrated by the Fleet Air Arm to this day. It was the first all-aircraft ship-to-ship naval attack in history and struck the Italian battle fleet while still at anchor in the harbour using torpedoes. In one night the Regia Marina lost half of its battleships, and the attack meant the surviving ships were transferred to Naples the following day to protect them from similar attacks. For his part in the reconnaissance of Taranto, Adrian Warburton was awarded the Distinguished Flying Cross.

After Taranto, Cunningham's belief that the Italians would be unwilling to risk their remaining heavy warships was quickly proven wrong. Just five days later, an Italian force comprising two battleships, six cruisers and fourteen destroyers were hassling a supply convoy to Malta. There was now a further problem, too. The Italians had laid mines off Malta, which provided another hazardous layer for ships to overcome when going in and out of the island, either to refuel or drop off supplies.

At this stage of the war no one side dominated the central Mediterranean but, in reality, it was proving far harder for the British to re-supply Malta than it was for the Axis powers to re-supply North Africa. After the earlier successful delivery of twelve Hurricanes off *Argus* in August, a second delivery was planned for mid-November. But unlike the previous delivery, the second, called Operation White, would end in disaster.

The *Argus* again sailed from Gibraltar with twelve Hurricanes and two Skuas on board, with a large escort of *Ark Royal*, three cruisers and seven destroyers. The Italian fleet was known to be at sea and so there was pressure to get the Hurricanes and Skuas off *Argus* as soon as possible. By dawn on 17 November, *Argus* was about 400 miles from Malta. If everything had been calculated correctly – wind, fuel, transit speed and altitude – the range

---

11. Holland, op. cit., p.75.

should have been sufficient for the fighters to make it safely to Malta with fuel to spare.

The plan was for the fighters to transit to Malta in two flights, each consisting of six Hurricanes led by a Skua. As things turned out, though, it took far too long to get the first flight airborne and then joined up heading for Malta. They also set off too low. The Hurricane's optimum cruising altitude was no lower than 10,000 feet but the formation set off at 2,000 feet and at 150mph, faster than the ideal speed for maximum range, and so the Hurricanes were already using more fuel. Furthermore, there was cloud and mist over the Med and the wind direction had changed, giving the fighters more of a headwind.

The Skua and Hurricanes pressed on but they were still forty miles from Malta when the first Hurricane ran out of fuel. The pilot baled out and was fortunate to be picked up by a Sunderland. Then a second Hurricane ran out of fuel, just minutes from reaching Malta. The pilot, Sergeant Bill Cunnington, was seen to bale out but he was never found. Only four of the Hurricanes and the Skua made it to Malta, although they all had just a few minutes of fuel remaining and the engine of one cut out before it even got off the runway.

But it was the second flight that suffered most. It had set off an hour after the first as Force H set course for Gibraltar at full speed. The flight missed an important navigational point, the Galite Islands off the coast of Tunisia, and so got hopelessly lost. One Hurricane after another fell out of the sky with the loss of all six pilots: 22-year-old Flying Officer Eric Bidgood; Flying Officer Pat Horton; 20-year-old Flying Officer James Walker; Flying Officer Raymond Clarke; 20-year-old Pilot Officer Robert Boret; and 20-year-old Pilot Officer James Horrox were all lost while the Skua crash-landed in south-west Sicily with the crew taken as prisoners.

With the second flight overdue, a Maryland, flown by Titch Whiteley, was sent from Malta to look for the aircraft but a five-hour search found no sign of any survivors. Operation White was a disaster and had resulted in a terrible loss of life. An official enquiry blamed the aircrew but it had been worse than that. The fleet's reluctance to take more risk and to get the aircraft closer to Malta was a factor, as was, of course, the bad weather. There had also been an obvious lack of co-ordination and co-operation between the RAF and the Royal Navy. It had cost Malta eight precious Hurricanes and, more importantly, the lives of seven pilots. The only positive thing to have come from Operation White was the fact that future ferry flights would never again be planned and conducted in such a manner.

Later that month there were, again, two large convoys sailing through the Mediterranean at the same time. These were the combined forces of Operation MB9 and Operation Collar. The main purpose of the eastern component, MB9, was to get three of Cunningham's ships – *Ramillies*, *Berwick* and *Newcastle* – all suffering from performance or technical problems, to the west of the Mediterranean while escorting four laden merchantmen of MW4 – *Memnon*, *Clan Ferguson*, *Clan Macaulay* and HMS *Breconshire* – as far as Malta. They set sail on 24 November, followed the next day by the battleships *Barham* and *Malaya*, the carrier *Eagle*, and the cruisers *Calcutta* and *Coventry* plus several destroyers. Cunningham sailed in *Warspite* with *Valiant* and *Illustrious* plus more destroyers, and the 7th Cruiser Squadron escorted a convoy to Suda Bay.

Simultaneously, Operation Collar, a small but fast three-ship convoy – *Clan Fraser* and *Clan Forbes* heading for Malta, and *New Zealand Star* heading for Suda Bay – set sail from Gibraltar on 25 November, escorted by two cruisers, *Manchester* and *Southampton*, with nearly 1,400 service personnel on board bound for Egypt, and the destroyers *Hotspur* and *Vidette* with four corvettes. Somerville sailed in *Renown* with his force made up of *Ark Royal*, the cruisers *Despatch* and *Sheffield*, and nine destroyers.

The Italians dispatched a strong naval force to intercept the eastbound convoy but were intercepted themselves by Somerville's fleet on 27 November in what later became known as the Battle of Cape Teulada (also known as the Battle of Cape Spartivento). The battle lasted an hour, although little damage was caused to either side, and by the following day, Somerville's ships were on their way back to Gibraltar, leaving the merchantmen and their escorts passing Cape Bon to rendezvous with Cunningham's ships.

The two Clan Line cargo ships, *Clan Fraser* and *Clan Forbes*, each grossing more than 7,500 tonnes, later sailed safely into Grand Harbour, and *Manchester* and *Southampton* joined Cunningham's fleet. The ships of MW4 also arrived in Malta unscathed, and another convoy of five empty merchant ships, ME4, including the patched-up *Cornwall*, headed east.

Meanwhile, in North Africa, the see-saw desert war between the British and Italians to gain control of the thousand-mile strip of sand between Alexandria and Tripoli had begun. Over the course of the next few weeks, the British Army would rout the vastly superior numbers of the Italian forces. As had been expected, Malta was now part of the desert war and it would remain so for the next two and a half years.

By the end of 1940, Malta's defenders had claimed thirty-one enemy aircraft shot down with many more claimed as either probably destroyed or damaged. Against these claims the Italian records confirm that twenty-seven aircraft (eighteen bombers and nine fighters) had been shot down by Malta's fighters and a further eight (five bombers and three fighters) by anti-aircraft fire; a total loss of thirty-five aircraft. For his contribution towards the island's defence, Flying Officer Timber Woods was awarded the Distinguished Flying Cross in December, his citation crediting him with five confirmed victories.[12]

There were now more than fifty aircraft based in Malta: sixteen Hurricanes and four Gladiators of 261 Squadron at Takali; sixteen Wellingtons of 148 Squadron at Luqa; four Sunderland flying boats of 228 Squadron at Kalafrana; twelve Swordfish of 830 Squadron at Hal Far; and four Marylands of 431 Flight at Luqa.[13]

The island had also been reinforced by the arrival of the 4th Royal East Kents, more guns and ammunition, as well as additional RAF ground crew. More than 3,500 men had arrived in Malta in the past few months. Although it would never seem to be enough, considering that Britain had been fighting for its own survival back home, it was a good start.

Malta had been given a chance. Furthermore, the sight of convoys arriving in Grand Harbour had raised the morale of the Maltese people. People had got used to, and adjusted to, the siege and their lives worked around the air raids, which, in the main, were now proving to be rather ineffective. The nightlife had returned and people were getting on with their lives, with the build-up to Christmas seeming almost like normal.

---

12. Shores and Cull with Malizia, op. cit., p.101.
13. Ibid, p.102.

HMS *Warspite* entered Grand Harbour on 22 December to a band playing and a guard of honour on the quayside. Cunningham stepped ashore to a hero's welcome. He was due to meet with Dobbie and Ford but he also wanted to see for himself just how the people of Malta were bearing up under the strain. Compared with the situation six months ago, there was cause for satisfaction and optimism. But that was soon about to change.

Chapter Six

The Illustrious Blitz

Hitler was becoming more than irritated at the way his ally, Italy, had failed to achieve success in North Africa and the Balkans, and had also failed to neutralize Malta's airfields and harbours. He was also concerned that a defeat of Italian forces in the desert would risk Italy making peace with the Allies or, even worse, changing sides.

Although he was initially reluctant to assist his ally, Hitler remained convinced that only German intervention in the Mediterranean and North Africa would keep the Italians in the war but, at this early stage, his initial plan was to send a small force to contain the situation rather than to expand it.

The first priority for the Germans was to neutralize Malta and the British Mediterranean Fleet to safeguard the Axis supply lines to Libya. Consequently, the Luftwaffe committed to the Mediterranean by transferring some 300 aircraft – Heinkel He111 and Junkers Ju88 twin-engine bombers, Ju87 dive-bombers and twin-engine Messerschmitt Bf110 fighters – from Norway to bases in Sicily and Libya to support the Italians.

It would not be long before the Luftwaffe was in action over Malta but the first air action over the island in 1941 took place on 9 January when Italian MC.200s carried out a low-level raid against Luqa. It was a clear attempt to destroy the Wellingtons of 148 Squadron that had been carrying out raids against the enemy harbours at Tripoli, Naples and Palermo. Also involved in the raid were Italian Ju87s, escorted by CR.42s, which attacked Kalafrana. The raiders were met by the Hurricanes of 261 Squadron from Takali. One successful pilot that day was 21-year-old Flight Lieutenant James MacLachlan. A former light-bomber pilot with a DFC, MacLachlan had arrived in Malta in November as the leader of the first wave of the ill-fated Operation White. He was flying one of the Hurricanes that engaged with the MC.200s attacking Luqa, and his two victims late that morning were his first two fighter successes of the war.[1]

Winston Churchill had always feared the Germans coming to the Italian's rescue by entering the Mediterranean war. The Luftwaffe's bombers were now settled at their new bases and ready to make their entry over the Mediterranean, and that appearance took place the following day, 10 January, when Ju87 dive-bombers crippled the carrier HMS *Illustrious*.

The carrier had been providing air cover for a convoy sailing to Greece and Malta as part of Operation Excess, a series of British supply convoys between Alexandria, Malta and Greece, when she came under attack during the early afternoon. Whereas all the convoyed freighters reached their destinations, *Illustrious* was hit six times in a matter of minutes and suffered severe damage when bombs penetrated the unarmoured aft lift, detonating beneath and causing devastation below and to the surrounding structure.

On the surrounding ships, men could only watch in horror as the great carrier took hit after hit, and often disappeared from view 'in a forest of great bomb splashes' as the near-misses pounded the water around her. With a fire having broken out and damaging the decks below, *Illustrious* was now dropping back from her station within the fleet, and also listing to starboard while steaming round in a circle.

On the bridge, Captain Denis Boyd and Rear Admiral Lumley Lyster, sent to the Mediterranean to take charge of Fleet Air Arm operations from the carriers, discussed the desperate situation. Knowing the Stukas would soon be back, they had no option other than to make for harbour in Malta nearly a hundred miles away; assuming, of course, they could first get the carrier back under control.

The first those in Malta knew of the attack on *Illustrious* was when a number of the carrier's Fairey Fulmar fighters, which had been airborne at the time of the attacks, arrived at Hal Far to refuel and rearm. One of the Fulmar pilots was Sub-Lieutenant Jackie Sewell of 806 Squadron. With his telegraphist air gunner, Denis Tribe, Sewell had shot down an SM.79 near the carrier earlier that morning but his Fulmar had been damaged by return

---

1. Shores and Williams, op. cit., p.418.

fire. Having landed back on *Illustrious*, he then changed aircraft and was back in action over the fleet again at the time the carrier had been hit.

After their stopover at Hal Far, Sewell and Tribe headed back out to sea to find their carrier, only to arrive in the area to find *Illustrious* with smoke pouring out of her as she limped towards Malta. Unable to do anything more, they returned to Hal Far once again. Another of the squadron's Fulmar pilots in action that day was 24-year-old Sub Lieutenant Stan Orr. The SM.79 he had shared to the west of Malta was his eighth success (five credited to him plus three shared), making Orr one of the Fleet Air Arm's most successful pilots in the Mediterranean; he would be awarded a Distinguished Service Cross (DSC) and Bar just a few weeks later after taking his total to at least six destroyed plus the same number again shared.

The *Illustrious* continued to make her way to Malta. She had suffered extensive damage to her steering gear and those below deck worked tirelessly and magnificently to combat the fires to ensure something of a steady course could be maintained, albeit at a reduced speed of 15 knots. *Warspite* and *Valiant* had also been hit but the damage was nothing compared to the carrier. With a second air raid detected by radar, and now with no air defence cover from *Illustrious'* fighters, Cunningham ordered his ships to close on the crippled carrier.

As enemy aircraft approached, the lookouts could see they were Italian SM.79s well above 10,000 feet. A huge barrage of anti-aircraft fire was thrown up from the fleet. Fortunately, the Italian pilots did not have the skill nor, perhaps, the courage to prosecute their attack to the level of the Luftwaffe's Stukas, and so the carrier escaped further damage.

Later that afternoon the Stukas were back but now the carrier's Fulmars had returned from Malta having again refuelled and rearmed. More determined than ever to protect their ship, the Fulmar crews fought magnificently to defend their carrier and only one Stuka made it through the gauntlet of fighters and heavy anti-aircraft fire. That one Stuka pilot, however, planted his 500kg (1100lb) bomb firmly into the aft flight deck. The bomb penetrated the armoured deck, bursting below and killing some thirty of the ship's company and reigniting the dying fires.

By early evening it looked as if all might be lost but Boyd refused to flood the magazines, an act that would have left the carrier utterly bereft of any defence. Boyd knew they were getting closer to Malta by the hour and even once there, the ship would still need to be able to fight. The Stukas would hardly go away just because the carrier was in harbour.

There was still time for one further air attack against the carrier before nightfall but the Italian SM.79s, this time carrying torpedoes, were gallantly driven off once more. Then, just before 10 pm, *Illustrious* limped into Grand Harbour, straddled by tugs and still burning in some parts of the ship, to undergo repairs.

Illustrious arrived alongside Parlatorio Wharf to the greetings of a large crowd and a band playing. It would have presented a marvellous sight but leaving the joy of having saved the mighty *Illustrious* to one side, it would have also been a sorry and morale-shattering sight. Fourteen aircraft had been destroyed, 126 men were dead and nearly a hundred more wounded and injured. As the carrier berthed, the lines of ambulances stood waiting with as many of the island's doctors and nurses that could be spared, while others waited in readiness at Malta's hospitals.[2]

It was a day that shook Malta. Until now, there had been some casualties along the way but nothing like this. Only two days before there had been joy when ships of the 3rd Cruiser Squadron, also part of Operation Excess, had safely dropped off 500 troops at Valletta who had arrived from Greece. But now that joy had turned to despair at the sight of the crippled carrier, with several of her crew dead and many more fighting for their lives.

It had probably been the deck armour that saved *Illustrious* from total destruction; few ships could have survived what the carrier had endured. But the carrier's fight for survival was far from over. With one of the Royal Navy's prize assets berthed in Grand Harbour and presenting itself as a relatively helpless target, particularly for enemy dive-bombers, those in Malta braced themselves for the onslaught that was surely to come.

The following morning there was no surprise when an Italian SM.79 appeared high above the harbour, presumably photographing the carrier, but it came as a welcome relief when no attacks took place that day. It appears the

2. Woodman, op. cit., pp.118–23.

carrier had remained undetected as the Luftwaffe mounted a raid against a Greek-bound convoy to the south-east of the island instead.

Those in Malta's dockyard worked tirelessly round the clock to repair *Illustrious*. She was a big and inviting target and so her upper surface was painted in an attempt to blend the ship in with the surrounding dockyard and to make her as difficult as possible to see from the air.

With the carrier hidden as best as possible, it took time for the Axis reconnaissance aircraft to spot her but once they did, on 13 January, bombs fell on her like never before when *Illustrious* came under an intense attack by Ju87s. But the defensive barrage put up by the anti-aircraft guns around the dockyard made accurate dive-bombing all but impossible. The bombs fell elsewhere and once again the carrier survived intact.

Three days later a much larger raid, consisting of nearly a hundred aircraft – Ju88s escorted by twenty Bf110s and Ju87s escorted by Italian CR.42s – took place. It was a huge attack and nothing like the people in Malta had experienced before. The raid took place mid-afternoon and was intercepted by just seven fighters (three Fulmars and four Hurricanes). Bombs rained down on the docks as the screaming sound of the Stuka dive-bombers brought more fear to those on the ground. Given the onslaught, it is remarkable that *Illustrious* was only hit twice. The ferocity of the anti-aircraft barrage and bravery of Malta's fighter pilots ensured that further damage to the carrier was limited, and ten enemy aircraft were claimed as destroyed.

The Germans returned in strength during the afternoon of 18 January. First they bombed Luqa and Hal Far in an attempt to destroy Malta's fighters, causing much damage to the airfields and the destruction of a number of fighters on the ground, before having another go at finishing off *Illustrious*.

The defenders launched eight fighters (five Hurricanes and three Fulmars) to intercept the main raid. George Burges, scrambled four times during the day, added a Ju87 to his total over Grand Harbour with two more reported as damaged. Two more Ju87s were shot down over the harbour by Eric Taylor, bringing his overall total in Malta to six and making him the island's top-scoring fighter pilot at the time, for which he would be awarded a DFC. There was also a Ju87 shot down by 21-year-old Sergeant Cyril Bamberger, his first victory over Malta, and another Ju87 was shot down above *Illustrious* by Sergeant Harry Ayre.[3]

It had been a remarkable effort by Malta's fighter pilots and anti-aircraft gunners to keep the raiders at bay, but it was not only *Illustrious* that was under attack in Grand Harbour. There was the Australian light cruiser HMAS *Perth*, sent into the harbour to provide additional anti-aircraft defence, and there was also the 11,000-tonne cargo liner *Essex*, part of Operation Excess, with her precious cargo including a dozen crated Hurricanes and 4,000 tonnes of ammunition. During one of the raids, a bomb passed through *Essex*'s deck, exploding in the engine room and killing sixteen of her crew, although, somewhat fortuitously, the unloaded ammunition did not explode.

Whether the Germans had become aware that repairs to the carrier were nearing an end is not known but the raiders returned again the following day, this time several times. The first raid, consisting of about forty bombers, took place early morning. Two hours later, twenty more Ju87s and a similar number of escorting CR.42s appeared to the north of Grand Harbour at about 10,000 feet. Then, soon after midday, a further formation of Ju87s were spotted to the north of Valletta at just 3,000 feet as they began their run-in to attack the carrier.

By now, Sergeant Fred Robertson was already flying his fourth sortie of the day. A former Fleet Air Arm pilot, Robertson had been in Malta five months having been among the first batch of Hurricanes to fly off *Argus* the previous summer. He soon spotted the enemy to the north of the harbour and picked on one of the Stukas, but it had already come off its target and was now running for home. Convinced he had shot it down, the first of four claims he made that day, Robertson was then pounced on by two escorting fighters. He promptly shot down one but a potential second success over Saint Paul's Bay could only be claimed as probable.[4]

The courage and determination of the Stuka pilots, as they dived relentlessly into the barrage of anti-aircraft fire over the dockyard, did not go unnoticed by the Hurricane pilots who were there to stop them from

---

3. Shores and Williams, op. cit., pp.103, 109, 159 & 581.
4. Ibid, p.520.

reaching their target. George Burges was in the thick of the action that day, adding two more Ju87s to his total over Grand Harbour, and like many of his colleagues could not help but admire the courage of the Luftwaffe pilots, later saying that the contrast between them and the Italians could not have been greater.[5]

Burges' claims that day were to be his last of the war. After a strenuous period of fighter operations he was transferred to Luqa to fly the Marylands before returning to the UK later in the year for a rest from operations. While flying from Malta he had been credited with seven enemy aircraft destroyed, two probably destroyed and six damaged.[6]

But the performance of that day, 19 January, belonged to James MacLachlan of 261 Squadron who was credited with four victories during the day, earning him a Bar to his DFC. Unsurprisingly, though, the Hurricanes had not had it all their own way and one aircraft was lost during the combat. Sergeant Eric Kelsey was last seen chasing a Ju87 into the anti-aircraft barrage but was not seen again; he was just 20 years old.

Remarkably, not one bomb hit *Illustrious* that day, despite the enemy's best attempts. However, being on the ground was not without its danger. After one attack an unexploded bomb lay in the rubble of Vittoriosa, and it was only the calmness and professionalism of a Royal Engineers bomb disposal expert, Sergeant R C M Parker, that prevented any further disaster; Parker was later awarded the George Medal.[7]

The air raids of 19 January were the last of a series of determined attacks against *Illustrious* that had spanned four days. Finally, on 23 January, under complete secrecy, and after a tremendous effort by the dockyard workers to complete the temporary repairs to her steering gear, *Illustrious* slipped out of Grand Harbour for Alexandria. She was escorted by four destroyers and was due to undergo further temporary repairs away from the barrage of air attacks. The Luftwaffe sent reconnaissance aircraft out over the Med to see if they could find the carrier but *Illustrious* escaped eastwards, arriving safely in Alexandria on 25 January. She would later sail to the United States for

---

5. Holland, op. cit., p.98.
6. Shores and Williams, op. cit., pp.158–9.
7. Shores and Cull with Malizia, op. cit., p.126.

permanent repairs and would be out of action for more than a year before resuming operations in the Indian Ocean; *Illustrious* would not return to the Mediterranean and Malta until mid-1943.

Although the mighty carrier had somehow survived all that the enemy had thrown at her, the loss of *Illustrious* was a huge operational blow for Cunningham. There had been further losses, too. The cruiser HMS *Southampton* was sunk off Malta on 11 January, with the loss of more than eighty lives, and the destroyer HMS *Gallant* was out of action having been towed into Malta after hitting Italian mines, with a further sixty-five lives lost.

The sustained period of enemy air attacks during the days before *Illustrious* left Grand Harbour had tested Malta's defences like never before. The dockyard had taken a pounding during the period that was later to become known as the *Illustrious* Blitz, but there seemed to be no limit to the degree in which the damaged dockyard could rehabilitate itself. The indefatigable and undefeated Wilbraham Ford and his men had done wonders.[8] However, the scene in and around Grand Harbour was one of devastation. Whether Malta could survive such an intense period of air raids again remained to be seen.

---

8. Woodman, op. cit., p.130.

Chapter Seven

Enter the 109s

The arrival in Grand Harbour of *Illustrious* on 10 January coincided with that of HMS *Upholder*, the fourth of the U-class submarines to arrive in Malta.

Commanded by the experienced submariner 29-year old Lieutenant Commander David Wanklyn, a tall, bearded and lean-looking man, *Upholder* sailed into Marsamxett Harbour to join *Upright*, *Utmost* and *Unique*. *Upright* had been the first of the new subs to arrive. Now under the command of 30-year-old Lieutenant Edward Norman, an experienced submariner with a DSC, she arrived a month before after a lengthy passage from the UK to Gibraltar and having completed her first Mediterranean patrol.

By the time *Upholder* sailed into harbour, *Upright* had already completed her first patrol from Malta and was now away again on a further patrol off Tripoli. *Utmost*, commanded by Lieutenant Commander Richard Cayley, had also arrived the previous month, but was undergoing repairs and would not be ready to undertake her first patrol until the beginning of February. Lieutenant Tony Collett's *Unique* had only just beaten *Upholder* to Malta by a few days. A fifth U-class sub, *Ursula*, commanded by Lieutenant Alex Mackenzie, was due to arrive in the next few days.

With the U-class submarines now arriving, things were looking up. George Simpson was already in Malta, having arrived from Alexandria just two days before *Upholder*, to take over command of the submarine base at Manoel Island, but there was still much to be done before it was ready to conduct operations. For the next few days Simpson's team scoured the naval base and dockyards to gather whatever equipment they could.

It was a quite remarkable effort and, on 24 January, *Upholder* set off for her first patrol. She returned just over a week later having expended all her torpedoes during three separate engagements against enemy supply ships heading for North Africa. Although her crew believed they had scored their first hits with two of the eight torpedoes fired, they had been unable to hang around to observe the results of their attacks. Like other submarine operations, *Upholder*'s stay in harbour would not last long as less than two weeks later she was back out at sea on her next operational patrol.

For those in Malta, the air raids were a daily occurrence again. The bombing had become so bad that Valletta and the Three Cities had again been evacuated, leaving only troops and members of the emergency services behind. Many of the locals found themselves back in one of the many shelters in the surrounding area. Every available space was used, even below ground in makeshift shelters cut into the rock.

Conditions in the caves were humid and damp, and with hundreds of people in one shelter, facilities were basic to say the least. The Maltese had done everything they could to improvise with beds and blankets, and there were occasionally electric lights rigged up in many of the shelters or candles flickering away, but there was no natural light, no running water and no toilets. The Maltese had to make the best of wherever they were sheltered but at least, in the main, they were safe.

The Maryland flight at Luqa had now been given squadron status and so Titch Whiteley's detachment became 69 Squadron, tasked with strategic reconnaissance missions over enemy ports and airfields in Sicily, Italy and Libya. Malta had also received additional reinforcements. Six Swordfish from *Ark Royal* were incorporated into 830 Squadron at Hal Far, and a further six Hurricanes and two Wellingtons of 38 Squadron arrived at the end of January.

There was also now a Spitfire on the island. It had landed in Malta following a photo-reconnaissance sortie over Turin and without enough fuel to return to England. With cameras fitted in the rear fuselage, the aircraft's wings had been modified and extra fuel tanks had been fitted, giving the aircraft a phenomenal range of 1,750 miles.

Maynard immediately made use of his latest asset by sending the Spitfire off on a reconnaissance sortie of Sicily two days later, although the aircraft's serviceability would be hampered because of a lack of spares. Unfortunately, the Spitfire would not last long as it was lost during a reconnaissance sortie over the Gulf of Genoa just two weeks after it had arrived in Malta.[1]

---

1. Shores and Cull with Malizia, op. cit., p.129 & p.139.

Meanwhile, the Wellingtons of 148 Squadron had continued to be a nuisance to the enemy. One notable raid was carried out on the night of 12/13 January against the Italian airfield of Catania, when ten Wellingtons pressed home a most determined attack from low level despite heavy anti-aircraft fire. One aircraft, flown by Flying Officer C M Miller, carried out four bombing runs over the target before returning to Luqa to refuel and rearm before heading back to the target for a second attack.

Two Wellingtons were lost that night and another crashed on landing back at Luqa, but the raid had caused significant damage to the enemy airfield with sixteen aircraft destroyed or severely damaged on the ground. Three of the Wellington crew members were awarded the DFC, including Miller, and so successful was the squadron proving to be that Wellingtons were being replaced when needed, with replacement aircraft flown in from other squadrons around the region.[2]

At the end of January 1941, Air Headquarters at Malta had more than seventy aircraft available on the island: twenty-eight Hurricanes and four Gladiators with 261 Squadron at Takali plus a detachment of Hurricanes at Luqa; nineteen Wellingtons of 148 Squadron, four Marylands and the one Spitfire at Luqa; twelve Swordfish of 830 Squadron and three Fulmars of 806 Squadron at Hal Far; and five Sunderland flying boats of 228 Squadron at Kalafrana.[3]

In the past four months more than forty enemy aircraft had been confirmed destroyed with many more claimed as probably destroyed or damaged. This brought the total number of enemy aircraft shot down since the start of hostilities over Malta to at least sixty-three destroyed.[4]

Little had been seen of the enemy during the last days of January, but February began with renewed air activity over Malta and so eight Hurricanes were moved to Hal Far. This not only spread the fighters across the three airfields to enable more to get in the air quicker but also reduced the risk of losing fighters on the ground.

_____

2. Ibid, p.119.
3. Ibid, p.134.
4. Ibid, p.143.

This new phase of aerial activity saw the introduction of the Messerschmitt Bf109 over Malta. Although it would be some time before the type would be introduced into the desert war in North Africa, a small detachment of 109s from the Luftwaffe's 7./JG 26 arrived at Gela in Sicily on 9 February under the command of its very capable young *Staffelkapitän*, 22-year-old Oberleutnant Joachim Müncheberg.

The vast combat experience of some of the 109 pilots, with men like Müncheberg, was completely at odds with many of the Hurricane pilots who were often experiencing air combat for the first time. Müncheberg, for example, had fought over southern England during the summer of 1940. He already had twenty-three victories to his name, for which he had been awarded the Knight's Cross, and was a masterful tactician.

The Bf109E would be a much more capable opponent than the Italian fighters had proved to be and when Müncheberg's yellow-nosed 109s first appeared over Malta during the late afternoon of 12 February it came as a surprise to the island's defenders.

One flight of Hurricanes, led by Flight Lieutenant Gerald Watson, had been scrambled to intercept what the pilots believed to be a handful of bombers approaching the island at 20,000 feet, but they suddenly found they were being bounced by three 109s. Led by Müncheberg, two Hurricanes were shot down in just a few minutes, one by Müncheberg, and a third returned to Malta badly damaged. One of the two Hurricanes shot down was that of Watson. His aircraft was seen to roll over on its back and plunge straight into the sea, killing Watson. The second pilot to be shot down, Pilot Officer David Thacker, was more fortunate. He baled out into Saint Paul's Bay and was later picked up by a motor launch; it had been his first encounter with the enemy.

The arrival of the 109s over Malta had an immediate and damaging impact on the moral of those defending the island. Although the Hurricane had proved more than a match for the Italian fighters, it was simply outclassed when it came to countering the 109s. Furthermore, Malta still had too few Hurricanes, as well as a shortage of fuel, to mount regular patrols and so the 109s climbed to height at leisure and arrived in the vicinity of Malta with height and tactical advantage. Even with the defenders having the benefit of radar, its limitations meant there was not enough warning time for the

Hurricanes to climb to sufficient height to engage the 109s before they arrived over the island.

The unwelcome yellow-nosed visitors were over the island again during the following two days. Then, on the morning of 16 February, James MacLachlan's luck ran out. He had added two more Ju88s to his score the week before, bringing his total to eight, but he now found himself bounced by an unseen opponent as he was pressing home an attack on four Messerschmitts. The 109 that had shot him down was flown by Müncheberg, the young German's twenty-sixth victim of the war. Fortunately for MacLachlan, he survived the encounter. He baled out of his Hurricane, but his left arm had been shattered by a cannon shell and so his forearm had to be amputated. As soon as he recovered, MacLachlan was evacuated back to England. He even returned to flying but was killed in 1943 at the age of just 24, by which time he had been credited with sixteen victories and had been awarded a second Bar to his DFC as well as a DSO.

The 109s had certainly made their mark. In what seemed like no time at all, 261 Squadron's strength was down to nineteen serviceable Hurricanes (from twenty-eight at the beginning of February) and thirty pilots available from a supposed squadron strength of forty-three. Then, during the early afternoon of 26 February, the Axis launched its biggest raid for more than a month when seventy aircraft – a mix of Junkers Ju87s and Ju88s, Heinkel He111s and Dornier Do17s – attacked Luqa.[5]

Scrambled to intercept them were eight Hurricanes led by Eric Taylor. The Hurricanes gained sufficient height to make their attack on the Stukas but the enemy fighters were soon on to them. These were Müncheberg's 109s and Italian MC.200s and as the main bomber force arrived over Malta virtually unscathed, four of the defending Hurricanes were shot down.

The attack against Luqa proved devastating. A number of Wellingtons were destroyed on the ground and there was extensive damage to hangars and other technical buildings at the airfield. It had also been a bad day for 261 Squadron. Pilot Officer Philip Kearsay was shot down and killed; he was just 20 years old. So too had 22-year-old Pilot Officer Charles Langdon.

---

5. Ibid, p.158.

But the biggest loss of all was 23-year-old Flying Officer Eric Taylor, Malta's leading ace with seven victories who had led the Hurricanes into action. He was last seen on the tail of a Stuka, although he was seen with a 109 on his own tail. Once again, the successful 109 pilot was Müncheberg; Eric Taylor was his twenty-eighth victim of the war.

For the next few days the defenders of Malta licked their wounds. The odds were heavily stacked against the Hurricane pilots whose chances of survival were now proving less than those who had fought the previous summer during the Battle of Britain. One *Staffel* of Bf109s was enough to cope with but then more 109s arrived over Malta during March. These were the 109s of Hauptmann Eduard Neumann's I./JG 27, which stopped off briefly in Sicily on their way to Libya and twice joined Müncheberg's 109s on operations over Malta.

The first time the two 109 units went into action together over the island was the afternoon of 5 March when they escorted a raid of sixty bombers. Once overhead Malta they engaged the defending Hurricanes before carrying out strafing attacks against any suitable targets they could find. Once again, the defenders fought hard but two Hurricanes were lost. In return, Hurricane pilots and anti-aircraft gunners made claims, and the wreckage of two Messerschmitt Bf110s spread over a wide area around Hal Far provided a welcome boost for all those who went to look.

More Hurricanes arrived later in the month to add to 261 Squadron's numbers. This time the new arrivals were from 274 Squadron based in Egypt and led by Flying Officer 'Imshi' Mason. These were welcome additions to Malta. Not only did it mean more Hurricanes but also the squadron had been involved in the First Libyan Campaign and so the pilots had already gained combat experience, with Mason, already wearing the ribbon of the DFC, being the leading scorer in the Middle East at the time, with at least thirteen confirmed victories.

But the new arrivals would find the fighting over Malta hard and one pilot, Flying Officer Johnny Southwell, was killed on 22 March, just five days after arriving on the island. That day also proved to be another bad one for 261 Squadron. The damage was done during the afternoon when ten Ju88s, escorted by a dozen 109s, approached Grand Harbour. Eight Hurricanes were scrambled to intercept the raid but five fell to the guns of the 109s. In addition to the loss of Southwell, Sergeant Richard Spyer, one of the pilots to have survived the disastrous Operation White in November, was also killed that day; he was aged 23. Also killed were Flying Officer Terry Foxton, Pilot Officer Tom Garland and 19-year-old Pilot Officer Dennis Knight.

Things were little better the following day. Capitalizing on their success the previous day, the raiders returned in force during the afternoon. Despite its losses the day before, 261 Squadron still scrambled fourteen Hurricanes, led by the squadron commander, Squadron Leader Robert Lambert, to intercept German Ju87s escorted by Italian MC.200s.

The Maltese watched anxiously as a fierce air battle raged above them once more. Lambert ordered his squadron into line astern and was the first to send one of the raiders, a Ju87, into the sea. Fred Robertson, awarded the Distinguished Flying Medal just four days before, shot down two more Ju87s over the village of Rabat but he had been hit by return fire and his Hurricane set ablaze, forcing him to bale out. He came down safely to the south of the village where he was greeted by triumphant locals; fortunately, his Hurricane was to be the squadron's only loss that day.

Although Robertson was out of the fight, the air battle continued to rage above as the Stukas were picked off by the marauding Hurricane pilots out for revenge from the day before. Among the pilots to make claims against the Ju87s were: Flight Lieutenant Teddy Peacock-Edwards, one of the flight commanders, with two; Pilot Officer Tony Rippon, who also claimed two; Sergeant Harry Ayre; and Pilot Officer Doug Whitney.[6]

With Malta struggling to survive, the war in the desert was about to take a dramatic turn following the arrival in North Africa of Major General Erwin Rommel. Rommel had arrived to take command of Germany's newly formed *Afrika Korps* to aid demoralized Italian troops after the British had driven the Italians out of Cyrenaica. In just two months, British forces had advanced more than 800 miles and destroyed an entire Italian army. But Rommel's forces had been allowed to build up rapidly, with most of the Axis convoys getting through to North Africa and then returning to their Italian ports unscathed.

---

6. Ibid, pp.171–3.

During the month of February 1941, the Axis landed nearly 80,000 tonnes of supplies, an increase of more than 60 per cent on the previous month, and this figure would improve yet again during the following month when nearly 93,000 tonnes of supplies were landed. Out of more than 230,000 tonnes of supplies destined for North Africa, only 5 per cent failed to reach their destination. Furthermore, during this same period, more than 50,000 enemy troops had gone ashore as part of Rommel's forces; 98 per cent of those who had boarded ships bound for North Africa had safely arrived.[7]

With the Luftwaffe continuing to build up its forces in Libya, most of its units left Sicily by the middle of March, leaving only Müncheberg's 109s to carry out nuisance raids against Malta. For the Malta-bound convoys, the departure of the German bombers was welcome news and meant the ships would get through to Grand Harbour largely unscathed.

On 19 March, four merchantmen – *Perthshire*, *Clan Ferguson*, *City of Manchester* and *City of Lincoln* – left Alexandria for Malta. They were given a large escort that now included the carrier HMS *Formidable*, which had arrived via the Suez Canal earlier in the month as a replacement for *Illustrious*. The convoy took place during the middle of Operation Lustre – the movement of 68,000 British and other Allied troops, vehicles and stores from Egypt to Greece – and all the merchantmen arrived safely in Malta, although two were attacked after their arrival in port.

Meanwhile, thousands of miles away at the UK's secret codebreaking centre at Bletchley Park, cryptographers had successfully broken the Italian naval codes for the first time and discovered that the Italian fleet, including one battleship and six heavy cruisers, plus a number of light cruisers and destroyers, was about to put to sea.

As with all Enigma codebreaking discoveries, the British were keen to prevent the enemy knowing that they had the ability to break codes. It was important, therefore, to ensure there was a plausible reason for the Royal Navy knowing just where and when the Italian fleet was putting to sea. In this case it was a carefully directed reconnaissance aircraft, and as a further piece of the deception plan, Cunningham had cleverly hidden his return to

7. Spooner, op. cit., p.36 & App IV.

Warspite before setting sail by making a surreptitious exit after dark from a golf club in Alexandria.

Trying to draw the Italian battle fleet out into the Mediterranean had always proved difficult but the skill of Bletchley's codebreakers now provided Cunningham with an opportunity to do just that. The major naval battle that followed, known as the Battle of Cape Matapan (because it was fought off the Cape on the south-west coast of Greece), was fought way to the east of Malta during March 27–29. The outcome was a resounding defeat for the Regia Marina; it was Italy's greatest defeat at sea with several ships sunk or severely damaged. The Royal Navy once again reigned supreme in the Mediterranean.

Naval personnel in Malta had little or no idea the battle was even taking place, such was the secrecy behind the discovery and the radio silence from Cunningham's ships, but news of the naval success soon spread across the island. The Maltese were in need of good news. There had been more than 200 air raid alerts during the past two months but news of the naval success coincided with a welcome lull in air activity over the island.

The reason for the lull was not immediately apparent but as it turned out, the Luftwaffe units in Sicily, including Müncheberg's 109s, were required to support Germany's invasion of Yugoslavia and Greece, which began on 6 April. The reduction in raids against Malta also coincided with the arrival of twelve more Hurricanes on the island. This time the aircraft were newer Mark IIs, flown off *Ark Royal* in early April under Operation Winch. In reality, the Mark II would offer the defenders little extra to what they had already and although it was more than a match against the MC.200, it was no better than the improved MC.202s that were now appearing over the island and made little difference against the 109s.

Among the new arrivals were Flight Lieutenant Peter 'Boy' Mould, who had led the first flight of six Hurricanes and would now lead 261 Squadron's C Flight. Mould had been credited with the RAF's first victory of the war in October 1939 while serving with 1 Squadron in France and had since added at least six more to his total, for which he had been awarded the DFC. Another to have arrived in Malta was Flying Officer Innes Westmacott, who had led the second flight of Hurricanes. With two victories while serving with 56 Squadron, he was now returning to operations having recovered from burns sustained the previous August during the Battle of Britain.

The new arrivals meant that 261 Squadron now gave a handful of pilots a rest and sent them to Egypt. But the air raids soon resumed and there were losses among the squadron, including five Hurricanes shot down on 11 April, with the loss of two pilots, as the Stukas and Müncheberg's 109s appeared over Malta once more.

The intense period of air attacks during the first quarter of 1941 had taken its toll but morale on the island was far from broken. A certain feeling of defiance had set in. In between the air raids people continued to go about their daily business as best they could. Malta's defences had been swelled by the arrival of more supplies and ammunition from two recent convoys. New anti-aircraft gun emplacements had been erected and the Royal Malta Artillery had incorporated local gun batteries, such as the Dockyard Defence Battery that had been established during the previous months. Furthermore, the Volunteer Force had become the Home Guard, based on the British organization back home, and all men between the ages of 16 and 56 were now liable for conscription, although, in reality, many had volunteered long before.[8]

Although Malta had a certain amount of food reserves, rationing was now introduced. Items such as coffee and sugar became luxuries and there was a severe lack of fuel. There was fruit, though, from the many citrus trees on the island, and farmers did what they could to produce large crops. But food had become a major concern. In fact, it was becoming the primary concern. Without food Malta could not survive and a lack of it meant the Maltese might give up their will to fight. After nearly a year of hostilities, Malta was now well and truly an island under siege.

8. Holland, op. cit., p.137.

Chapter Eight

The Arrival of 249

While food was desperately needed in Malta, so too was oil and fuel. On the evening of 19 April 1941, four empty Merchantmen – *Clan Ferguson*, *Perthshire*, *City of Lincoln* and *City of Manchester* – slipped out of Grand Harbour with their four-destroyer escort and bound for Alexandria once more. Inbound was the fast supply ship *Breconshire* laden with much-needed oil and aviation spirit for Malta.

At the end of April, Grand Harbour was suddenly full of ships when the 5th Destroyer Flotilla, commanded by Captain Lord Louis Mountbatten in HMS *Kelly*, arrived. With *Kelly* were five other destroyers, a light cruiser and a minelayer, all carrying supplies for Malta.

The presence of Mountbatten's ships highlighted both the problem and the value of Malta. It underlined the utility of the island as a strategic oiling port for naval ships to stop and refuel but the cost of maintaining that facility was extremely high in resources. The Malta convoys, although vital to the island's defenders and the Maltese people, were simply part of a far greater convoy system, and Mountbatten's destroyers provide timely evidence that Malta seemed to be sliding down the list of priorities. His ships were intended to relieve the Malta Strike Force but were soon diverted elsewhere and so their brief presence at Valletta merely attracted more heavy bombing raids.[1]

Not all attempts by merchant ships to reach Malta were successful, nor were they part of large convoys. Such was the desperate state of Malta that it was decided to try to supply the island by means of a clandestine passage by unescorted merchant ships. There were always several small vessels passing along the North African coast and so the idea was possible but also extremely risky.

---

1. Woodman, op. cit., p.164.

Sadly, the first of these daring passages, called Operation Temple, ended in disaster. The plan was for the steamer *Parracombe* to travel unescorted from Gibraltar under the disguise of a Vichy French merchantman. The hope was that she could slip unnoticed through the western Mediterranean by hugging the French North African coast, as if bound for Sfax. She would then pass the Cape Bon peninsula in north-eastern Tunisia and make a final dash for Malta, receiving fighter protection for the last fifty miles.

It was a risky and, with hindsight, careless plan. Tragedy struck east of the cape in the early hours of 2 May when *Parracombe* struck a mine, detonating the ammunition being carried on board for Malta. Although some of the crew survived and were later picked up as prisoners of war, many had been killed. Not only was the ammunition bound for Malta lost but also *Parracombe* had taken with her to the bottom her vital cargo, including twenty-one crated Hurricanes with all their spares.

Fortunately, though, more Hurricanes had made it safely to Malta as the re-supply runs to the island, known as Club Runs, were generally proving a success; albeit, they were proving heavy on resources. This time twenty-four of the fighters had flown off *Ark Royal* on 27 April under Operation Dunlop, led by the extremely experienced Wing Commander 'Bull' Halahan. All but one of the fighters arrived safely.

Also arriving in Malta that day were six Blenheim light-bombers from 21 Squadron, led by Squadron Leader Les 'Attie' Atkinson, an experienced pilot with a DFC and Bar. The Blenheims arrived from England via Gibraltar. They had come from 2 Group, Bomber Command, on a trial basis to see whether they could operate effectively from the island. The man behind the idea was the group's senior air staff officer, Group Captain Hugh Pughe Lloyd. These new and welcome additions were to operate from Luqa and it now meant that Malta had a daytime anti-ship capability.

The Blenheims were briefly joined by thirteen Beaufighters of 252 Squadron. The Beaufighters were on their way to Egypt but were temporarily held on the island to work with the Blenheims. One example of the two units operating together was on 7 May. An Axis supply convoy bound for North Africa had been spotted by one of Malta's Marylands and was successfully attacked by a mixed force of three Beaufighters and five Blenheims.

Apart from being horrified at the conditions on the island, compared to their purpose-built airfields back home, the Blenheim crews returned to England to report that it was perfectly feasible to operate from Malta. The Blenheims had taken part in a number of raids from the island, losing just one aircraft, and the post-detachment report led to two important decisions. One was that various Blenheim squadrons from 2 Group would take it in turns to spend a nominal two months or so in Malta. The second was that Hugh Pughe Lloyd would be promoted direct to the rank of air vice-marshal and sent to Malta as the new air officer commanding. With Atkinson promoted to wing commander and given command of 82 Squadron, it was understandable that his squadron would be the first to provide aircraft and crews. And so in early June, his squadron picked up some tropicalized Blenheims and headed for the Med.[2]

For 261 Squadron, the new arrivals allowed further changes to be made to the squadron's establishment so that some of the long-serving pilots could be given a rest. Robert Lambert handed over command to Squadron Leader Charles Whittingham and Sergeant Reg Hyde, a Kiwi with five confirmed victories over Malta, was rested and posted back to the UK. Also to be rested from operations was Fred Robertson, still recovering from his injuries sustained a couple of weeks before; he was also to return to the UK via Egypt. Robertson had performed magnificently over Malta, having taken part in nearly 200 interceptions and credited with ten victories.

With so many Hurricanes now on the island, about fifty in all, 185 Squadron was re-formed at Hal Far under the command of Boy Mould on his promotion to the rank of squadron leader. His pilots were largely taken from C Flight of 261 Squadron with its Hurricanes spread between Hal Far and Takali.

For a brief period in May, Malta had two Hurricane squadrons until 185 took over responsibility for Malta's air defence from 261 Squadron; the latter briefly disbanding before being resurrected in Iraq two months later. However, the change in number plate was purely academic. The fact that it was now 185 Squadron defending Malta rather than 261 made no

---

2. Spooner, *Faith Hope and Malta GC*, p.39.

difference to the air war over the island. The Axis raids were relentless and the skirmishes with Müncheberg's 7./JG 26, and other Luftwaffe units stopping off briefly in Sicily, would continue until late May and would only end when the 109s were transferred to North Africa.

Elsewhere for the British, the campaigns in the rest of the Mediterranean and North Africa were, on the whole, not going well. Germany had invaded Greece but the British intervention there had been a disaster. This, in turn, impacted on the war in the desert. With so many British forces transferred to the Greek campaign, the British Eighth Army in North Africa had been weakened to the point that Rommel's forces had surrounded the vital port of Tobruk and had succeeded in pushing back the depleted British forces to Sollum on the Egyptian border.

Cunningham felt that he was fighting the war on two fronts. Fighting the Axis forces in the Mediterranean was relatively clear and straightforward but the battle with the key decision makers back in London, less so. With Malta reasonably safe, he was under increasing pressure to score greater success against the Axis convoys re-supplying Rommel's forces in North Africa.[3]

Cunningham knew the best way of achieving this was from Malta but his surface ships lacked air cover to protect them by day, although they did enjoy some success at night. For example, one night in mid-April the 14th Destroyer Flotilla, operating out of Malta under the command of Captain Philip Mack, attacked an escorted enemy convoy of five merchant vessels, mainly German, and sank the lot, although one of Mack's destroyers was lost during the attack. There were also the RAF Wellingtons and Blenheims, as well as the Fleet Air Arm's Swordfish, all doing their bit. Carrying a combination of bombs, mines and torpedoes, they struck at the convoys, and Malta's submarines were also making their mark against the Axis ships sailing between Italian ports and North Africa.

However, successes had been relatively few and far between. *Upholder*, for example, only scored its first sinking on 25 April, an Italian freighter of 5,000 tonnes, three months after it had arrived in Malta. But the Tenth Flotilla had now expanded to include Lieutenant Ed Tomkinson's HMS *Urge*, HMS *Union*

---

3. Holland, op. cit., p.141.

(Lieutenant Robert Galloway), HMS *Undaunted* (Lieutenant James Livesey), HMS *Usk* (Lieutenant Godfrey Darling) and HMS *Unbeaten* (Lieutenant Edward Woodward). The subs would need to up their game but, to be fair to the commanders and their crews, they had up to now been restricted in where they could carry out operations. Furthermore, the U-class subs had many disadvantages, not least their lack of speed, and so they struggled to catch convoys if unable to carry out a perfect interception. And even when the subs had got into a position to fire, hits did not always result in a sinking.

As the submarine crews became more familiar with operating in the region and the pattern of the Axis convoys, as well as working to the submarine's advantages, rather than to be limited by its disadvantages, more successes followed. On 1 May, Wanklyn's *Upholder* sank two German freighters totalling 10,000 tonnes, although both were northbound and on their way home at the time.

Wanklyn's patience and persistence would pay off soon after when, late on 24 May, *Upholder* was patrolling off the coast of Sicily. Wanklyn sighted a southbound enemy troop convoy strongly escorted by destroyers. The fading light made observation by periscope difficult but a surface attack would have meant his submarine would easily have been seen. Furthermore, *Upholder*'s listening equipment was out of action, but in spite of these handicaps he pressed on with his attack at short range.

Having worked the submarine into a favourable position, Wanklyn took *Upholder* closer to make sure of his target. Fully aware of the risk of being rammed by an escorting destroyer, he continued to press on towards the enemy troop ships. Picking one, the 18,000-tonne *Conte Rosso* with nearly 3,000 enemy troops on board, he fired his torpedoes. The troop ship sank with the loss of nearly half of those on board. The enemy destroyers at once made a strong counter-attack and during the next twenty minutes dropped thirty-seven depth charges in an attempt to destroy the submarine. It was hard to get away but with greatest courage, coolness and skill, Wanklyn took *Upholder* clear.[4]

4. Citation for Victoria Cross awarded to Lieutenant Commander Malcolm David Wanklyn RN, 3rd Supplement to *London Gazette* 35382 Page 7103 dated 12 December 1941.

It had been a brilliant and daring night attack by Wanklyn. The troop ship had been travelling at more than 20 knots, twice the speed of *Upholder*, and had been escorted by a number of destroyers. Wanklyn could proudly take his submarine and crew back into Marsamxett Harbour with her 'Jolly Roger' flag blowing in the breeze, to the delight of those who were there to welcome her home.

But it was not all good news for the submarine crews; far from it. Operating in the Mediterranean was extremely hazardous and there were soon losses among the U-class community. Both *Usk* and *Undaunted* were reported missing in May after failing to return from patrols.

The number of Luftwaffe aircraft in Sicily peaked during May 1941 with nearly 250 on the island[5] but there was welcome news when Malta's Maryland crews reported them leaving their bases on the island. The reason for their departure this time was because the Luftwaffe's units in Sicily were needed to support Hitler's invasion of the Soviet Union, now just a month away.

In Malta, the news of the Luftwaffe's departure from Sicily was most welcome and coincided with the planned arrival of more RAF fighters on the island as more reinforcements were already on their way to the Mediterranean and Middle East. Furthermore, the reinforcements this time were three well-established fighter squadrons – 213, 229 and 249 – with many pilots with combat experience, and they were due to arrive in Malta from two carriers, *Ark Royal* and *Furious*, sailing from Gibraltar.

The carriers, with forty-eight Hurricanes on board, were part of a big convoy provided by Force H, under Operation Splice, which included a third carrier, HMS *Eagle*. Not all the Hurricanes were destined to stay in Malta. Only 249 Squadron, led by Squadron Leader 'Butch' Barton, was earmarked to stay on the island (to replace 261 Squadron), and the other two squadrons were to carry on to Egypt after a quick stopover. In addition to 249, the guiding Fulmars would also be staying in Malta; their role to carry out night intruder operations over Sicily.

---

5. Shores and Cull with Malizia, op. cit., p.106.

249 Squadron boasted some of the RAF's most experienced fighter pilots, many of whom had been with the squadron for a year or so and had fought during the Battle of Britain. Barton, a 24-year-old Canadian with a DFC for at least six confirmed victories, had been in command for six months. Also going to Malta was one of the RAF's finest young fighter pilots, Flight Lieutenant Tom Neil. Known as 'Ginger', 20-year-old Neil was already one of the squadron's flight commanders with a DFC and Bar for his eleven victories so far. Other long-term squadron pilots on their way to Malta were Flying Officer John Beazley, aged twenty-four with two victories, Flying Officer Pat Wells and Pilot Officer John Crossey, both South Africans. All three had been with the squadron throughout the Battle of Britain. Then there were others who had joined 249 after serving with other squadrons during the hectic summer of 1940. These included Flying Officer Ernie Cassidy, Pilot Officer Tommy Thompson and newly commissioned Pilot Officers Charlie Palliser and Jack Mills. With two victories already, Palliser was now with his third fighter squadron, having served as a sergeant pilot during the Battle of Britain, and Mills had also served as a sergeant pilot during the battle and credited with three victories. And so the list went on.

For 249's pilots, the journey had started at North Weald more than a month before after being warned to prepare for service in the Middle East. At that stage Malta had not been mentioned but the pilots were told to prepare to fly their Hurricanes, fitted with long-range external fuel tanks, off an aircraft carrier.

Flying a Hurricane off a carrier and then transiting over a long distance in a hostile environment was to be a new experience for them all. To prepare the pilots, two Hurricanes equipped with external fuel tanks, giving the aircraft an extra eighty-eight gallons of fuel, arrived at North Weald so that the pilots could become familiar with the fit before leaving for service overseas. Then, after a period of leave, the pilots were told to report to London's Euston railway station for the journey to Liverpool where they boarded HMS *Furious* for the passage to Gibraltar.

The pilots arrived in Gibraltar on 18 May. Meanwhile, the squadron's ground crew were on their way to Egypt via the Cape of Good Hope and the Suez Canal. At Gibraltar the Hurricanes and pilots were transferred to

Ark Royal and the force soon set sail. By dawn on 21 May the ships were in a position for the fighters to fly off for Malta.

The first group, led by Barton, initially had to turn back after the oil tank of the guiding Fulmar split but a relief aircraft was flown off the carrier and the formation reached Malta safely. The second group was led by Ginger Neil. With the first group on their way, his gaze was fixed on the flight deck mechanic holding the all-important wand. He later recalled what it was like to take off from a carrier for the first time:

> *'Then the wandsman again, waving urgently and beckoning in exaggerated gestures. My turn! My mouth dry, I opened up and taxied forward, straightening up on the centre-line. The wands gyrating, urging me to rev up. Up! Up! Then suddenly, with a sweep of the arm – Down! I was off! I set off down the deck at a smart walking pace, my Hurricane feeling ridiculously light. The island drifted by, faces gawping. At this rate I would be airborne in seconds. This really was a stroll! A moment later I was in the air, despite the extra 88 gallons of fuel, the deck dropping away beneath.'*[6]

Neil was on his way but his formation had problems from the start. While transiting at low level, they had lost sight of their guiding Fulmar as it suddenly pulled up and accelerated away. At that stage they had already been airborne for nearly an hour. Neil decided to orbit for a few minutes and after it became obvious they would not resume visual contact with their guide, he took the formation back west, either to resume contact with the fleet or, if that was not possible, then he would take them back to Gibraltar. As it happened, the ships were sighted and a second guiding aircraft launched but the Hurricanes were now a hundred miles further from Malta than they should have been and on the extreme limit of their range. Fortunately, the rest of the transit went well and after five and a half hours in the air, all the Hurricanes reached the island safely, with Neil taking his section to Luqa and the others landing at Takali and Hal Far.[7]

---

6. Cull, *249 at War*, p.66.
7. Ibid, pp.65–7, and taken from memoirs and log book of Squadron Leader P.H.V. Wells DSO.

The Hurricanes had landed in the middle of an air raid and it was only then that 249's pilots learned they were to stay on the island. As with ferry pilots before them, the news came as a shock. With their ground crew and equipment on their way to Egypt, the pilots had nothing with them. Worse news was to follow after the pilots had been taken by bus to Takali where they found out that the Hurricanes they had so carefully nursed all the way to Malta were to be flown on to Egypt by others and that they would be taking over 261 Squadron's old and rather battered Hurricanes instead.

The pilots had arrived at Takali to find the facilities basic to say the least: a few chairs and a couple of tents with a telephone providing the only link to Lascaris and the outside world. The squadron was then split into two flights, with Barton leading one and Neil the other, and a roster arranged with 185 Squadron so that pilots could be given rest in between their periods of standby.

The new arrivals were still getting used to life on the island when Müncheberg's 109s carried out a strafing attack against Takali during the early afternoon of 25 May. It came at an unfortunate time for 249 as it was the squadron's first period of readiness on the island, and the first the pilots knew of the attack was when the airfield's air raid siren started wailing. Pat Wells later recalled:

> '*This was our first readiness in Malta and whilst sitting in the crew room were astonished to hear the air raid sirens howling. In the UK we had always been airborne before the sirens sounded. We rushed out to our aircraft and got ready for the scramble, which never came. I noticed Ginger Neil get out of his aircraft obviously to go to the telephone. I am fundamentally lazy and decided that we would inevitably be scrambled, so it was less effort to remain in my aircraft and wait for it, helmet on and listening to the R/T. The next thing I saw was people running. I could still not hear anything due to my helmet, and on looking round saw the 109s starting their dive on the airfield.*'[8]

---

8. Ibid, pp.68–9, and taken from the personal memories of Squadron Leader P.H.V. Wells DSO.

One of the 109s was heading straight for Wells but it was too late for him to do anything. While his ground crew fled, Wells was left stranded in his cockpit:

'I tried to start the engine but the airman on the starter battery trailer had fled, so I could not do a thing except huddle in the cockpit, waiting for the sensation of being hit.'[9]

His Hurricane was hit and in no time at all was on fire. The burning and the sound of ammunition exploding hastened his exit from the aircraft but it was only when he fell to the ground that he realized he had been hit. Wells recalled:

'Only when I got to the ground and tried to walk off did I realise that I had a bullet through the top of my right ankle. The ambulance came and I was filled with delicious brandy, but was instantly sick when I got to hospital.'

Pat Wells' war in Malta started in a hospital bed at Imtarfa Hospital and he would not fly again for two months. The raiders had arrived undetected, having flown in beneath Dingli's radar cover, and caught 249's pilots by surprise. Two of the Hurricanes were destroyed and two more had been left burning and irreparable. It had been a bad start to 249's war in Malta.

Fortunately, though, it would be the squadron's only encounter with Müncheberg's crack unit as it was to be the latter's last appearance over Malta; 7./JG 26 was the last fighter unit to leave Sicily, although they were destined for North Africa rather than the Eastern Front. During its time operating from Sicily in the air war over Malta, Müncheberg's small force had been a complete nuisance to the island, claiming nearly fifty victories without a single loss.

Elsewhere, Hitler had launched Operation Mercury, his assault on Crete, during the morning of 20 May. The fact that the Germans carried out an airborne invasion of Crete was, for Malta, a stroke of luck. An

---

9. Ibid.

airborne invasion of Malta had been considered alongside Crete but, for the Germans, it could only be one or the other at that time. Many within the German High Command had favoured an assault against Malta because of its strategic importance. But Crete was also strategically important and seemingly favoured by Hitler.[10]

The Battle of Crete was unprecedented for a number of reasons, largely because it was the first mainly airborne invasion in military history and, therefore, the first time that German paratroopers had been used on a large scale. During the days that followed, Cunningham's fleet took a pounding. The Luftwaffe reigned supreme over Crete and its surrounding waters, and the decision to evacuate Allied troops from the south of the island at the end of the month resulted in the loss of a number of the Royal Navy's ships.

But despite its successes in Crete, heavy casualties suffered by the German paratroopers led to Hitler forbidding any further large-scale airborne operations. This meant that Malta was safe from any future airborne assault, not that anyone on the island would have known that at the time. But for the Axis convoys it meant they no longer had to run the gauntlet past Malta. The ships could instead head eastwards and then swing south towards their destination under the Luftwaffe's protective umbrella from Crete.

There was now little Cunningham could do to prevent enemy supplies from reaching Rommel's forces other than to rely on Malta's aircraft and submarines. Furthermore, the Luftwaffe's presence in Crete gave him the additional problem of having an enemy aerial threat on Malta's eastern flank, with the sea route from Alexandria now enfiladed by enemy air bases in both Crete and North Africa. To send convoys to the besieged island from the east would surely court disaster.

---

10. Holland, op. cit., p.157. The supreme command of the German Armed Forces, the *Oberkommando der Wehrmacht* (OKW), had considered an airborne invasion of Malta during the spring of 1941.

Chapter Nine

Hitting Back, June to November 1941

The beginning of June saw Sammy Maynard replaced by Hugh Pughe Lloyd as air officer commanding Malta. Lloyd's military career had started as a Royal Engineer sapper during the First World War but he had been with the RAF as a bomber pilot since its outset in 1918, and by the outbreak of the Second World War he was a group captain. As a staff officer within Bomber Command it had been his idea to send Blenheims to Malta and he was now the ideal man to take over the running of the island's air war.

Lloyd arrived in Malta facing a quite different task to his predecessor. Whereas Maynard had started from a position of nothing, the combination of Malta's build-up of aircraft and the departure of the Luftwaffe from Sicily meant that Lloyd's units would now take a more offensive role in the Mediterranean. Furthermore, even more fighters were on the way to Malta with the next Club Run, called Operation Rocket, essentially a re-run of Splice, taking place during the first week of June.

The operation brought thirty-five more Hurricanes and eight Blenheims to Malta at a time when air-to-air activity over the island had reduced. The Luftwaffe's departure for the Eastern Front had left the Mediterranean air war in the hands of the Italians, for the time being at least. Nonetheless, there were still raids and 249 Squadron's first victory in Malta was claimed by Butch Barton on 3 June; his victim, an SM.79 near the island of Gozo, was the first of his five victories while in Malta.

Little was seen of the Italians over the next few days and this valuable respite gave 249's pilots the chance to settle down. As well as mounting the fort by day, 185 Squadron took over defence of the island at night with some degree of success. During the early hours of 6 June, 21-year-old Flight Lieutenant Pat Hancock, one of 185's flight commanders, was patrolling between Grand Harbour and Kalafrana at less than 2,000 feet when he spotted an enemy bomber part-illuminated by Malta's searchlights and part-silhouetted by the moonlight. Hancock identified the intruder as a Heinkel He111 and manoeuvred to attack. His tracer rounds struck his target, but the raider was not seen to crash and so he could only make a claim of having probably shot it down.

In addition to 185 and 249 Squadrons, Lloyd now had Hurricanes of 46 Squadron to add to his order of battle. The new squadron, led by Squadron Leader Sandy Rabagliati, another veteran of the Battle of Britain with a DFC, had been on its way to Egypt but its fighters were retained in Malta and spread between Hal Far and Takali.

Rabagliati was soon adding to his seven earlier successes of the war. During the squadron's first encounter with the Italians in the early morning of 11 June, he shared the destruction of an SM.79 to the east of the tiny outcrop of Filfla. Unfortunately, though, one of the squadron's long-term and most experienced pilots, Flight Lieutenant Norman Burnett, was shot down and a subsequent search as far as the coast of Sicily failed to find him.

Rabagliati added a CR.42 to his total the following day, a day during which two engagements were fought over and around Grand Harbour. In the early morning eighteen Hurricanes were scrambled, nine each from 46 and 249, to intercept a reconnaissance SM.79 escorted by fifteen MC.200s. Then, during the early afternoon, CR.42s were intercepted near the harbour and it was during this raid that Rabagliati made his claim, although one of his pilots, Sergeant Norman Walker, was lost during the action. As soon as Rabagliati had landed and refuelled, he was off again to search for Walker but could find no trace.

Sandy Rabagliati was an excellent squadron commander and would become one of Malta's finest fighter pilots of the war. Despite these early losses, he was fortunate to have so many good young pilots around him. Two of them had arrived in Malta with him. These were 21-year-old Pilot Officer Jack Kay, with three victories already, and Flying Officer 'Chips' Carpenter who had just celebrated his twentieth birthday. Carpenter had earlier flown Gladiators off HMS *Furious* during the Norway campaign and then Spitfires during the Battle of Britain, being credited with at least three enemy aircraft destroyed, and scored his first success over Malta on 30 June: an MC.200 to the north of Valletta.

Admiral Sir Andrew Browne Cunningham, widely known as ABC, took command of the Royal Navy's Mediterranean Fleet just before the outbreak of the Second World War. He led British naval forces to victory in several key Mediterranean battles before handing over command in March 1942. (*IWM*)

Lieutenant General William Dobbie, a Scot and engineer by background, took over as governor and commander-in-chief of Malta at the end of April 1940. Knighted the following year, Dobbie held the post for two critical years until relieved in May 1942. (*IWM*)

When Italy entered the war in June 1940, Malta's defence was in the hands of a few ageing Gladiator biplanes flown by volunteers. The aircraft had been found in crates and this one, N5519, was one of the first four erected and delivered to Hal Far during April. In the cockpit on readiness is George Burges who had been serving as personal assistant to Air Commodore Sammy Maynard, the air officer commanding Malta. (*AHB*)

Malta's capital, Valletta, receives another hit during one of the countless air raids against the island during the siege. The first bombs fell during the early morning of 11 June 1940 and the last air raid against the island took place just over three years later. (*IWM*)

The first Italian air raids quickly led to the bolstering of Malta's defences, including more anti-aircraft guns set up around key areas such as Grand Harbour and the island's airfields. (*AHB*)

An early picture of a Hurricane at Hal Far. One of Malta's immediate priorities was to improve the island's air defence and the first Hurricanes arrived on the island towards the end of June 1940. They had left the UK bound for Egypt but were instead retained on the island to boost Malta's defence. (*AHB*)

The improved anti-aircraft defences surrounding Grand Harbour included 40mm Bofors guns; this gun emplacement overlooks Senglea. (*IWM*)

A U-class submarine of the Tenth Flotilla at Lazaretto Wharf. At a little over 500 tonnes, and with a surface speed of just 11 knots, the U-class was neither big nor fast compared to the Axis submarines but was ideal for disrupting the Axis supply lines to North Africa. (*IWM*)

Lieutenant Commander David Wanklyn, the skipper of HMS *Upholder* and one of the Allies' most successful submariners. *Upholder* arrived in Malta in January 1941 and while operating from the island Wanklyn was awarded the Victoria Cross, the highest and most prestigious award for gallantry, before he and his crew disappeared without trace while on patrol in April 1942. (*IWM*)

Joachim Müncheberg, the 22-year-old *Staffelkapitän* of 7./JG 26, at Gela in Sicily at the end of his 200th combat sortie in March 1941. His yellow-nosed Messerschmitt Bf109s had first appeared over Malta the previous month, marking a new phase of intense aerial activity over the island. The vast combat experience of men like Müncheberg, who already had twenty-three victories to his name, was completely at odds with many of Malta's Hurricane pilots who were experiencing air combat for the first time. (*Bundesarchiv-Bildarchiv 427-408-19*)

The arrival of the Luftwaffe's 109s over Malta meant that aircraft on the ground had to be better protected against low-level strafing attacks against the airfields. All hands were used to construct improved aircraft pens for Malta's precious fighters. (*Via Tony Spooner*)

Three of 249 Squadron's Hurricane pilots, taken at North Weald shortly before their departure for Malta. On the right is Pat Wells and it has been his memoirs, log book and photographs that have contributed to this book. In the centre is Tommy Thompson who went on to serve with the Malta Night Fighter Unit, and on the left is a Rhodesian, Roich Munro, who was killed within days of arriving in Malta. (*Via Pat Wells*)

The new arrivals of 249 Squadron had no time to settle in to their new surroundings at Takali. This was the result of their first period of standby during the early afternoon of 25 May 1941, following a low-level strafing attack by Joachim Müncheberg's 109s. (*Via Pat Wells*)

Just moments before, Pat Wells had been sitting in this Hurricane awaiting the order to scramble. No order came and the first Wells knew of the raid was when he saw the 109s running in to attack. With no option other than to huddle into his cockpit and wait for the hits, Pat Wells was fortunate to escape with just a cannon shell through his foot. (*Via Pat Wells*)

Leading Stoker Charles Jacobs, the author's father, pictured at Gibraltar during 1941 while serving in the destroyer HMS *Wishart*. His diary and photos kept while escorting the Malta convoys provided the inspiration behind this book. (*Author's collection*)

HMS *Wishart* shown alongside a support vessel at Gibraltar. In the left of the picture can be seen a number of RAF flying boats. (*Author's collection*)

Royal Navy destroyers return to Gibraltar at the end of another Malta convoy. (*Author's collection*)

The aircraft carrier, HMS *Ark Royal*, pictured during Operation Halberd in September 1941, the largest re-supply of Malta at the time. (*IWM*)

HMS *Nelson*, one of two large battleships of its class built after the First World War, was assigned to Force H for escort duties in the Med. She was damaged when torpedoed by Italian aircraft on 27 September 1941 during Op Halberd. After returning to the UK for repairs, *Nelson* returned to the Med the following summer. (*Author's collection*)

Tony Spooner arrived in Malta during September 1941 and led the ASV-equipped Wellingtons of the Special Duties Flight at Luqa. His memoirs and photos have provided a valuable contribution to this book. (*Via Tony Spooner*)

When the first Wellington VIIIs arrived in Malta they were immediately dubbed as 'Sticklebacks' because of the rows of additional ASV aerials on top and along each side of the fuselage as well as under the wings. But when on the ground they were targeted during enemy air raids and suffered extensive damage as a result. (*Via Tony Spooner*)

Commanded by Captain William Agnew, the cruiser HMS *Aurora* arrived in Grand Harbour on 21 October 1941 as the lead element of Force K. With another cruiser, HMS *Penelope*, and two destroyers, HMS *Lance* and HMS *Lively*, Force K became Malta's small surface strike force. (*Via Tony Spooner*)

Two ships of Force K – *Penelope* (left) and *Lance* – pictured in Grand Harbour on 10 November 1941 after returning from the highly successful attack on the enemy Duisburg convoy two nights earlier. Nine of the ten Axis merchantmen were sunk, as were three Italian destroyers, and the tenth merchant vessel, a tanker, was left ablaze. (*IWM*)

Disaster during the late afternoon of 13 November 1941. Having successfully delivered more Hurricanes to Malta, the carrier HMS *Ark Royal* was on her way back to Gibraltar when she was torpedoed by the German submarine *U-81*. The mighty *Ark* was struck amidships, causing her to list in just a matter of minutes. The scene is captured from *Wishart* as the destroyer HMS *Legion* is seen alongside taking crew off the carrier while a second destroyer, HMS *Laforey*, stands by to assist. (*Author's collection*)

The last moments of *Ark Royal* captured from *Wishart*. For those who witnessed the loss of such a great ship, and one that had played such a key role in the re-supply of Malta, it was a terrible and demoralizing sight. Remarkably, though, of the *Ark*'s complement of 1,487 officers and men, only one life was lost. (*Author's collection*)

Built before the war as a fast passenger and cargo liner, HMS *Glengyle* was used in the Mediterranean as a commando landing ship before she was briefly allocated to Malta convoy duties before returning to the UK. In January 1942 she arrived in Grand Harbour laden with oil, food and ammunition after making a daring dash through the eastern Med from Alexandria. (*IWM*)

Spitfires heading for Malta aboard HMS *Eagle*, and looking back to the flat-topped HMS *Argus* and the light cruiser HMS *Hermione*, during Operation Picket in March 1942. (*IWM*)

The use of smoke screens was used to hide the convoy's merchantmen when evading Italian warships or when under attack. The cruiser HMS *Cleopatra* can be seen 'smoking' during Operation MG1 in March 1942. (*GCIA*)

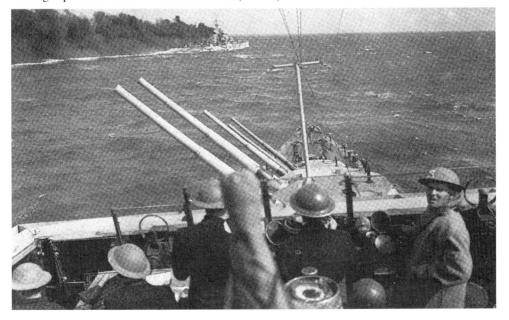

Merchant vessels heading for Malta had to run the gauntlet of the Mediterranean and so were fitted with a variety of anti-aircraft guns manned by servicemen; a term known as DEMS (Defensive Equipped Merchant Ships). This Bofors gun is fitted aboard the Blue Star liner *Melbourne Star*. (*GCIA*)

Most of 46 Squadron's pilots were then transferred to form the nucleus of 126 Squadron, which re-formed at Takali at the end of June for the defence of Malta, and 46's ground component continued by sea to Egypt, taking the 46 Squadron number plate with them.

Malta had now been at war for a year, during which an estimated hundred-plus enemy aircraft had been shot down with nearly the same number again claimed as either probably destroyed or at least damaged. More Hurricanes had arrived on the island during June. First, on 14 June, forty-three arrived under Operation Tracer, flown off *Ark Royal* and *Victorious*. Although thirty-four soon left for Egypt, nine were kept on the island. Then, at the end of the month, Operation Railway, mounted in two parts and involving *Ark Royal* and *Furious*, saw thirty-five more Hurricanes and six Blenheims arrive in Malta.

It was a monumental effort to re-supply the besieged island, and these new arrivals again allowed some of the longer-serving pilots to rest. One was George Burges. He had more than done his bit since his first victory on the opening day of the campaign a year before. On promotion to the rank of squadron leader, Burges returned to the UK. Another to leave Malta was Titch Whiteley; he was replaced by Squadron Leader Russell Welland.

Strengthened by the new arrivals, 185 Squadron moved back to Hal Far and resumed daylight operations, and 249's pilots took their turn at providing night defence. Even though the air raids had far from dried up altogether, Malta was enjoying a period of relative calm. Living conditions were tolerable and there was an adequate supply of water and food. People got out and about once more. Some would take a daytime stroll high up on Dingli Cliffs in the sun, and in the evening uniforms of all ranks and services were seen in Sliema's many popular clubs and bars. Romances blossomed and, for now, life on the island returned to something approaching normality.

But at sea, Axis supplies were still getting through to North Africa. Although Malta's subs and aircraft had accounted for more than 8,000 tonnes of enemy supplies sunk during June 1941, the month proved to be another record for the Axis with more than 125,000 tonnes reported to have arrived at their destination; mostly at Benghazi and Tripoli. Furthermore, nearly 13,000 enemy troops successfully crossed the Mediterranean during the month, without any losses reported.[1]

However, the reduction in daylight raids against Malta's airfields and Grand Harbour, combined with the arrival of more offensive aircraft on the island, meant that a renewed campaign against the Axis convoys could begin. Malta's aircraft and submarines would soon be sinking three-quarters of supplies destined for Rommel's *Afrika Korps*.

The newly arrived Blenheims of Attie Atkinson's 82 Squadron took part in their first operation from Malta on 22 June. The squadron had only arrived two days before and was tasked with attacking an enemy convoy heading for Tripoli. Both merchant vessels and their destroyer escort were off Lampedusa and put up a hail of defensive flak as the six aircraft attacked at low level. One of the air gunners, Sergeant Eric Chandler, later recorded:

'It was soon made very clear that, despite hugging the sea we had been sighted. Black puffs of smoke could be observed and after an interval, which seemed like ages, the sea both ahead and to each side of us started to erupt, as heavy shells hit the water.'[2]

The formation evaded left and then right, rising and falling to deceive the enemy gunners. The leading three Blenheims turned to port and the rear formation turned starboard. Chandler first saw one aircraft hit and then another. He continued:

'A sharp jolt to our own machine not only indicated that we also had been hit but threw me violently against the side of my turret. An unbelievable pain paralysed my right arm. I ducked down to check the arm, quite expecting to find it had been blown off! As I did so, a snaking line of Bofors tracer

---

1. Spooner (*Supreme Gallantry*), op. cit., pp.50–5. These are official Italian figures for losses in June 1941. Many British strikes against enemy convoys were reported during the month and suggest that Axis losses could have been higher.
2. Spooner (*Faith Hope and Malta GC*), op. cit., pp.39–41.

played across the aircraft, passing through the Perspex cover of my turret. This brought me to life with a vengeance and a determination to fight back.'[3]

The Blenheim pressed on, passing at deck height between two destroyers. Chandler opened up with his two Brownings. Then, climbing up along the deck of the 6,000-tonne merchantman, the crew released their four eleven-second delayed bombs as the aircraft struggled to clear the superstructure and funnels. The Blenheim kept climbing. The pilot, Flight Lieutenant Tom Watkins, had been wounded by a shell, tearing away the calf of his right leg and almost severing it from the knee downwards. The observer, Sergeant Jim Sargent, rushed to his aid and to prevent the aircraft climbing further to the stall. Once clear of the convoy, the crew headed for Malta. Watkins was at risk of bleeding to death but it was then that there was further mayhem. Chandler recalled:

'It was at this point that my radio exploded into my lap and I observed a CR.42 curving in for a second attack. I took my time lining up my sights, allowing the necessary deflection, and opened fire at almost the precise moment that he recommenced firing at us. At once his nose went up, then he seemed to slide down, tail first, then turning over, slid into the sea below.'[4]

The two enemy merchant vessels had both been badly damaged during the attack. Part of the joint citation for the award of the DSO to Watkins and the DFM to Sargent states what happened next:

'On the return journey, Flight Lieutenant Watkins fell into a stupor as a result of his wounds and Sergeant Sargent, who was unable to call the air gunner as the intercommunication gear was out of order, removed the wounded pilot from his seat, took over the controls and flew the aircraft back to base. During this period, Flight Lieutenant Watkins had momentary periods of consciousness and, when informed the aircraft was over base,

---

3. Ibid.
4. Ibid.

insisted on taking control. Although in intense pain and very weak from loss of blood, by a supreme effort, he regained his seat and made a landing without damaging the aircraft. Throughout, Flight Lieutenant Watkins displayed the highest courage and devotion to duty while Sergeant Sargent displayed courage and resource in difficult circumstances.'[5]

Back at Luqa help for the crew soon arrived, although Watkins would not return to operational flying. For his part in the attack, Chandler would also later be awarded the DFM.

July began much the same with a series of hard-fought successes by the Blenheims, particularly during a daylight raid against Palermo, led by Atkinson, where two merchant ships at 10,000 tonnes and 5,000 tonnes were sunk. Another large ship of 10,000 tonnes was left with a broken back and three other vessels damaged. All the Blenheims returned safely on this occasion but the fact was that the anti-shipping strikes from Malta were proving to be harder fought than might have been expected, and so 82 Squadron had to be relieved well under the two months that had been planned.

In the same *London Gazette* that had announced the award of the DSO to Tom Watkins, there was also a DSO to Attie Atkinson. His lengthy citation included:

'This officer has proved himself to be a fearless operational pilot, and has been responsible for the destruction of many thousands of tons of enemy shipping. He is a magnificent leader whose courage and determination have been of the highest order.'[6]

A detachment of Beaufighters from 272 Squadron had also been in action from Malta, and the island's resident Wellingtons and Swordfish were also getting in on the act during their frequent night raids. Meanwhile, at sea, the U-class submarines were now achieving regular success.

---

5. Supplement to the *London Gazette*, dated 15 August 1941.
6. Ibid.

This new and determined offensive by Malta's aircraft and submarines meant that during the month of July 1941, only 62,000 tonnes of Axis supplies reached their destination; less than half the tonnage that had arrived during the previous month.[7] The British offensive was beginning to count and every effort to keep Malta topped up with supplies was put in place. Hardly a ship or submarine sent through the Mediterranean failed to stop off in Grand Harbour to unload supplies, no matter how small or seemingly insignificant they may have appeared to the crew.

These supply runs included so-called Magic Carpet runs from Alexandria to Malta by the Porpoise-submarines *Cachalot* and *Rorqual*, which bravely carried on their re-supply of the island despite the German presence in Crete. However, for Lieutenant Hugo Newton's crew of *Cachalot*, their luck ran out on the night of 30/31 July. After delivering more supplies and personnel to Malta, the submarine was on her way back to Alexandria when Newton was ordered to a patrol position off the Libyan coast. Having sighted an enemy tanker heading for Benghazi, *Cachalot* was taking up a position on the surface to mount an attack when she was rammed and sunk by an escorting destroyer. Fortunately, though, all of *Cachalot*'s crew were saved to be taken as prisoners of war. Notwithstanding this loss, the Magic Carpet runs to Malta during July alone carried more than 84,000 gallons of petrol, 83,000 gallons of kerosene, six tonnes of munitions, thirty tonnes of other supplies, 126 personnel and twelve tonnes of morale-boosting mail for those serving on the island.[8]

With the Italian air raids taking place mostly at night, the Malta Night Fighter Unit (MNFU) was formed at Takali. With a dozen all-black Hurricanes and ten pilots, the flight was set up under the command of Squadron Leader George Powell-Shedden. He had arrived in mid-July on board a Blenheim from Gibraltar. Arriving with him, and soon to join the MNFU as a flight commander, was Flying Officer Donald 'Dimsie' Stones with at least seven victories and a DFC. Others to join the MNFU from 249 were Ernie Cassidy, who became the other flight commander, Tommy Thompson and Jack Mills.

7. Spooner (*Supreme Gallantry*), op. cit., pp.57–8.
8. Woodman, op. cit., p.184.

The tactic employed by the Hurricanes at night was to use two aircraft backed up by the searchlight batteries to illuminate their target. The preferred route for the Italian intruders was to fly a lengthy sea-route to approach Malta from the south, and to avoid over-flying the island until making their attack. Running in to their target on a northerly heading meant they were already heading back towards Sicily and so would not have to spend valuable time, or speed for that matter, turning off-target and taking up a heading for safety.

Knowing this, pairs of searchlights were set up at both ends of Malta. The Hurricanes would circle these in the hope that an enemy bomber could become 'coned' by the lights. Using the combination of fighter controllers acting on the radar return of the incoming intruders and the searchlights with their own lookouts, the two night fighters would position themselves above the intruder and then attack it from each side simultaneously. There was, however, always a risk of collision between the two fighters and so tail lights were usually kept on to prevent the likelihood of this happening.[9]

It was estimated that Malta now had enough supplies and equipment to keep the island going for at least eight months.[10] Although no Club Runs had been possible during the first three weeks of July, more Blenheims arrived in Malta and the continued re-supply of Malta meant that its garrison now stood at more than 22,000, including three battalions of the King's Own Malta Regiment. The island's defences also included nearly 250 anti-aircraft guns (an even mix of heavy and light guns), plus more than another hundred guns used for ground and coastal defence; all manned by the Royal Malta Artillery and backed up by searchlights.

There were also seventy-five Hurricanes on the island plus a range of bombers. These, in particular, enjoyed much success during August. Malta's Wellingtons (now including aircraft of 38 Squadron), Blenheims (soon to include aircraft of 107 Squadron), Beaufighters and Swordfish operated more freely from the island's relatively undisturbed airfields, and carried out attacks against enemy shipping, ports and airfields, almost at will.

---

9. Shores and Cull with Malizia, op. cit., pp.270–1.
10. Ibid, pp.269–70.

Even the Hurricanes started to be used as fighter-bombers. They were fitted with temporary racks for four small 40lb (18kg) bombs beneath each wing so that they could carry out offensive raids and strafing attacks over Sicily. Furthermore, two newly arrived Swordfish were equipped with Air-to-Surface Vessel (ASV), essentially a radar. Because it was difficult, suicidal even, for the 100mph (160km/h) Swordfish biplanes to attack enemy shipping in daylight, virtually all Swordfish attacks had to be made at night and this led to the crews finding a novel way of attacking ships under the cover of darkness; hence ASV. The ASV equipment was housed in a radome between the legs of the main undercarriage and gave the operator a detection range of about twenty-five miles against ships. In good sea conditions, even a U-boat could be detected, albeit at a much reduced range.

Meanwhile, the crews of 69 Squadron continued to conduct valuable reconnaissance missions buoyed by the addition of a Hurricane to add to the squadron's Marylands. The squadron would also soon include a Blenheim and a Bristol Beaufort among its ranks. It was now time for Adrian Warburton to be given a well-earned rest from operations but not before the announcement of a Bar to his DFC for his excellent work while operating from Malta.

As far as the air war over Malta was concerned, this was the quietest period since the outbreak of hostilities. There were no major aerial engagements during the first half of August, although the MNFU claimed its first victory when an Italian intruder was shot down by two Hurricanes during a night raid against Valletta.

The Italians did not appear over the island again until 19 August when a dozen Hurricanes were scrambled to intercept a dozen Italian fighters. One pilot from 126 Squadron to achieve success that day was Flight Lieutenant 'Pip' Lefevre. He was one of the former members of 46 Squadron and the MC.200 he shot down that day was his third victory. Another of the squadron's pilots claimed his first successes of the war that day. This was Pilot Officer Pat Lardner-Burke, a South African, who shot down two MC.200s over Cap Passero and damaged another. These victories were the first of five Italian fighters he would shoot down over Malta, for which he would later receive the DFC.[11]

---

11. Shores and Williams, op. cit., p.388 & p.396.

Meanwhile, at sea, Malta's submarines were still enjoying success. On 18 September, *Upholder* sent two large Italian troop ships to the bottom. They were the *Neptunia* and *Oceania*, each just short of 20,000 tonnes and carrying between them some 6,000 enemy troops to North Africa. This attack was another example of the vital role played by the codebreakers back home as word had been received that four enemy troop ships were attempting to reach Tripoli. With three other U-class subs – *Unbeaten*, *Upright* and *Ursula* – *Upholder* had been rushed to the area of probable interception. By skilful manoeuvring in poor light, and despite his submarine yawing badly due to more technical problems, Wanklyn fired his torpedoes at both his targets with devastating accuracy as they overlapped.

In addition to these two prize targets, *Upholder* had sent three more enemy ships to the bottom since its success against the *Conte Rosso* in May and had damaged three more, earning David Wanklyn the Distinguished Service Order; one of eleven awards to the crew. A few weeks later came the announcement of the award of the Victoria Cross, Britain's highest award for gallantry, for Wanklyn; his citation including all of his great feats so far and making Wanklyn the first submariner to be awarded the VC during the Second World War.

But while Malta's aircraft and submarines were making severe dents into the Axis convoys, the island remained in constant need of its own re-supply. During July 1941, 65,000 tonnes of supplies had arrived in Malta from Gibraltar under Operation Substance, with six merchant ships making it safely to Grand Harbour. The vital supplies included three months of food for Malta's inhabitants, but the convoy had come at a cost to the Royal Navy with one destroyer lost, and a cruiser and another destroyer were damaged.

The Italians sought desperate new ways of attacking the British merchantmen and one audacious attempt to attack the ships in Grand Harbour took place on the night of 26 July. An Italian sloop, with two escorting vessels, had left the port of Augusta on the east coast of Sicily the evening before. She was carrying eight small explosive motor boats, each with a single-man crew and the bow bearing an explosive charge, and in tow was a barge carrying two human torpedoes, each with a two-man crew.

Having arrived at a position about five miles from Grand Harbour, the explosive craft and human torpedoes were launched. The plan was to first blast an entry into the harbour, and for the remaining explosive craft and human torpedoes to then attack the merchant ships and the submarine base at Manoel Island.

But the harbour's defences were thorough in their design to deter such surface or underwater attacks. The entrance was closed by a manoeuvrable boom and the mole across the entrance to the harbour was connected to the foot of Saint Elmo by a steel viaduct. The design had allowed peacetime passage of small craft between Grand and Marsamxett Harbours but these were closed for the duration of the war by heavy steel wire nets.

The Italians knew this and so the explosive craft had meant to clear the obstructing net, but the first craft had impacted so violently that the steel span above the net was dislodged and blocked the entrance into the harbour. The sound of the impact had alerted the defences at Saint Elmo and searchlights soon picked up the Italian craft waiting offshore, and within minutes the would-be attackers had been destroyed.[12]

As dawn broke, Hurricanes took off to look for the raiders. They spotted four of the motor boats and attacked them offshore, all of which were claimed as destroyed. Italian fighters arrived soon after, to escort any survivors from the raid back to friendly waters, but they arrived too late to save the stricken motor boats that were already under attack, although they did shoot down one of the Hurricanes; the pilot baled out into the sea. It had been a bold plan but it was one that had ended in disaster for the Italians, with fifteen dead and eighteen captured.[13]

A further convoy arrived in Malta on the first day of August. This was Operation Style from Gibraltar, a fast convoy of three naval minelayers, each laden with fuel, ammunition, food and personnel, and escorted by two destroyers and covered by Force H. The three minelayers all arrived safely and after a quick turn round in Grand Harbour were on their way back west again.

But nothing else arrived in Malta during August and so the following month, a second unescorted merchantman made a dash for the island.

12. Woodman, op. cit., pp.210–11.
13. Shores and Cull with Malizia, op. cit., pp.264–5.

This time, though, and unlike the poor *Parracombe* before her, the freighter *Empire Guillemot* arrived in Malta safely during the early morning of 19 September. During her long passage from the UK and through the Straits of Gibraltar, she had been transformed from being British to then wearing the disguise of a Spanish freighter, and then a French one before she became Italian as she headed north towards Sicily. Then, finally, she returned to flying British colours for the final dash to Malta.

Malta's crews had been well briefed not to attack a single merchantman approaching the island during the previous night and, at last, the plan to risk an unescorted merchantman to Malta had worked. Safely in harbour, *Empire Guillemot* unloaded her cargo of fodder. This might seem an unusual cargo to carry but transport in Malta had largely reverted to the use of horses and donkeys, which also provided a food reserve, and so fodder was vital to keep the transport system going.

If the arrival of a single merchantman had come as a surprise and, perhaps, a disappointment to the locals who had turned out in their numbers, the disappointment was not to last for long. Nine days later, Malta welcomed the ships of Operation Halberd from Gibraltar, the largest re-supply of Malta to date.

The convoy consisted of nine merchant ships escorted by an aircraft carrier and three battleships to deter any interference from the Italian fleet, and a close escort of five cruisers and seventeen destroyers provided an anti-aircraft screen. As things turned out, the Italian fleet did approach but then turned away once the strength of the Royal Navy escort became known, although Italian bombers attacked the ships from the air. The large battleship *Nelson* was torpedoed and damaged, and several more naval ships also suffered damage. One of the merchant vessels, *Imperial Star*, had to be scuttled because she could not maintain convoy speed, although fortunately without any loss of life. But the rest of the convoy – *Breconshire*, *Ajax*, *City of Calcutta*, *City of Lincoln*, *Clan Ferguson*, *Clan MacDonald*, *Dunedin Star* and *Rowallan Castle* – all arrived safely in Grand Harbour during the morning of 28 September to deliver 85,000 tonnes of supplies to the island.

Re-supplying Malta remained a huge drain on the Royal Navy's resources in the Mediterranean but these two latest main convoys, Operation Substance and Operation Halberd, had kept Malta afloat. The latter had also coincided with another lull in air activity over the island with only a dozen night raids during the month.

September was also significant because of the arrival in Malta of the first Wellington VIIIs equipped with ASV. The new arrivals soon became dubbed as 'Sticklebacks', because of the rows of additional ASV aerials on top and along each side of the fuselage as well as under the wings. A new unit was formed, called the Special Duties Flight (SDF), under the command of Flight Lieutenant Tony Spooner, with the ASV-equipped Wellingtons being used for night reconnaissance to supplement the Marylands of 69 Squadron.

October began with a sad loss for 185 Squadron when its squadron commander, Boy Mould, was killed. Only days before Mould had been awarded a Bar to his DFC, but after being scrambled to intercept an incoming raid his formation were jumped by MC.202s. It was the first time the 202s had been seen over the island and Mould fell to the guns of one; he was just 24 years old.

It was also during October that the MNFU suffered a notable loss. Pilot Officer David Barnwell was Malta's most successful night fighter pilot at the time with at least three night victories, for which he had just received news that he was awarded the DFC. But Barnwell was lost just before dawn on 14 October when Luqa was strafed by low-flying MC.202s. The raid took the island's defences by surprise but five of the unit's all-black Hurricanes and six Hurricanes from 185 and 249 Squadrons were scrambled to intercept the raiders. Exactly what happened to Barnwell is unknown. He was heard to have claimed to have shot down one of the Macchis but he was not heard or seen again. David Barnwell was just 19 years old.

The expansion of British forces in the Mediterranean and Middle East gave Cunningham the opportunity to set up a new and small surface strike force in Malta. Called Force K, it comprised two cruisers, *Aurora* and *Penelope*, and two destroyers, *Lance* and *Lively*. Although fuel on the island remained a problem, it was estimated there was enough to operate a small strike force for up to two months without further re-supply.[14]

---

14. Holland, op. cit., p.198.

The passage of Force K to Malta took place in mid-October as part of Operation Callboy, another Club Run to fly more Swordfish and Fairey Albacore torpedo-bombers to Hal Far. It would also allow the remaining empty merchantmen from Operation Halberd, as well as *Empire Guillemot*, to leave the island under the loose cover of naval protection.

The four ships of Force K sailed into Grand Harbour on 21 October while the merchantmen slipped independently away from Malta to head back to Gibraltar. The faster ships, *City of Lincoln* and *Dunedin Star*, arrived back at Gibraltar four days later, despite the efforts of the Italians to stop them. They arrived to find that *Clan MacDonald* had also arrived back safely, having set off from Malta a few days earlier. The *Clan Ferguson*, however, would be less lucky. She was the last of the Operation Halberd merchantmen to sail from Grand Harbour on 24 October but was spotted and then attacked by Italian aircraft soon after, and so she ended up returning to Malta.

But the poor elderly *Empire Guillemot* would not make it back. Her speed of just 11 knots meant that she would have to return to Gibraltar much the way she had come, keeping close to the Tunisian coast and round Cape Bon, and then staying close inshore wearing different nationalities as she went. But it soon became apparent that she was overdue and despite the best efforts of the RAF's long-range Catalina flying boats operating over the western Mediterranean from their base in Gibraltar, nothing was seen.

It turned out the unescorted *Empire Guillemot* had been attacked and sunk by Italian aircraft off the Galite Islands. With nothing more than a single Lewis machine gun, the crew were helpless and could do nothing to prevent the attack. One engineer officer was killed, although the remaining forty-four crew members took to the life boats. However, nine men were lost when their boat was wrecked in surf off the North African coast, although the survivors made it to shore and were taken as prisoners of war.

And so the first two unescorted merchantmen to have run the gauntlet of the western Mediterranean between Gibraltar and Malta – *Parracombe* and *Empire Guillemot* – had both suffered the same fate, with the tragic loss of both ships. The next unescorted attempt to re-supply Malta from the westward was by two ships, *Empire Defender* and *Empire Pelican*, in Operation Astrologer. They passed independently through the Straits of Gibraltar in early November, two days apart, and followed the same route that *Empire Guillemot* had taken before. But neither ship made it to Malta. Both were sunk by Italian aircraft off the Galite Islands, with the loss of five lives.

The Italians may have found out details of these solo runs from the survivors of the two previous attempts, or they may have simply become familiar with the route and pattern of these unescorted merchantmen. Either way, these latest setbacks ended unescorted sailings from the west for a year. Worse still, they were to be the last merchant ships sent from the west to relieve Malta for six months.

Meanwhile, Force K had been preparing to make its mark. The ships were led by *Aurora*'s skipper, 42-year-old Captain William Agnew, a tall, lean and quietly spoken man. He had commanded his ship for a year and his task now, quite simply, was to sink the merchant ships supplying Rommel's forces in North Africa.

Aided by Britain's codebreakers back home, Agnew would also need the help of the ASV-equipped Wellingtons to locate the enemy convoys and so he called Tony Spooner to his ship to be briefed with his radar officer on the aircraft's capability. In his book, *In Full Flight*, Tony Spooner recalled:

> '*This was music to my ears. Someone at last wanted to know both the potential and the limitations of the device my plane carried. He listened and he asked a few direct questions. I was left with the impression that during the next fifteen minutes he mastered all that I had ever learnt about the use of airborne ASV. He, in his turn, then launched into a concise and clear description of his purpose on that bombed and battered island.*'[15]

A typical Force K operation would start when intelligence was received (either from codebreakers in the UK or from an aerial reconnaissance photograph) that an enemy supply convoy was due to pass through the Straits of Messina or leave port at Naples or Palermo. Navigators would then work out where the enemy was likely to be at certain stages through their passage to North Africa, and from these calculations they would work out where Force K was

---

15. Spooner, *In Full Flight*, pp.172–3.

most likely to carry out its night attack, typically at a distance of about 150 to 200 miles from Malta. Then, an hour before dusk, Force K would leave Grand Harbour and in line astern formation head towards where the enemy convoy would be. At much the same time, the Wellington, loaded with fuel and flares, would get airborne and head for the same area of interception. Once there, it would commence the lengthy drawn-out search using ASV. Then, having located the enemy ships, Agnew would lead Force K into the attack, fighting at close stations as one ship and maintaining a fighting speed of 28 knots throughout.[16]

The plan worked particularly well on the night of 8/9 November when a large enemy convoy, the Beta Convoy, otherwise known as the Duisburg Convoy, was spotted by a Malta Maryland off the toe of Italy. The convoy was heading east across the Ionian Sea and on its way to North Africa. Because of the mauling suffered by the Tripoli-bound convoys during recent weeks, the enemy routed the convoy the long way round Malta's attackers by first heading eastwards for the Greek coastline and its islands, and then heading south towards Benghazi before finally turning west to Tripoli; twice the distance of the normal direct route across the Med.

The four ships of Force K and an ASV Wellington left Malta immediately and in the early hours of the following day intercepted the convoy of ten merchant ships and six destroyers. After a brief but violent action, nine merchantmen were sunk and the tenth, a tanker, was left ablaze. Three Italian destroyers were also sunk. It was carnage for the Italians.

In a matter of just a few months, Malta had become an island from where successful offensive operations were being carried out. Every day, small formations of aircraft, ships or submarines were seeking ways of harassing the Axis supply lines. Between them all – the Royal Navy, the RAF and the Fleet Air Arm – Malta's forces were crippling the Axis supply chain between Italy and North Africa as never before. During November 1941, 77 per cent of all Rommel's supplies were sunk,[17] and when the Allies launched Operation Crusader on 18 November, their first major offensive in the

16. Spooner (*In Full Flight*), op. cit., pp.173–7.
17. Holland, op. cit., p.205.

desert, they achieved quick and substantial gains, and lifted the long siege of Tobruk.

The pendulum in North Africa had swung in favour of the Allies as the Luftwaffe could no longer operate freely over the desert as the lack of fuel and supplies took effect. November had been a critical month in the Mediterranean war, and especially for Malta. The fortunes of the land war in the desert and those in the air and sea war being fought above and around Malta were irrevocably intertwined. But never again would Malta's forces achieve so much success. The period of calm, during which Malta had taken the opportunity to hit back, was about to come to an end.

The devastation caused by Malta's Force K, a relatively small naval force, had caused repercussions among the Axis command and resulted in swift action by the Germans. The combination of a prolonged campaign in North Africa and the onset of winter on the Eastern Front led to Hitler ordering one of his air fleets back to Sicily to increase its effort in the Mediterranean once more. Among his top priorities was the neutralization or conquest of Malta, once and for all; something the Italians had failed to do.

Hitler also ordered half of his Atlantic U-boat submarines to the Mediterranean, much to the annoyance of his senior naval commanders who believed that Britain was on the brink of starvation. But Hitler's decision would immediately bear fruit when the *U-81* torpedoed *Ark Royal* on 13 November.

The *Ark* had been on her way back to Gibraltar with *Argus* having delivered thirty-four more Hurricanes to Malta under Operation Perpetual. Somerville had received word that U-boats were operating off the Spanish coast and had warned his ships to be vigilant. But *Ark Royal* was struck amidships between the fuel bunkers and bomb store, and directly below the bridge island. A massive hole was on the starboard side, causing severe flooding of the starboard boiler room and causing the ship to list in just minutes.

It was late afternoon when the attack took place and every effort was made throughout that night to save the carrier and tow her into Gibraltar, but further flooding caused the ship to list further. Remarkably, there was only the loss of one life. The rest of the 1,487 officers and crew were offloaded and transported back to Gibraltar. By dawn the following morning, the list had reached 45 degrees and then, finally, the mighty *Ark Royal* rolled on her side, held that position for a few minutes before inverting and breaking in two, the aft sinking first and then the bow.

For those who witnessed the final moments of such a great ship, and one that had played such a key role in the re-supply of Malta, it was a terrible and demoralising sight. It was the darkest of days and brought an end to Club Runs until early the following spring.

News of the loss of *Ark Royal* soon reached Malta and came as a tragic reminder of just how quickly the tide in the Mediterranean could change. The Regia Aeronautica now stepped up its attacks on Grand Harbour and once again Malta's fighter pilots found themselves in air battles over the island.

Although recent successes against Axis supply convoys had brought optimism to Malta, the future did not look quite so bright as far as the defence of the island was concerned. In truth, the Hurricanes had become outdated and tired. The pilots had performed magnificently but being at the end of a supply line had always been a problem. Furthermore, Malta appears to have slipped down the priority list again and support from senior air commanders back home seemed, to those on the island at least, to be disappearing.

With hindsight, this frustration is fully justified. During 1941, Britain had only been fighting on two fronts: at home and in the Mediterranean/ Middle East. With the Battle of Britain won and the nation safe from Nazi invasion, for the time being at least, it would be quite reasonable for those in Malta to expect Spitfires to be sent to the island, as well as Egypt, to bolster the second front. After all, more Spitfires had been built and introduced into service during the year than Hurricanes. Yet, in that same period, newer and improved marks of the Bf109 had been introduced into service but even the Hurricane Mark II would be no match for them should they suddenly appear over the Med.

But no Spitfires were sent to Malta, much to the annoyance and frustration of those defending the island. For Hugh Pughe Lloyd, a man of bomber origins, things had gone relatively well since he had arrived in Malta and maybe he felt optimistic for the future, even without Spitfires. Equally, it may be that no Spitfires were sent to Malta because, back home, things were seen to be going well in the Mediterranean, and so it provided the RAF with an opportunity to offload the ageing Hurricanes without compromising its home defence. But it was now only a matter of time before the Luftwaffe returned and Malta needed Spitfires.

Chapter Ten

Return of the Luftwaffe

In the desert war, the newly formed British Eighth Army launched Operation Crusader, a bold thrust to relieve the vital port of Tobruk, on 18 November. Crusader also involved Gibraltar's naval ships and merchantmen when Operation Chieftain, a phoney and decoy Malta convoy, sent ships into the western Mediterranean to draw off enemy aircraft to the west. The idea was that the convoy would set sail from Gibraltar but, under the cover of darkness, the merchantmen would return to Gibraltar leaving the Royal Navy out in the Med.

Malta's Force K also participated in the phoney plan. The ships set sail from Grand Harbour on the opening day of the offensive and headed west as if to rendezvous with the convoy. They then turned round under the cover of darkness and returned to Malta before sailing east to carry out a second diversionary operation, called Landmark, to give the appearance of heading east to Alexandria.

With Rommel's forces in retreat and short of supplies, particularly fuel, Axis commanders were forced to send more ships out into the Med to make the crossing to Libya. While the British deception plan was underway, the Axis, in desperation, put two small convoys to sea from Naples bound for Benghazi. One of the convoys was soon spotted by Malta's Marylands and ASV-equipped Wellingtons, and Force K was ordered to intercept. The engagement that followed left two Italian freighters ablaze.

Cunningham sent his ships to look for the second convoy but the enemy ships were never found. Tragically, though, the battleship *Barham* was torpedoed and sunk on 25 November by the German submarine *U-331*. Three torpedoes had been fired from just 750 yards, giving no time for evasive action. As the battleship rolled over to port, her magazines exploded and she quickly sank with the loss of nearly 850 lives, more than two-thirds of the ship's crew.

Cunningham's Force B, consisting of the light cruisers *Ajax* and *Neptune* with the destroyers *Kingston* and *Kimberley*, was now sent to Malta as a second surface strike group to supplement Force K. The two surface groups were soon hassling more Axis convoys. But the cruisers and destroyers were depleting Malta's fuel and oil stocks to a critical degree. Efforts to obtain a fast tanker to ease the constraints imposed by the shortage of fuel failed, and so *Breconshire* was converted at Alexandria to become a naval auxiliary, with her deep tank capacity enlarged to take 5,000 tonnes; less than a tanker but the best that could be achieved given the circumstances.[1]

Breconshire put back to sea bound for Malta in mid-December carrying her precious cargo of urgently needed boiler oil. Her escort was commanded by Rear Admiral Philip Vian in the cruiser HMS *Naiad*. Vian, aged 47, was a destroyer man by background and a specialist in naval gunnery. He had served at Jutland during the First World War and had been involved in the boarding of the German supply ship *Altmark* in a Norwegian fjord in early 1940 when commanding the destroyer *Cossack*. Fast-tracked to flag rank, Vian was to become a key naval figure in Malta's survival, proving to be totally committed to the fighting ships and crews he commanded. The escort he was leading that day, which consisted of another two cruisers, *Euryalus* and *Carlisle*, and eight destroyers, was large for a single cargo-carrying ship, such was the importance of *Breconshire* getting through to Malta.

While *Breconshire* was starting her journey west with her escort, Force K slipped out of Grand Harbour and headed east to meet up with her and to take over the escort from Vian. Coincidentally, a large Axis convoy was heading for Tripoli at the same time. They were first spotted by one of Malta's patrolling submarines and with *Breconshire* and her escort heavily outnumbered to the south of the enemy convoy, Cunningham ordered all available ships to sail from Malta. He also ordered Vian to maintain escort of the auxiliary until relived by Malta's warships; *Breconshire* was not to be left alone.

With *Ajax* defective, *Neptune* led *Jaguar* and *Kandahar* out of Grand Harbour to meet the incoming convoy. By now Force K had met up with

---

1. Woodman, op. cit., p.263.

Breconshire, and the combined force of cruisers and destroyers, surrounding the auxiliary, steamed rapidly west towards Malta. But they had been spotted by an Italian reconnaissance aircraft and were being shadowed constantly from above, and throughout that afternoon the ships had to endure bombing and torpedo attacks by Italian SM.79s and German Ju88s that had returned from the Eastern Front. The air attacks were relentless but only one torpedo-bomber penetrated the defensive screen and was promptly shot down.

The Italian warships escorting the Axis merchant ships now turned towards the small British convoy. By late afternoon on 17 December the Italian ships were closing in and shortly before 6.00 pm the two fleets sighted each other. Vian, wishing to avoid combat, ordered *Breconshire* and two destroyers to the south-west, away from the enemy threat, and the rest of his warships turned to face the Italians.

The engagement that followed took place to the south-east of Malta, in the Gulf of Sirte, and lasted only minutes. The battle itself was relatively uneventful but Vian's tactic had worked and *Breconshire* got away with relative ease. Vian then took his ships back to Alexandria while Force K caught up with *Breconshire* and the two destroyers. They then met up with *Neptune* and the two destroyers rushing to them from Malta. More attacks by Ju88s followed but once the ships were within range of the island, Malta's Hurricanes broke up the bombers. Finally, during the afternoon of 18 December, *Breconshire* sailed into Grand Harbour. As soon as she was alongside, her tanks of precious oil were emptied. It had been a magnificent effort to get her there.

Breconshire's safe arrival had proved the value of prioritizing in the Mediterranean. In the surface action later to be called the First Battle of Sirte, Vian had shown discipline in avoiding a direct confrontation with the enemy convoy. Although it was disappointing the enemy supplies were still on their way to Rommel, the safe arrival of *Breconshire* had been a higher priority. Malta's survival depended on it.

With *Breconshire* safely in port, the seven warships of Force K, which now included the cruiser *Neptune* and the destroyers *Havock* and *Kandahar*, went straight off in pursuit of the Axis convoy still out at sea and heading for Tripoli. Meanwhile, at Hal Far, the Swordfish and Albacore crews waited, their aircraft armed, ready to join the attack.

Wellingtons had already taken off from Luqa to lay mines in the approaches to Tripoli and Force K soon caught up with the convoy off the Libyan coast. The enemy ships had come to a halt, having been unable to go into port because of the mines. The torpedo-carrying Swordfish and Albacores took off from Malta and made an attack but it was late in the day and almost dark, and so no hits were seen.

In the gloominess off Libya, Force K then ran into the enemy's coastal mines. One was detonated by *Neptune* and then the same happened to *Aurora* and *Penelope* following in her wake. As a rescue effort got underway, *Kandahar* had her stern blown off and *Neptune* detonated further mines. By the early hours of the following morning, 19 December, *Neptune* began to capsize as water poured into her hull. Only about thirty of the ship's complement of 767 are believed to have survived the initial sinking but only one of those was still alive when the lifeboat was picked up several days later. With *Kandahar* drifting helplessly, the five remaining ships headed back to Malta, arriving there about midday. An attempt was made to recover the stricken destroyer but she had to be scuttled by HMS *Jaguar* the following day; seventy-three lives had been lost.

The damage to Force K had been devastating, with *Aurora* and *Penelope* out of action for some considerable time. It had been Force K's last operational sortie and not until the Tunisian campaign, more than a year later, would an effective Royal Navy force be based in Malta.

These losses added to what had been a disastrous month for the Royal Navy in the Mediterranean, which had also seen two great battleships, *Queen Elizabeth* and *Valiant*, mined and seriously damaged by Italian frogmen riding human-torpedoes while in harbour at Alexandria, with the loss of nine lives and putting both ships out of action for several months. On the plus side, though, the siege of Tobruk had been lifted during Operation Crusader. After a hard and costly fight the Axis forces withdrew. It had been a bold thrust to end the siege and was the first British victory over German ground forces of the war.

But there had been an increase in German activity over and around Malta once more, and this period coincided with changes in the fighter component of Malta's defences. The MNFU was renamed 1435 Flight with Innes Westmacott taking command on promotion, and George Powell-Shedden, now with a DFC, was promoted and appointed wing commander Takali. Powell-Shedden would soon be replaced by Wing Commander 'Jack' Satchell, and Sandy Rabagliati was rested from operations to become a staff officer with HQ Mediterranean.

Desperate for all the help he could get, Hugh Pughe Lloyd continued to hijack aircraft and crews transiting through Malta to the Middle East. Fortunately for Lloyd, he seemed to have the backing of his own superior in Cairo, Air Marshal Arthur Tedder. As air officer commander-in-chief Middle East, Tedder had overall command of air operations in the Mediterranean and North Africa, and would have had every reason to be angry at Lloyd's constant waylaying of aircraft destined for his own Desert Air Force, but, instead, Tedder displayed remarkable tolerance as far as Malta was concerned.[2]

The Blenheims, in particular, were a prize asset for Lloyd and his keen eye to identify the right people to command his units was one of his great fortes. In the same way that he had shown belief and trust in Adrian Warburton, Lloyd's decision to elevate one young sergeant pilot, 21-year-old Ivor Broom, to lead the Blenheims was inspired.

Broom would have gone on to serve elsewhere had it not been for Lloyd's decision to retain some Blenheims in Malta. The young pilot's leadership qualities had already surfaced during raids carried out from the island, but the Blenheims had incurred heavy losses while attacking Axis shipping and targets in Italy and North Africa. With 107 Squadron having lost its officer pilots, it left Broom and another young sergeant pilot, 20-year-old Ron Gillman, as the two most experienced Blenheim pilots on the island.

Lloyd instructed Broom to move into the officers' mess and the paperwork could be sorted out later. And so Ivor Broom became an officer and was soon leading low-level attacks on heavily escorted Axis shipping. One raid of note took place on 17 November when Broom bombed and set ablaze a 4,000-tonne enemy ship in the Gulf of Sirte and helped attack a destroyer. Broom would go on to carry out forty-three operational sorties before returning to the UK for a rest, earning him the first of his three DFCs while

---

2. Spooner (*Supreme Gallantry*), op. cit., p.143.

in Malta, to which he would later add a DSO, and would go on to reach the rank of air marshal.[3]

Although the entry of the United States into the war during December 1941 meant that Britain was no longer fighting alone, things were looking bleak for Malta once more. The Axis had surpassed previous efforts to re-supply Rommel, the number of U-boats in the Mediterranean had continued to rise and fast German S-boats had laid mines around the approaches to Grand Harbour. Then, on 20 December, the Luftwaffe commenced its new campaign against Malta when Ju88s, escorted by newly arrived Bf109Fs, attacked Allied shipping in Grand Harbour.

The return of the Luftwaffe in considerable strength over the island had been a most unwelcome sight for the defenders. Not only had the RAF suffered losses in the air but there were also significant losses on the ground with eleven Hurricanes destroyed during the attack.

The raiders returned the following day. This time the Hurricanes were airborne in greater numbers but still the 109s came out on top. As well as providing escort for the bombers, once over the island the 109 pilots were given the freedom to attack whatever they could. Descending to low level, the raiders strafed anything and everything they could find, including flying boats moored in the bays around the island and any vessels in and around Grand Harbour.

During the last days of 1941, Malta's defenders suffered several losses in the air. Furthermore, a large part of the island's defences and infrastructure was destroyed on the ground as the airfields came under repeated attack from the Luftwaffe. At night, Ju88s carried out regular bombing raids against the island.

The Luftwaffe, in particular, were very accurate when it came to bombing, especially by day. The Ju87 Stuka's technique of near-vertical dive-bombing was by far the most accurate way of putting a bomb on target. Even the Ju88s, using a technique of diving at 45 degrees, were accurate. The Luftwaffe's pilots also seemed to be more courageous than their Italian

---

3. Obituary Sir Ivor Broom, *The Telegraph*, 28 January 2003.

colleagues and would fly through any barrage thrown up against them to deliver their bombs on target.[4]

The fiercest day of air action since the Luftwaffe's return to Sicily occurred on 29 December and it proved to be a costly one for the defenders. There were five scrambles during the day, three of which turned into major air combat. The first, during mid-morning, when thirty-six raiders approached the island, was intercepted by sixteen Hurricanes. The second raid took part in the afternoon when eighteen Hurricanes were scrambled to intercept another twenty-four raiders. Then, just an hour or two later, four Hurricanes were scrambled to intercept a raiding force of 109s attacking shipping. During the day's fighting, five Hurricanes were lost as, once again, the 109s reigned supreme.

There had, however, been some brief cheer for those in Malta over Christmas 1941. A convoy bound for Alexandria had stopped off on Christmas Eve to deliver supplies to the island. Rather frustratingly for the islanders, though, was the sight of empty merchantmen stuck in Grand Harbour and unable to get away. There was little that could be done other than to keep moving them around to deceive the enemy's reconnaissance aircraft and make it harder for the enemy bomber crews to carry out their attacks.

Malta had now been under siege for more than eighteen months, during which the island's defenders had claimed 199 enemy aircraft destroyed. Against this claim, actual Italian losses appear to be 105 aircraft (fifty-nine bombers and forty-six fighters) and Luftwaffe losses from Sicily alone (all types) were eighty-one. Malta's losses were at least ninety Hurricanes, three Fulmars and one Gladiator, as well as eight Marylands, one Spitfire and one Hurricane lost during reconnaissance operations; forty-seven pilots had been killed in action with a further fifteen lost while ferrying aircraft to the island. Of the other visiting squadrons and detachments, three Beaufighters and one Blenheim had been lost, with the loss of nine lives, although this list is probably far from complete.[5]

---

4. Spooner (*Supreme Gallantry*), op. cit., p.96.
5. Shores and Cull with Malizia, op. cit., pp.362–3.

At the end of 1941 the fighter strength in Malta was three squadrons of Hurricanes at Takali (126, 185 and 249 Squadrons) plus the night fighters of 1435 Flight. There were also two squadrons of newly arrived Hurricanes (242 and 605 Squadrons) spread between Luqa and Hal Far, although they were on their way to the Far East. Other RAF and Fleet Air Arm aircraft on the island were: a squadron plus two detachments of Wellington bombers at Luqa (104 Squadron plus detachments from 40 and 221 Squadrons); two detachments of Blenheim light bombers from 18 and 107 Squadrons, also at Luqa; Swordfish of 830 Squadron and Albacores of 828 Squadron at Hal Far; reconnaissance Marylands and Hurricanes of 69 Squadron at Luqa; and two Beaufighters of 252 Squadron, also at Luqa.[6]

The war in the Mediterranean had now reached a critical point but with the Luftwaffe back on the scene, and with Germany's U-boats harassing the Royal Navy with relative freedom, the strategic balance in the Mediterranean was swinging back to the Axis.

---

6. Ibid, p.341.

Chapter Eleven

A Desperate Situation

Hitler knew that Malta held the key to the door of North Africa and re-supplying Rommel's forces in the desert could only be achieved by either capturing Malta or destroying the island's offensive forces based there. Hitler did, of course, have a third choice. He could have abandoned his effort in North Africa altogether and leave the region to the Italians. This would enable him to extricate the *Afrika Korps* and Luftwaffe to fight elsewhere but given his usual unwillingness to give up ground gained, even when all seemed lost, this was never likely to be a realistic consideration.

There were even plans drawn up for an invasion of Malta, involving hundreds of aircraft and gliders, probably sometime during the summer of 1942. New parachute units were formed and production of new assault craft initiated. There was even some urgency within the Italian leadership to bring the invasion date forward to June but the Germans ruled out the idea on the grounds that priorities lay elsewhere.[1]

And so, for now, the German High Command opted for defeating Malta's offensive forces and to gradually wear down the island's defenders by massive air attacks, and to use famine as a weapon of war. Hitler knew that Malta could not survive without the convoys, and without food the island would have to surrender. And with Malta out of the war there would be little or nothing to get in the way of the Axis convoys reaching North Africa. On the other hand, if Malta remained in Allied hands then the Axis forces would never be able to assume that sufficient supplies and reinforcements would arrive in North Africa to drive the Allies out of the desert and ultimately out of Egypt.

---

1. Ibid, pp.92–3.

But there was now a clear divide in opinion among Hitler's military hierarchy. The Luftwaffe's commander-in-chief south, Albert Kesselring, who commanded all forces operating in the Mediterranean and North Africa, wanted to launch an airborne invasion of Malta whereas Rommel wanted the resources to launch a new offensive in the desert and to push on into Egypt.

Whether to allocate vital resources to Kesselring or to Rommel would be Hitler's most strategically important decision of the Mediterranean and desert war. Hitler, with the heavy cost of capturing Crete still very much in his mind, ruled in favour of Rommel. It was a decision that would ultimately lead to Malta's survival, not that anyone on the island knew it at the time.

Since the return of the Luftwaffe, the number of air raid warnings in Malta had significantly increased. There had been 169 reported air raids during December 1941, more than the combined total recorded for the three months before, and, had it not been for poor weather, the number might well have been even more.[2]

After further attacks by the Luftwaffe during the opening days of 1942, the weather turned bad and brought a temporary lull in the air war over Malta. There had been so much rain that the island's airfields had, in places, turned into a bog. Takali, in particular, after several days of torrential rain, was so waterlogged that fighters had to be moved to Luqa. But although the number of air raid warnings continued, and even exceeded the high figure recorded the previous month, as far as the air war over Malta was concerned, little or nothing happened during much of January.

Apart from the conditions, the break from enemy air raids had been welcome and by the time 1435 Flight's Hurricanes did resume operational flying, some had been fitted with long-range fuel tanks to enable them to fly long offensive missions at night. Given that so many raids against Malta were taking place at night, this made perfect sense. The extra fuel enabled the night fighters to hit the enemy bombers as they took off from their

---

2. Spooner (*Supreme Gallantry*), op. cit., p.95. (The actual number recorded in 1941 were: thirty-one air raids in September, fifty-seven in October and seventy-six in November.)

airfields, rather than wait for them to arrive overhead Malta, or otherwise hit them as they returned to their airfields before landing.

This idea was far from new. The Luftwaffe had been employing such tactics over Bomber Command's bases in England and it had worked to some degree. The idea was first tried from Malta on the night of 25 January 1942 and proved relatively successful when an enemy bomber was destroyed at Comiso airfield in Sicily.

However, this same date will also be remembered for the heavy losses suffered earlier in the day when Malta's Hurricanes provided air cover for two supply ships leaving Grand Harbour. The Hurricanes had only just got airborne and were struggling to gain height when they were jumped by 109s. Seven Hurricanes were shot down and three more were subsequently destroyed on the ground when the 109s strafed Hal Far.

It had been a brief but extremely costly encounter for Malta's defenders and things were about to get worse as the Luftwaffe's attacks against the airfields intensified. During January, some fifty Hurricanes were either destroyed or severely damaged on the ground to add to the eight shot down over the island. The few surviving Hurricanes of 249 Squadron were forced to move to Luqa because their own airfield at Takali had been so frequently bombed.

It had been quite a turnaround for those on the island who, only weeks before, had been enjoying a period of calm. The war had seemed manageable but now the relative peace and quiet of the previous few months had disappeared.

Malta, once again, lacked fighters. It seems almost unbelievable that nearly 350 Hurricanes had either been sent to Malta or passed through the island over the past eighteen months, yet there were now fewer than thirty serviceable on the island. With every available aircraft needed to counter the daylight raids, the pilots of 1435 Flight reverted to daytime defence.

Hugh Pughe Lloyd repeatedly asked for more fighters to be sent to Malta but his pleas fell on deaf ears.[3] But there was, perhaps, some hope when Group Captain Basil Embry arrived in Malta at the end of January to assess

---

3. Holland, op. cit., p.214.

the situation on behalf of the recently knighted C-in-C, Sir Arthur Tedder. Embry was soon convinced. He could see just how the morale of the fighter pilots had dipped because of the lack of support from back home and wasted no time putting forward his recommendation that every possible step should be taken to reinforce Malta with Spitfires with the least amount of delay.[4]

Not only was it vital to build Malta's fighter strength in the air but it was also vital to build Cunningham's surface fleet once more. The loss of *Ark Royal* and *Barham*, plus others, had left the Royal Navy in the Mediterranean short. Furthermore, the virtual destruction of Force K in one bad encounter with the enemy off Libya had left Cunningham starting the year without a strike force in Malta.

The ASV-equipped Wellingtons, which had proved to be such a valuable asset since arriving on the island, had also suffered losses. Luqa had become a priority target for the Luftwaffe's bombers and of the three special duties aircraft that had been given to Tony Spooner for the SDF, only one was still available at the end of January. His flight had been so devastated that his crews had to move out from Luqa to live temporarily at Kalafrana.

The SDF continued as best it could with its one remaining aircraft. The crews had to endure patrols of more than ten hours at a time, but they were not helped by the bad weather as the aircraft's aerials were affected by icing and moisture, often giving the crew false signals. Although the Maryland crews continued to provide aerial reconnaissance as best they could through the period of bad weather, tracking an enemy convoy once at sea was far from simple, and even when a convoy was spotted, there was often little that could be done to stop it.

And so it was left to Malta's bombers and submarines to continue the fight as best they could to prevent the Axis convoys from getting through to Rommel. But the submarines of the Tenth Flotilla had now been at sea for almost a year, with little or no rest. Stress and fatigue was setting in among the crews. Simpson faced little choice other than to give his crews the rest they desperately needed and so a number of subs came into Manoel Island

---

4. The National Archives, AIR 23/1200 (Embry also recommended that Malta should receive Curtiss P-40 Kittyhawks).

for a refit and to give the crews a break. But for *Upholder* and her crew there would be no rest. After a quiet end to 1941, *Upholder* was soon back to winning ways during the first week of January 1942 when she crippled an Italian merchantman of more than 5,000 tonnes and sank an Italian submarine.

The Fleet Air Arm's torpedo-bombers were hard at it too, despite the appalling weather, and continued to harass the Axis supply convoys with some success. But the loss of so many sorties to the bad weather in the early weeks of the year meant that most of Rommel's supplies were getting through. A large Axis convoy in early January, for example, consisting of six merchant vessels with a large Italian naval escort including submarines, had got through to Tripoli unscathed. Not everything, though, got through to Rommel's forces. Swordfish of 830 Squadron succeeded in penetrating the outer defences of one convoy in the approaches to Tripoli and had contributed towards the sinking of a large transport merchantman, the 13,000-tonne liner *Victoria*, regarded by the Italians to be the pearl of their merchant fleet.[5] This rare British success during January was followed up by the sinking of two more Italian supply ships by the submarines *Ultimatum* and *Umbra*.

Now with the supplies he needed, Rommel counter-attacked in the desert during January 1942 and forced the British Eighth Army all the way back across Cyrenaica. The pendulum in the desert had swung once more. Not only was this bad for the British Army in North Africa but it was also bad for Malta. Although supplies were reaching British forces in Egypt by the long route round the Cape, getting them to Malta was another matter. Any convoys bound for the island from the east would no longer get air cover from the RAF in Libya. One attempt by three merchantmen had to return to Alexandria after the ships came under repeated attacks from the Luftwaffe based in North Africa.

Running a convoy to Malta from the east would soon be all but impossible but every effort was made to get supplies through. The Magic Carpet runs from Alexandria continued as best they could. The submarine *Talisman* made

---

5. Spooner (*Supreme Gallantry*), op. cit., p.107.

it into Grand Harbour during January, and an exchange of fast transports was instigated involving *Breconshire* and her sister ship, the 10,000-tonne *Glengyle*.

The *Glengyle* had been operating in the Mediterranean as a landing ship for commandos but was briefly allocated to Malta convoy duties before returning to the UK. While *Breconshire* left Malta with her escort of four destroyers, *Glengyle*, laden with oil, food and ammunition, and escorted by two cruisers and five destroyers, made a dash through the eastern Med. The plan worked and it got *Glengyle* with her precious supplies safely into Grand Harbour. Then, on 27 January, *Breconshire* sailed fully laden back into Grand Harbour once more at the end of another daring dash through the Mediterranean, and *Glengyle* and *Rowallan Castle* sailed the other way, taking with them more service families off the island.

Despite the hazards of operating in the eastern Med, there was a well-oiled system in place for the exchange of naval escorts between Vian's Alexandria-based ships, consisting of four cruisers and eight destroyers, and those Malta-based ships comprising the cruiser *Penelope* and five destroyers: *Lance*, *Lively*, *Legion*, *Maori* and *Zulu*. The handover of escort responsibilities took place to the south-west of Crete with naval submarines providing picket duty to warn of any enemy intervention.

At the other end of the Mediterranean in Gibraltar, James Somerville was replaced by Edward Neville Syfret, the former naval secretary. Somerville had returned home on promotion before taking up his next appointment in the Far East. He had done his bit as far as the re-supply of Malta was concerned. The Club Runs had kept the island topped up with RAF fighters and the huge naval support for the Malta-bound convoys had kept the island afloat for the past eighteen months.

For Cunningham, though, the desperate fight in the Mediterranean continued. He again found himself going into bat, calling for more reinforcements to be sent from the UK. But there was now also a war in the Far East to consider. From now on, it would be difficult enough for Cunningham and Lloyd to hang on to what they already had, let alone get anything more, as many of those assets currently in the Mediterranean and Middle East were now required in the Far East.

The last few runs through the eastern Med had been helped by the January weather, although the fortune would not last. With better weather came more air raids as Malta's airfields again took a pounding, sometimes several times a day. Takali, in particular, resembled something out of a disaster film with buildings flattened and laying derelict. Aircraft were left in ruins despite the protective pens that had been rapidly constructed around the airfield.

The Luftwaffe's raids against Grand and Marsamxett Harbours, as well as against the submarine base at Manoel Island, had also intensified with the Royal Navy also suffering losses. The destroyer *Maori*, for example, had succumbed to bombs during an air raid while moored alongside a merchant vessel, although, fortunately, most of her crew had been ashore at the time.

Royal Navy ships arriving in Grand Harbour continued to bring in whatever supplies they could, as did the submarines, but the fact was that a submarine could only carry, at best, about 1,000 tonnes of supplies; and even that was at risk to the crew because it made the sub difficult to trim. Furthermore, the passage from Gibraltar could take a submarine several days and meant navigating through hazardous minefields. Then, having reached harbour, they had to surface to unload. This was usually done at night because of the relentless air raids by day and so it was not unusual for a submarine crew to sit on the bottom in Marsamxett Harbour, still at risk from falling bombs, just waiting for darkness when they could surface to offload. All this took up valuable time that should have otherwise been spent on patrol.

It was a tremendous effort by all those involved but despite all the bits and pieces going ashore from the ships and submarines, the fact remained that it was not enough. Shops, restaurants and bars closed one by one, and, for the Maltese, life was getting harder by the day. Although morale had been dented, people still refused to give up. At the airfields, for example, each air raid was followed by the normal pattern: a working party to fill in the craters to keep the airfield open, followed by repairs to the buildings and protective shelters being erected. Others had the unpleasant task of tending to any bodies.

For the island of Malta, the situation was desperate once more, bordering on hopeless. One of many bad days was Friday, 13 February. First the submarine *Tempest* was lost having been forced to surface after repeatedly being attacked by an Italian torpedo-boat. While the Italian commander tried to tow his prize into harbour at Taranto, the British submarine sank and took with her thirty-nine members of her crew. Then, during the afternoon, convoy MW9 from the east was spotted by an Axis reconnaissance aircraft and during the inevitable bombing attack later in the day, *Clan Campbell* was so severely damaged that she had to make for Tobruk under the escort of two destroyers.

Early the next morning the Luftwaffe returned. This time it cost the convoy the merchant vessel *Clan Chattan*. Meanwhile, further to the west, *Rowallan Castle* was running at full speed towards Malta but being the only merchantman among her small convoy she was an obvious target. She was singled out by the attacking Ju88s and although she avoided receiving a direct hit, a stick of bombs fell just off her port side and caused significant damage. With her speed down to no more than 4 knots, the destroyer *Zulu* took her in tow.

Although nightfall brought some relief for those on board, they knew they would be a sitting duck for the Luftwaffe when the bombers returned at dawn, which they surely would, and so the decision was reluctantly made to sink *Rowallan Castle*.[6] It was a desperate decision to have to make. Although it would deny the enemy the satisfaction of sinking the stricken vessel, or capturing its cargo, it also denied Malta more essential supplies.

There was more disappointment for Malta when a Club Run from Gibraltar at the end of February, called Operation Spotter, had to be aborted. It was a desperate shame because on board the carrier HMS *Eagle* were sixteen Spitfire Mark Vs, the first Spitfires for the island. It was only when a defect in their auxiliary fuel tanks was spotted at the last minute that the operation had to be cancelled, and so the carrier had to return to Gibraltar so that the defect could be rectified. Although the defect would soon be put right so that the Spitfires could get back on their way to Malta, Cunningham was now advised by the chiefs of staff that he could no longer expect to be replenished with other supplies from Gibraltar.

---

6. Woodman, op. cit., pp.284–7.

Without food, fuel and ammunition, Malta would soon be in crisis. The island was threatened with starvation and was facing the unthinkable prospect of surrender. It could only be a matter of time. The situation in Malta had become grave.

Chapter Twelve

At Last – Spitfires!

Fearing an invasion was always likely, Malta's defenders prepared as best they could. Word had spread as to how the Germans had carried out their airborne invasion of Crete the year before and just how important the capture of the island's airfields had been to the success of that operation. Consequently, more anti-aircraft gun emplacements and machine-gun posts were set up at Malta's airfields and at other key positions across the island. Rifles and ammunition were spread around the island's servicemen, regardless of which service they belonged to, and techniques such as close-quarter fighting and hand-to-hand combat were taught. More slit trenches were built as everyone pulled their weight, regardless of rank.

Following the aborted Club Run at the end of February, a revised effort, Spotter II, was mounted in early March. Once south of the Balearics, fifteen of the sixteen Spitfires destined for Malta were launched; one had suffered a technical problem. With a transit of nearly 700 miles, and escorted by seven Blenheims from Gibraltar, the Spitfires flew in two formations, one of eight and the other of seven, led by Squadron Leader Stan Grant and Flight Lieutenant Norman McQueen respectively. After a flight of four hours, they approached the island with Malta's Hurricanes providing fighter cover during the final part of the transit. Fortunately, there was no sign of the Luftwaffe and all the Spitfires landed safely at Takali. It was mid-morning on Saturday, 7 March.

The new arrivals were the first Spitfires to see action outside of Britain. They were given to 249 Squadron as the squadron's Hurricanes had been mauled by the 109s. The Spitfires were immediately stripped of their external fuel tanks, repainted with a more appropriate camouflage scheme and their guns harmonized in preparation for commencing operations as soon as possible.

The arrival of Stan Grant meant there was a brief period when 249 had two squadron leaders. At the time of Grant's arrival, the squadron was under the command of Stan Turner, a stocky Canadian and one of the RAF's most experienced fighter pilots at the time, who had arrived in Malta just the month before. With a DFC and Bar for his twelve victories, Turner had earlier served as a flight commander with 242 Squadron during the Battle of Britain, under the legendary Douglas Bader, and had then commanded 145 Squadron and 411 Squadron RCAF before flying out to Malta.[1]

The squadron's two flight commanders were, at that stage of their combat careers, still reasonably inexperienced. One was Percy Lucas, known as 'Laddie', a 26-year-old graduate from Cambridge University and an excellent golfer, having before the war been a member of the English International and Walker Cup Team. The other was Robert McNair, a tough 22-year-old Canadian from Nova Scotia and known to everyone as 'Buck'. Both Lucas and McNair had arrived in Malta in mid-February on board the same Sunderland flying boat from Gibraltar that had brought Stan Turner to the island, and both would quickly prove themselves to be outstanding flight commanders.

Stan Turner's impact on the daytime fighter operations in Malta had been immediate and lasting, and his achievement was even more remarkable given that he had arrived on the island when the squadron's fortunes had reached an all-time low. The few Hurricanes that had remained serviceable had seen better days although, in the right hands, they still had an effective part to play. But, tactically and speed-wise, the brutal fact was the Bf109Fs had the measure of them.[2]

Although the Hurricanes could not have saved Malta, they had gallantly held the fort until better fighters could arrive. There were many Hurricane pilots who had played their part: Fred Robertson, Sandy Rabagliati, James MacLachlan, George Burges, Eric Taylor and Pat Lardner-Burke plus many more.

---

1. Shores and Williams, op. cit., pp.597–8.
2. Lucas, *Five Up*, p.88.

News that Spitfires had finally arrived on the island spread around Malta in no time. Three days later, on the morning of 10 March, the new arrivals were in action over the island for the first time. Seven Spitfires were scrambled with eight Hurricanes of 126 Squadron to intercept a force of nine Ju88s escorted by 109s.

The Spitfires were led by Stan Turner. He took a section of three aircraft up to 19,000 feet, followed by a section of four led by Flight Lieutenant 'Nip' Heppell. The superior performance of the Spitfire Mark V over the Hurricane Mark II meant the defenders were above the raiders as they coasted in towards their target of Luqa.

The RAF's tactics when operating a mixed Spitfire-Hurricane force in Malta were much the same that had been used earlier in the war during the Battle of Britain. The Spitfires would deliberately target the fighter escort, leaving the Hurricanes to attack the bombers.

Because the 109s had become used to engaging Malta's Hurricanes while they were still climbing for height over the island, the 109s were beneath the bombers during their final run-in towards Luqa. This would normally make the task of the fighter escort easier than to have to attack through the height of their own bombers. But, on this occasion, the escorting 109 pilots were to get a shock and their position suggests that they had not received news of the arrival of Spitfires in Malta. Either that or they were aware of the Spitfires but chose to ignore the superior performance of the Spitfire V.

Heppell struck first, bouncing the unsuspecting fighter escort and firing a long and deadly burst into a Bf109F, sending the German into the sea. It was the squadron's 100th victory of the war. Other 109s were attacked and claimed as damaged during the encounter, although none of the bombers were shot down. One Hurricane was lost.

There were further raids during the day, including a raid late in the afternoon against the airfields of Luqa and Hal Far. Four Spitfires joined eleven Hurricanes to intercept the raid but it was to end in the first loss of a Spitfire over Malta, flown by 20-year-old Pilot Officer Kenric Murray, an Australian. The Spitfires had been attacked at high level by 109Fs of II./ JG 3 led by Hauptmann Karl-Heinz Krahl, an experienced Luftwaffe ace with eighteen victories. Laddie Lucas was flying one of the Spitfires that afternoon and later recorded the horror of what he saw:

'We spotted, far away to port, a single Spitfire obviously looking for a mate. As we turned to go to his aid, a lone 109, diving very fast out of the sun, pulled up unseen, under the Spit. From dead astern, the pilot delivered a short, determined burst. Relieved, we saw a parachute open. As we watched the silk canopy floating down in the distance, with the pilot swinging on its end, another single 109, diving down out of broken cloud, made a run at the 'chute, squirting it as he went and collapsing it with his slipstream as he passed by. The canopy streamed, leaving the pilot without a chance.'[3]

Murray's Spitfire crashed near Rabat. Since it was believed that Murray had come down in the sea, three Spitfires went out to cover the area where he may have come down, and a launch was sent out to pick him up but, although the young Australian was found, Kenric Murray died of his injuries.

Lucas made his first claim of the war that day, a 109, but nothing was confirmed and it is recorded as damaged; it was the first of many claims he would make while flying over the island. One of the Hurricanes was shot down by Krahl. It was the German's nineteenth victim of the war, but such was the ferocity of the air war being fought over Malta that it was to be his last; Krahl would be killed a month later when he was shot down by the island's anti-aircraft defences during a low-level strafing attack against Luqa.

Now with Spitfire Vs, Turner was quick to adapt the squadron's tactics. The effect upon him having earlier seen Hurricanes clambering up in a straggling 'V' formation, with the 109s thousands of feet above, had been profound. Within a week of his arrival, pairs and fours in line abreast had become the only battle formation flown. The 'V' and line astern, both popular formations back home where the RAF had the luxury of numbers to sustain them, were out. Lucas later explained:

'With the odds we were dealing with in the Mediterranean, we couldn't afford them. And anyway, if we had tried leaving a sergeant pilot out in the cold, flying in line astern as tail-end Charlie at the back, protecting some of the more senior and commissioned backsides in the front, I wouldn't have given too much for their chances.'[4]

---

3. Cull, op. cit., pp.92–3.
4. Lucas, op. cit., p.90.

In his short time on the island, Turner had already achieved so much. He had taken Malta's flying apart and given it a refit in readiness for the major battles ahead. Four days after the Spitfire's combat debut over Malta, he handed over command of 249 Squadron to Stan Grant, with Turner deservedly promoted and appointed as wing commander flying at Takali.

Stan Grant would also be a great success and prove to be one of the RAF's most effective squadron commanders in the battle for Malta. Finely trained before the war, he knew how to run and lead a squadron. He retained firm overall control but delegated detail to his two flight commanders, Lucas and McNair, and proved to be an excellent officer to serve under and thoroughly proficient in the air.[5]

The air raids against Malta intensified once more and now regularly involved large raiding forces of up to fifty aircraft or even more. The number of air raid warnings had also risen to an average of about seven alerts every day, with any one warning lasting for up to several hours. This made it difficult for the RAF to hit back and so the procedure at the airfields was for the airmen to ignore the persistent general warning and to carry on work until the local airfield alarm could be heard.[6]

The Luftwaffe launched another blitz against Malta on 20 March, further reducing the island to even more rubble. Takali, in particular, took yet another pounding and was so obliterated that, at times, the fighters could not operate. When the raids were over, work started immediately to clear up the mess but early the following morning the raiders were back again with an estimated 200 aircraft delivering another devastating attack.

More than a thousand bombs had fallen on Malta in just two days.[7] With the submarine base at Manoel Island also being high on the Luftwaffe's list of targets, combined with subs being lost at sea, there was doubt as to whether the Tenth Flotilla could even remain there.

This was a crucial part of the war and there was little good news for those in Malta. In addition to the grim accounts coming from the desert war, news received from elsewhere hardly brought any joy or encouragement. Britain had suffered a humiliating defeat in the Far East with the surrender

---

5. Ibid, p.103.
6. Spooner (*Supreme Gallantry*), op. cit., p.96.
7. Holland, op. cit., p.252.

of Singapore, the Germans had pushed the Russians back to within miles of Moscow, the U-boats were winning the Battle of the Atlantic and the United States was still lickings its wounds suffered at Pearl Harbour.

All Malta could do was to struggle on and be grateful for any reinforcements that could be spared. The arrival of the Spitfires had given Malta hope and reminded the Maltese that, despite all that was going on elsewhere in the war, the island had not been forgotten. The Spitfires had, in fact, arrived in the nick of time but whether they could make the difference in the air war, and enable Malta to survive, remained to be seen.

Everyone was delighted to see a second flight of nine Spitfires, destined for 126 and 185 Squadrons, arrive at Luqa on 21 March from the carrier *Eagle*. This delivery was completed under Operation Picket with the Spitfires led by Squadron Leader Edward 'Jumbo' Gracie, another experienced pilot with a DFC and at least five victories.

Gracie was sent to Malta to take command of 126 Squadron. While leading the squadron he would add two more victories to his total before he was promoted and appointed wing commander flying at Takali, replacing Stan Turner who was to be rested from operations. Gracie would soon take over command of Takali airfield from Wing Commander Jack Satchell. Although he had been station commander for the past four months, Satchell had flown whenever he could and had achieved three victories while in command to bring his overall total to six while flying from the airfield.[8]

Jumbo Gracie was just the man needed in a crisis and immediately proved to be a very popular figure at Takali, often walking around amid the air raids. He was an exceptional organizer with drive and purpose, and within days the spirit of the station, and the morale among pilots and ground crew, had been transformed.[9]

Meanwhile at sea, the latest convoy from Alexandria, MW10, comprising four merchantmen – the naval auxiliary *Breconshire*, the patched-up *Clan Campbell*, and a Norwegian vessel called *Talabot* as well as the Royal Mail Line's *Pampas* – was desperately trying to reach Malta covered by the largest

---

8. Shores and Williams, op. cit., pp.532–3.
9. Lucas, op. cit., p.95.

escort Vian could muster. Between the four vessels they were carrying a total of 29,000 tonnes of supplies for the island. *Breconshire*'s tanks had been refilled with 5,000 tonnes of boiler oil and her decks were laden with ammunition and other munitions as well as grain, coal, kerosene and other essential stores. With the exception of the boiler oil, the other three vessels were carrying a similar cargo, as well as service personnel bound for Malta. All the merchantmen were well armed with various defensive machine guns manned by servicemen, a term known as DEMS (Defensive Equipped Merchant Ships).

The convoy set sail at first light on 20 March under the close escort of the cruiser *Carlisle* and six destroyers of the 22nd Destroyer Flotilla, covered by three cruisers of Vian's 15th Cruiser Squadron and four destroyers of the 5th Destroyer Flotilla. There was always the possibility the Italian fleet would mount a surface attack, and the Axis submarines always posed a threat from beneath the surface. And so there was further protection out in the Med, involving three of Malta's U-class submarines and two P-class, to provide early warning of any enemy surface vessels manoeuvring to intercept. Also out to the west were the cruiser *Penelope* and the destroyer *Legion*, the remnants of Force K, from Malta.

The whole operation was given the codename MG1. The convoy simply had to get through and the stakes were desperately high. The air threat would come from the Luftwaffe's airfields in Crete and Libya and so the complex plan involved specialist army units and land-based RAF and Fleet Air Arm aircraft mounting diversionary attacks against enemy airfields in North Africa, in the hope it would keep aircraft such as the Luftwaffe's Ju88s grounded, or at least distracted.

Once underway, the differing speeds of the merchantmen made station-keeping difficult and reduced the convoy's mean speed of advance. About 8.00 am on 22 March, *Penelope* and *Legion* joined up with Vian's fleet. It was a beautiful Sunday morning with good visibility and clear skies, and so their arrival was both timely and welcome. Vian had just been informed from the outer submarines that a powerful Italian fleet, comprising a battleship, two heavy cruisers, a light cruiser and eight destroyers, were seen heading for the convoy.

By now the convoy was passing clear of the first area of high risk, the stretch of water between Crete and Cyrenaica, known to the naval crews as 'bomb alley'. Fortunately, the wind was picking up with the visibility reducing by the hour and by midday the convoy was heading past Libya's Gulf of Sirte. Meanwhile, far to the north, the Italian warships were racing towards the convoy at a speed in excess of 20 knots, although the building headwind and increasing swell were making conditions difficult.

With the Italian fleet in pursuit, the convoy came under repeated air attacks from Italian torpedo-carrying aircraft and German Ju88s. During the early afternoon, Vian positioned his ships in readiness for the anticipated surface battle about to follow. *Carlisle* and a number of destroyers were to remain with the merchantmen, laying smoke across the convoy's rear and using the strong breeze to their advantage, while his remaining warships formed five strike groups to confront the Italian fleet.

Unlike the previous action, to be remembered as the First Battle of Sirte, this encounter, later dubbed the Second Battle of Sirte, saw a more determined effort by the Italian fleet to reach and engage the convoy's merchantmen. Adopting the overall tactic of threat and concealment, by using smoke screens to cover his ships, Vian's force of cruisers and destroyers held off two Italian attacks during the course of the afternoon while the convoy escaped. After these two attempts to break through Vian's defences, the Italian fleet gave up and broke off the attack.

The naval action was portrayed as a tactical success for the British against a greatly superior enemy, although the convoy had been forced to change course several times, delaying its progress and leaving it vulnerable to further air attacks. As expected, the air attacks resumed later that day. The *Clan Campbell*, struggling to keep up, attracted more than its fair share of bombs. Bombs rained on her but every time the great gouts of water settled, she could be seen to reappear from a curtain of water in one piece.[10]

The weather continued to deteriorate throughout the day, causing the convoy and her escort to bounce around in the swell. With *Clan Campbell* struggling to keep pace, she was ordered to make directly for Grand Harbour while the other three merchantmen were to make a southward

---

10. Woodman, op. cit., p.306. (Taken from a report by Captain Edkins of the Hampshire Regiment aboard the *Talabot*).

leg as a diversionary manoeuvre. The idea was that the convoy would join together again during the early hours of the following morning for the final run through the swept channel into Grand Harbour, under the protection of the close escort. But, as things were to turn out, this would prove a fatal decision for *Breconshire*, which, at 17 knots, could probably have easily reached Grand Harbour before daylight the following day.

The lack of refuelling facilities at Malta meant that Vian's force could only escort the convoy for the first three days. As darkness fell on the evening of 22 March, his covering force turned back for Alexandria, leaving the convoy to complete its dash to Malta and to hopefully arrive before dawn.

Soon after 9.00 am the following morning, *Talabot* and *Pampas* sailed into Grand Harbour, accompanied by two damaged destroyers, *Havock* and *Kingston*. Both merchant ships had narrow escapes during their final run-in to Malta. *Pampas*, in particular, had been fortunate to survive an air attack at first light when two bombs hit her but failed to explode, and *Talabot* had to endure a final low strafing and single-bomb attack by an enemy 109 near the harbour.

But things had not gone so well for the other two merchant ships. *Clan Campbell*'s slow speed had cost her dearly and she fell further behind. By daylight she was still fifty miles from Malta with her escort, HMS *Eridge*, a Hunt-class destroyer. They were both getting closer to Malta by the hour and by mid-morning they were just twenty miles away. Then came another air attack, this time from low level and with devastating accuracy. The two ships could provide little or no opposition and the poor *Clan Campbell* did not stand a chance. Within minutes she had gone to the bottom, taking with her all of her precious cargo and six of the crew, and the survivors were taken on board *Eridge*.

Closer to Malta, but still eight miles away from Grand Harbour, *Breconshire* was also in trouble. She had been spotted at first light and attacked by Ju88s. This time, though, she was to be less lucky than before. A bomb hit her, causing severe damage to the engine room and bringing the merchantman to a halt. Two naval destroyers tried as best they could to tow her into Malta but bad weather and a heavy swell made it impossible. As the stricken *Breconshire* drifted towards shore, protected by three destroyers and a smoke screen, she dropped anchor and spent the rest of the day wallowing helplessly in the swell waiting for Malta's tugs to arrive.

With *Carlisle* and two Hunt-class destroyers, *Southwold* and *Dulverton*, remaining in the vicinity to provide as much protection as they could, that night was spent restoring power to the stricken *Breconshire*. The following morning proved difficult. Tugs that had arrived on the scene could not get alongside because of the swell. Then, during the afternoon, air attacks from Ju88s and Bf109s sent *Southwold* to the bottom.

Fortunately, *Breconshire* had survived further damage but, despite her two anchors, she had been slowly drifting towards a minefield. By midnight she was successfully under tow and the following day, 25 March, *Breconshire* finally arrived in a sinking state in Marsaxlokk Harbour, a traditional home to fishing vessels in the south-east of the island.

Meanwhile, the damage to Malta's quaysides and wharves, the result of the past three months of air attacks, meant that *Pampas* and *Talabot* had to be moored in the middle of Grand Harbour rather than docked alongside the Corradino Heights in French Creek. Consequently, the two merchantmen had remained exposed and making the whole unloading process difficult and slow. Supplies had to be taken off the ships and then ferried to the quayside on barges, which, in turn, had to be unloaded before returning to the two vessels to be loaded with more supplies. But, because of the blackout, no cargo was unloaded at night. For those who could only stand and watch, it was a painfully slow process. Fortunately, though, the weather was in Malta's favour. Low cloud made it difficult for any raiders to attack the ships and when any enemy aircraft were seen, an accurate barrage of anti-aircraft fire meant that neither ship was hit during the day.

With so many bombers and dive-bombers now based in Sicily and Italy, the Luftwaffe was able to attack Malta at will and, consequently, the bombers returned with a vengeance the following day.[11] The *Breconshire* had been spotted at Marsaxlokk and was bombed by Ju88s. With no real defence, the merchantman had not stood a chance. Hit yet again, the poor

---

11. At the time there were a reported 172 Ju88 bombers plus thirty-two Ju87 dive-bombers based in Sicily and Italy, as well as 137 Bf109s. See Spooner (*Supreme Gallantry*), op. cit., pp.115–6 (figures taken from records held at the Air Historical Branch (RAF) at RAF Northolt).

old *Breconshire*, a ship that had done more than any other vessel to bring relief to Malta, rolled over.

Meanwhile, in and around Grand Harbour, *Pampas* and *Talabot* were also hit during the heavy raids. Both ships caught fire before *Pampas* sank and *Talabot*, with the risk that her ammunition supplies might explode, had to be scuttled.

The scuttling of the burning *Talabot*, with her explosive cargo and in a busy harbour, was a hazardous operation. It was led by 27-year-old Lieutenant Dennis Copperwheat, a torpedo and explosives officer from HMS *Penelope*. His group laid scuttling charges as the fires caused ammunition stored on the deck to explode around them and prevented the charges being laid in the hold. The charges had to be draped over the sides of the stricken vessel, which lay just 40 yards from the shore and, as the electric cables required to fire the charges could only just reach the shore, Copperwheat took it upon himself to fire the charges after seeing his men safely to cover. He was, therefore, exposed to the full force of charges he had laid but was successful in sinking the ship. Had the ship been left to burn, the inevitable explosion from the burning ammunition would have caused grievous damage to Valletta's harbour. That possibility had now been averted and for his extreme heroism, Dennis Copperwheat was awarded the George Cross.

Of all the supplies on board *Pampas* and *Talabot*, a total of more than 16,000 tonnes, less than 2,000 tonnes had been taken off the ships since they arrived in harbour. Furthermore, all the supplies on board *Breconshire* were lost, in addition to those already lost on *Clan Campbell*.

It was a devastating blow for everyone involved with the convoy and those on the island of Malta. Four merchant ships had set out from Alexandria but all four were now lost. Three of those ships had bravely run the gauntlet of the eastern Med and had sailed into harbour, only then to be sunk while unloading.

It had been an extremely costly attempt to run a small convoy from Alexandria. Calling the convoy a disaster seems harsh on all those who had fought so bravely to get the convoy through to Malta. There had, after all, been a tactical success by the escorting ships against an Italian fleet determined to prevent the convoy from reaching the island. Calling the operation a disaster is also harsh on all those in Grand Harbour who worked tirelessly to do what they could to get the supplies ashore from *Pampas* and *Talabot,* despite being constantly harried by the German bombers.

But the fact was the convoy was a disaster. Mistakes had been made at sea, particularly the decision to disperse the merchantmen during the final run-in towards Malta, and then once in harbour the unloading of the precious cargo had been poorly managed. After all the effort, the harsh reality was that Malta was only marginally better off at the end of MG1 than it had been before the convoy had sailed from Alexandria.

All sorts of discussions and debates, arguments even, began in the aftermath of MG1. Questions were understandably asked about why the unloading had not been better managed. After all, the weather had been generally poor and so the blackout during the two critical nights before *Pampas* and *Talabot* were sunk in harbour could have been lifted to aid the unloading of supplies.

As things were to turn out, though, the wrecks of *Breconshire* and *Talabot* were in shallow water and so further salvage operations could take place with some of the supplies rescued and taken ashore. In the end, just over 5,000 tonnes of the possible 29,000 tonnes were saved.[12]

Nonetheless, the arguments and discussions went on among Malta's top administrators, which included the governor, Sir William Dobbie, and his deputy, Vice Admiral Sir Ralph Leatham, who had taken over from Wilbraham Ford just weeks before. The discussions went on but the fact was that such an outcome should never be allowed to happen again. The fortress island of Malta was now sinking.

---

12. Holland, op. cit., pp.259–60.

Chapter Thirteen

George Cross Island

The disastrous convoy MW10 at the end of March was the last operation to take place under Cunningham's direction; it was time for him to rest. On 1 April 1942 he handed over temporarily to Henry Pridham-Wippell until Cunningham's appointed successor, Vice Admiral Sir Henry Harwood, could arrive.

It had been a hard three years for Cunningham, particularly the last two, but he had led the Mediterranean Fleet to victory in several critical naval battles, including the air attack against Taranto in 1940 and the Battle of Cape Matapan in 1941. He had also controlled the defence of the Mediterranean supply lines through Alexandria, Gibraltar and the key chokepoint of Malta. Cunningham was off to Washington in the United States as head of the Admiralty delegation there, and would later replace Sir Dudley Pound as first sea lord, but he would have been disappointed to depart the Mediterranean Fleet at a time when it was at its lowest ebb.

Just when it seemed like the Luftwaffe could do no more to Malta, more bombs were dropped on the besieged island. During March 1942, more than 2,000 tonnes of bombs fell on Malta, twice that of the previous month, with an average of nearly ten air raid alerts every day.[1]

But there was worse to come. The Luftwaffe launched another assault against Malta on 2 April. The main priority was to neutralize the island's fighters with specific targets again being Malta's airfields, its harbour installations and shipping. During that morning, a large raid of more than a hundred aircraft attacked the airfields and harbour. But Malta's defenders were waiting for them. The island had been further reinforced by sixteen

---

1. Ibid, pp.261–2.

more Spitfires at the end of March following the resumption of Club Runs from Gibraltar.

The Spitfires and Hurricanes were airborne in reasonable numbers and the anti-aircraft gunners presented the raiders with an intense barrage of accurate fire. The Ju87 Stukas proved a relatively easy target as the raiders suffered without loss to the RAF. Nonetheless, there was only so much the defenders could achieve against such a mass raid and the island, in particular the airfields, still took a pounding.

The raids continued and damage to the airfields was again significant. It was not long before there remained just a few fighters left. Even with the newly arrived Spitfires, there were some days when just ten serviceable fighters were available and on five separate occasions during the month, there was only one Spitfire available. There was a further problem, too, as losses meant there were now just sixty or so fighter pilots spread across the squadrons.[2]

The Luftwaffe and Regia Aeronautica had almost gained air superiority over Malta. The bombing campaign was intense and those ships fit for sea left Malta to take their chances elsewhere, although a number of smaller vessels – oil lighters, water boats, tugs, fire floats and drifters – did not escape in time.

The extent of the damage to Malta's dockyard was highlighted in a signal from Naval HQ Malta to the Admiralty, dated 7 April 1942, which included:

'*No 2 and 3 boiler yard machinery shop demolished. Santa Teresa tunnel completely wrecked. Church tunnel partly collapsed and completely blocked. Sewage system and water supplies almost completely out of action. Drawing offices and many other offices and storehouses have been destroyed. Residences completely wrecked. Numerous large craters in roadways and on wharves. At present there is practically no light in the dockyard except in 4 and 5 dock area.*'[3]

2. Ibid, p.265.
3. NA, WO 106/2113, Situation Reports and Operational Messages: Mediterranean Area: Malta 1 January - 30 September 1942.

And so it went on. With the harbour in ruins, the resilient light-cruiser HMS *Penelope*, a stalwart of Force K, slipped out of Grand Harbour on the night of 8 April. She had been hit so many times that she earned herself the now legendary name of HMS '*Pepperpot*', and so her many holes had been patched up as best as possible to enable her to get out to sea. Although *Penelope* suffered a further air attack the following day, she eventually made it to Gibraltar to undergo extensive repairs.

Not only had the harbour and dockyards been extensively damaged but the surrounding areas had also suffered once again. According to the Luftwaffe's bombing strategy, the built-up areas of Valletta, Sliema and the Three Cities were supposed to be avoided, but the Maltese would always maintain there was a deliberate intent to bomb them into submission, in the same way the Luftwaffe had launched the Blitz on London and other cities on the home front. Homes and churches were destroyed and the number of civilian casualties mounted. Even the hospital at Imtarfa did not escape the bombing, despite a large red cross being painted on the adjacent sports field.

The rest of the island suffered too, with electricity, water and telephone lines often cut off. What little food there was on the island could not always be distributed as there was little or no transport available due to the shortage of fuel. There was not even transport to ferry the fighter pilots between their digs in the local villages and towns to the airfields, and so the fighter pilots tended to stay at their base.

Although the struggle in the air was every bit as desperate as some of the pilots had endured during the Battle of Britain before, life on the ground in Malta was a very different existence altogether. With hardly any bowsers left, and aircraft dispersals surrounded by craters, pilots would often help carry the fuel by hand around the airfield. And even then, with the aircraft refuelled and rearmed, it was all but impossible to rest. Furthermore, the food was awful and the dreaded Malta Dog, with a combination of high temperature, stomach pains, sickness and diarrhoea, plagued almost everyone at some point. There was hardly ever any mail and life in general was many times worse than what pilots had been used to back home. Conditions were so bad that the tour of duty for a fighter pilot, whenever possible, was reduced to just three months from the recommended six months made earlier in the year.[4] But everyone had to contribute, and everyone suffered together, to give the island the chance to survive.

Malta's offensive air power, once so effective, had now all but gone. The two Fleet Air Arm squadrons, 830 and 828, were so depleted that they were formed into a single unit. Most of the Wellingtons and Blenheims had gone, having suffered appalling losses in the air and on the ground. Those that had not been destroyed had left for the relative safety of Egypt. With the exception of the fighters, there were just two RAF units still in existence on the island. The SDF was still at Luqa, as were the reconnaissance aircraft of 69 Squadron.

One pilot who had got away for a rest, although he would later return, was Adrian Warburton. He had left Malta at the end of his second operational tour with a DSO to add to his two DFCs. During his time on the island, Warburton had tested the patience of his superiors and had taken to flying in almost any clothes, provided they were not the official ones. He would often be found playing cards with airmen at the dispersal rather than socializing with his fellow officers at Luqa.

While on detachment in Egypt Warburton had even 'acquired' a Beaufighter. Stripping the aircraft of all its guns and armour, he equipped it with cameras and took the aircraft back to Malta. Owing to its size, there was ample room in the Beau for additional crew and so Warby flew with two of his airmen – Ron Hadden and Norman Shirley – rather than qualified aircrew; one to change the camera spools and the other to look out for enemy fighters. Although somewhat unorthodox, both airmen displayed great courage flying with Warby for which both were awarded the DFM. Away from the stressful world of operational flying, Warburton lived in Valletta with the charming and beautiful music hall cabaret artiste, Christina Ratcliffe, a member of a dance troupe and assistant to the RAF controller in the ops room at Lascaris.[5] Warby attracted either hero worship or occasionally dislike.[6] But he was liked by the airmen and, perhaps more importantly, the senior

---

4. Holland, op. cit., pp.330–1.
5. Spooner (*In Full Flight*), op. cit., pp.203–6.
6. Spooner, *Warburton's War*, p.111.

officers because he was an outstanding reconnaissance pilot and delivered vital intelligence time and time again.

With Malta's offensive capability depleted, the Axis convoys again sailed largely unmolested to North Africa. Of 151,578 tonnes of supplies sent by sea to North Africa during April 1942, more than 150,000 tonnes arrived. Moreover, every one of the 1,349 personnel scheduled to join Rommel's forces reached their destination. These figures reported for the month had never been achieved before, nor would they ever be reached again.[7]

The Axis bombing of Grand Harbour and its surrounding area had also caused devastation among the submarines of the Tenth Flotilla. *Pandora* was sunk while unloading at the end of another Magic Carpet run and *P.36* was sunk the same day while berthed at Lazaretto Wharf. Simpson's force was diminishing fast and conditions had become so bad that the submarine base at Manoel Island was no longer tenable. The submarines of the Tenth Flotilla, what was left of them, fled east for Alexandria.

Even *Upholder*, which had now completed twenty-four patrols from Malta, was in need of a rest but she was forced to escape the carnage and had put to sea yet again for what should have been the submarine's last patrol before returning to the UK. The crew had done their bit. Wanklyn, now with two Bars to his DSO for further successes since the announcement of his Victoria Cross, was in particular need of a rest, even though he had often refused to return to the UK.

But, tragically, *Upholder* and its crew of thirty-two would never be seen again. She was tasked with dropping off two agents on the coast of North Africa and then deliver their escorting army officer to *Unbeaten*, which was on her way back to the UK ahead of *Upholder*. The drop-off of agents went as planned, as did the transfer of the army officer to *Unbeaten*, after which *Upholder* was then tasked to a patrol line with two other submarines, *Urge* and *Thrasher*, to intercept an Axis convoy.

Whether Wanklyn received the signal to proceed to the patrol line or not is unknown, and the exact circumstances of the loss of *Upholder* is unclear,

---

7. Spooner (*Supreme Gallantry*), op. cit., p.119. (According to the official post-war Italian figures).

as there was no receipt of the signals sent. *Upholder* was declared overdue on 14 April. She may have been depth-charged by an Italian torpedo boat or she may have struck a mine, or she may have been lost in some other way. But the fact was the *Upholder* and her gallant crew, including her courageous skipper, Lieutenant Commander David Wanklyn VC DSO and two Bars, were lost without trace.

David Wanklyn was one of the Allies' most successful submariners in terms of tonnage sunk. In all, *Upholder* was credited with having sunk or damaged nineteen supply ships, amounting to 119,000 tonnes, as well as sinking two U-boats, plus a third damaged, and damaging one cruiser and a destroyer. When the Admiralty later announced the loss of *Upholder*, the communiqué carried with it a rare tribute to an individual and his men:

> '*It is seldom proper for Their Lordships to draw distinction between different services rendered in the course of naval duty, but they take this opportunity of singling out those of HMS Upholder, under the command of Lieutenant Commander David Wanklyn, for special mention. She was long employed against enemy communications in the Central Mediterranean, and she became noted for the uniformly high quality of her services in that arduous and dangerous duty. Such was the standard of skill and daring set by Lieutenant Commander Wanklyn and the officers and men under him that they and their ship became an inspiration not only to their own flotilla, but to the Fleet of which it was a part and to Malta, where for so long HMS Upholder was based. The ship and her company are gone, but the example and inspiration remain.*'[8]

Sadly, the loss of *Upholder* would soon be followed by the loss of *Urge*, commanded by Ed Tomkinson. *Urge* was second only to *Upholder* in terms of enemy tonnage sunk and Tomkinson, with a DSO and Bar, was one of the Tenth Flotilla's best submarine commanders. Only earlier that month he and his crew had added the Italian tanker *Franco Martelli* and the Italian light cruiser *Giovanni delle Bande Nere* to their lengthy list of victims. But having

---

8. De la Billière, *Supreme Courage*, p.174 (Taken from Submarine Museum Archive).

left Malta on 27 April, HMS *Urge* failed to arrive at Alexandria. It was later determined that she had been lost, with all hands, during an air attack two days after leaving Malta. In the space of just a couple of weeks, Shrimp Simpson had lost his two best submarine commanders and their crews.

April 1942 has been described by some as 'the cruellest month'. It had been a month that had seen more than 6,700 tonnes of bombs dropped on the island. The airfields of Luqa and Takali had each been on the receiving end of more than 800 tonnes of bombs dropped during the month, more than the previous two months put together. But it was the dockyard that had, perhaps, suffered the most. More than 3,000 tonnes of bombs were dropped against the docks during April, a ten-fold increase on the previous month and twenty times that of February. No other month would approach this intensity and ferocity of attack.[9]

To make matters worse, there were no signs of a convoy that month. Plans to run one from Gibraltar had been shelved and then, too, was the idea to send one from the east. Furthermore, even trying to get one together for May was unlikely and it was increasingly looking like Malta would get no more supplies until June.

Malta could simply not wait so long to be re-supplied, particularly as more fighters were needed more than ever before. But Churchill was determined not to abandon Malta. With a shortage of British carriers, he turned personally to the American President, Franklyn D Roosevelt, for help.

The result of Churchill's plea was Operation Calendar, an Anglo-American operation involving the American carrier USS *Wasp*, a ship that had the capacity to carry more than eighty fighters. However, the most that could be prepared in time were forty-eight Spitfires, which the *Wasp* picked up from the King George V Dock at Shieldhall in Glasgow in mid-April before setting sail for the Mediterranean.

Escorted by two American destroyers, USS *Lang* and USS *Madison*, and with two squadrons of pilots on board (from 601 and 603 Squadrons), *Wasp* was joined by the battlecruiser HMS *Renown* and her escort destroyers. In the early evening on 17 April, the force was joined by the cruisers *Cairo* and

---

9. Shores and Cull with Malizia (The Spitfire Year), op. cit., p.227.

Charybdis plus their destroyer escort in preparation for the passage into the Mediterranean. A diary kept by Charles Jacobs, the author's father, then a leading stoker aboard the destroyer HMS *Wishart*, records:

> '*Picked up force from England consisting of Renown, American carrier Wasp and American destroyers Lang and Madison, British cruisers Cairo and Charybdis, and destroyers Echo, Ithuriel, Partridge and Inglefield. All destroyers and cruisers carried on to Gib to oil, intending to pick up force again later. Our force of destroyers take over escort of Renown and Wasp, which are going direct into the Med to fly off Spitfires from Wasp for Malta. Then going into Gib but we may oil at sea.*'

Designated Force F, the ships passed Gibraltar overnight. By first light on 19 April the ships were heading east into the Med and now rotating their escort to maintain suitable protection for the carrier and main fighting ships, and also carrying out essential oiling. The diary of Charles Jacobs continues:

> '*Heading east through Straits. 0700 – destroyers which went into Gib to oil with cruisers have returned to force. We left force at 0800 with Westcott, Wrestler and Antelope, each ship headed for Gib at full speed. Wishart arrived first having beaten all ships and did 31 knots. Vidette remained with force and will head back to Gib at night. 1545 – left Gib harbour with Wrestler; Antelope and Westcott had gone half hour before. Headed east with Wrestler at 27 knots. 1730 – caught up with Westcott and Antelope. Headed flat out to pick up force.*'

With daylight on 20 April approaching, eleven of *Wasp*'s Grumman Wildcats took off to patrol overhead while the Spitfires prepared to take off. The Spitfires to be flown off *Wasp* that day were armed for the first time with four 20mm Hispano cannons and four 0.303-inch Browning machine guns, and each aircraft was fitted with external fuel tanks, which all added extra weight to the aircraft.[10]

---

10. Ibid, p.200.

Malta's fighter reinforcement operation from the carriers was under the direction of Wing Commander John McLean, a Gibraltar-based fighter pilot. McLean, described as a crisp, plain-spoken and positive New Zealander, had earlier commanded 111 Squadron and was now spending a tour of duty on board the aircraft carriers as they shuttled between Gibraltar and their flying-off positions for Malta. Following earlier losses, McLean's job was to ensure that aircraft weights and fuel loads were correct, and that flying-off points had been correctly calculated. He was also responsible for ensuring the pilots were carefully briefed so that the RAF fighters would have every chance of reaching Malta safely. McLean's uncomplicated methods and instructions were always tailored to the need for each re-supply. He did not underrate the hazards but his good sense and balance allowed them no more than their appropriate weight, and seemed to allay the worst apprehensions of those who were new to flying aircraft off carriers.[11]

Just before 6.00 am, it was time for the Spitfires to get airborne. Because there were so many to fly off, the plan was for them to form four groups. The first group was to be led by Jumbo Gracie, who had been flown back to Gibraltar from Malta to lead the Spitfires to the island, and the second group was to be led by the commanding officer of 601 Squadron, Squadron Leader John Bisdee.

One of those pilots in the second group was Denis Barnham, then a young and relatively inexperienced flight lieutenant serving with 601 Squadron. In his book *Malta Spitfire Pilot*, Barnham recalls what it was like below deck in the large aircraft hangar, strapped into his Spitfire and just waiting for his turn to take off:

'I can feel the heaving and shuddering of the ship's engines racing more vigorously than they have ever raced before: our carrier must be moving at full speed so that the Spitfires, whose engines I can already hear roaring from the flight deck above, are able to take off. There goes the first, passing slowly across the space where a panel has been removed in the side of the

---

11. Lucas, op. cit., p.95.

huge hangar, a tiny aircraft low over the framed strip of dark water, almost invisible in the grey light of dawn.'[12]

With the first group on its way, it was then the turn of the second group to be lifted up onto deck. First Bisdee's aircraft was wheeled back, engine running, onto the lift. Barnham watched it all in his mirror as he was unable to turn round to watch. Next up was the second aircraft, that of Pilot Officer Scott, an Australian, and then a third. Then it was Barnham's turn. Having started his engine, he arrived up on deck to see the flight deck stretched out in front of him and the superstructure halfway down on the right. Remembering all that he had been briefed, and keeping his gaze fixed on a young American flight mechanic wearing a red skull cap and goggles, Barnham waited his turn. Then, it was his time to go. Barnham described what it was like:

'*I open the throttle. The engine is roaring, brakes are slipping; a chequered flag falls: release brakes, throttle wide open, gathering speed, tail up, looking over the nose: deck's very short. Going faster. The overhanging bridge on the superstructure sweeps towards me. Grab the stick again – end of the deck. Grey waves. Keep her straight – stick back. Out over the sea. Waves nearer. Stick further back – at last she begins to fly.'*[13]

It took an hour to get all but one of the forty-eight Spitfires off and on their way. While *Wasp* and her escort headed west towards safety, the Spitfires landed at Luqa and Takali four hours later.

The Spitfires would be seen as saviours to the Maltese but unlike previous reinforcements, many of the new pilots arriving in Malta lacked combat experience; more than half had never flown in action. Malta was not the place for a new fighter pilot to learn his trade and many would arrive to find they were unprepared for the conditions on the island.[14]

No sooner had the Spitfires arrived, the airfields were under attack. The German intelligence and reporting system along the western Mediterranean

---

12. Barnham, *Malta Spitfire Pilot*, pp.43–4.
13. Ibid.
14. Holland, op. cit., pp.297–8.

had been as sharp as usual. The Luftwaffe had clearly been expecting the Spitfires and the first raid against the airfields by Ju87s and Ju88s took place just as the first were arriving.

It was the first of many raids in what turned out to be a horrendous day for Malta, with some 300 enemy aircraft over the island during the course of the day. Many of the new Spitfires were destroyed before they even had a chance to get back into the air, several of which had been destroyed within minutes of landing.

The following day, only twenty-seven Spitfires were available to face the anticipated onslaught on the airfields. Some of the new pilots were involved in operations that day and, for them, it was to be a real baptism of fire. They had been given no time to familiarize themselves with their new surroundings, either on the ground or in the air.

It was during the second raid of the day, just after noon, that newly arrived John Bisdee and Denis Barnham found themselves airborne to meet the attack. Led by Jumbo Gracie, the three Spitfires attacked a formation of up to thirty Ju88s. Barnham picked on one and as he closed in he opened fire again and again. He last saw it close to the water and pouring black smoke. Then, black smoke puffs and orange fire flashed past his own cockpit, crackling in his ears, telling him he had been hit. Looking over his shoulder, Barnham spotted two 109s and after a few hard manoeuvres, got on the tail of one and fired a long burst into it. The 109 toppled sideways, pouring black smoke, but more Messerschmitts then appeared and his Spitfire was hit again, this time in the engine. In his book, *Malta Spitfire Pilot*, Barnham described what happened next:

> '*My Spitfire vibrates violently and the sea changes place with the sky. I'm spinning. Opposite rudder and stick forwards – I'm level again. Two more from the right. Once again my Spitfire flicks upside down, Steep cliffs and yellow ground hang above my head….Explosion from my engine – smoke bursting back into the cockpit. Upside down, spinning again. Cliffs very close. Controls don't answer. All gone slack. Can't stop spinning – Spitfire burning…out of control. Too low to bale out. Might just make it. Bale out quickly.*'[15]

---

15. Ibid.

Just at that point, Barnham regained enough control of his aircraft to make a crash-landing at Hal Far. And so ended Denis Barnham's first operational flight from Malta; a crash-landing, a Ju88 claimed as probably destroyed and a Bf109 damaged.

Meanwhile, John Bisdee had also run into trouble after attacking the Ju88s. Having succeeded in shooting one of the bombers down, he had also been jumped by the 109s. As bits flew off his Spitfire, Bisdee baled out. However, his webbing harness had torn from his shoulders and he was lucky to hook his legs around one of the loops, otherwise he would have fallen to his death. Bisdee came down in the sea headfirst and was fortunate to survive. Semi-conscious, it took him six hours to get into his dinghy and he eventually washed ashore beneath the cliffs near Hal Far, where he was spotted and helped to safety, although his injuries would keep him off flying for several weeks.[16]

With his two wingmen gone, Gracie had done well to survive the melee. After landing, he had to report the loss of both Bisdee and Barnham, believing them both to have been killed, but several hours later news filtered to the squadron that Barnham had crash-landed at Hal Far and Bisdee had been found. For the two new arrivals, it had been an unforgettable first day.

Within just forty-eight hours of the new Spitfires arriving in Malta, only seven were left. The airfields and everyone there seemed to have been inadequately prepared, and considering all that had gone into getting the Spitfires to Malta, it was yet another disaster for the island.

Germany's plan to bomb Malta out of the war was succeeding. In North Africa, with reinforcements and more supplies, Rommel mounted a further push towards Egypt. April 1942 was, indeed, a bad month and it was yet another one of those periods that very nearly broke Malta. Nearly 5,000 Axis sorties had been flown against the island and more bombs fell on Malta during the month than had been dropped on London during the entire Blitz. Most fell in the vicinity of the harbours, causing widespread damage across Valletta, Sliema and the Three Cities.

---

16. Shores and Cull with Malizia (*The Spitfire Year*), op. cit., pp.209–10.

The Maltese had now suffered 117 continuous days of attacks, double anything London had ever endured. The damage, of course, was widespread and devastating, and the loss of civilian life recorded as 300 for the month, with a further 330 seriously injured. The Axis were now dropping twenty-one tonnes of bombs for every Maltese civilian killed, an enlightening figure and further proof, as seen in London before, that dropping large numbers of bombs was never likely to defeat a civilian population. But from the Axis perspective, the bombing campaign was extinguishing Malta's offensive capability, reflected in the amount of supplies reaching Rommel's forces in North Africa.[17]

But among all the carnage and losses that had gone with April 1942, the month should be best remembered for a letter sent to Malta's governor, Sir William Dobbie, informing him of the award of the George Cross to 'The Island of Malta', dated 15 April 1942, so as to 'bear witness to the heroism and devotion of its people' during the great siege; the letter, signed by the king, George VI, stated:

> *'To honour her brave people I award the George Cross to the Island Fortress of Malta to bear witness to a heroism and devotion that will long be famous in history.'*

Dobbie replied:

> *'By God's help Malta will not weaken but will endure until victory is won.'*

The *Times of Malta* reported the news on 17 April, although the Maltese would have to wait until a public ceremony was held in Valletta on 13 September 1942 to see the award. It was the most remarkable honour and the highest possible recognition for all that the island had endured for nearly two years under siege.

The fortitude of the population under sustained enemy air raids and a naval blockade, which almost saw them starved into submission, won

---

17. Terraine, *The Right of the Line*, pp.365–9 (taken from Richards & Saunders, The Royal Air Force 1939–45).

widespread admiration in Britain and other Allied nations. It brought the Maltese a great boost at the most difficult of times and was the first time the George Cross had been awarded on a collective basis.

From that moment on, Malta was known as the George Cross Island.

Chapter Fourteen

An Island Facing Starvation

The situation in Malta, as described by Sir William Dobbie, had become worse than critical. The debacle following Operation Calendar, and that of convoy MW10 before it, was inexcusable. The time had come for Dobbie, now showing the strain of all that had gone on during the past couple of years, to be replaced.

A fresh man was needed and that man was Lord Gort, a highly decorated and greatly respected army officer who, on the Western Front during the First World War, had won the Victoria Cross, the Distinguished Service Order with two Bars and a Military Cross. A tough and uncompromising man, Gort had been the head of the British Army from 1937 until the outbreak of the Second World War, and had then led the British Expeditionary Force to France. After the evacuation at Dunkirk he was made an aide-de-camp general to the king before being appointed the governor of Gibraltar, a post he held for a year before arriving in Malta.

And so in the space of just a month both Dobbie and Cunningham had gone. Although changing the top leadership at such a critical time was undoubtedly a risk, Gort was the ideal man to replace Dobbie. He arrived during the evening of 7 May, typically in the middle of another raid, as Dobbie and his family boarded the same flying boat bound for Gibraltar to leave the island without any fuss or attention.

Malta was still on its knees. Following the loss of so many Spitfires after Operation Calendar, a second convoy to get more Spitfires to the island was quickly put together under Operation Bowery. The *Wasp* had returned to Scotland to pick up another forty-seven Spitfires and sailed back to the Med with her fresh cargo in what was, effectively, a re-run of her first Club Run. In addition to *Wasp*'s cargo of Spitfires, seventeen more of the fighters, delayed from previous Club Runs in Gibraltar, were transported to HMS *Eagle*, which then joined up with *Wasp*.

Days earlier, a group of 249 Squadron's most experienced pilots had left Malta in Hudsons to fly back to Gibraltar. They were to lead in the reinforcement flights from the carriers. Led by Stan Grant, the pilots included Laddie Lucas and Buck McNair. Also with them were newly promoted Flight Lieutenant Ron West, who had arrived from 126 Squadron earlier in the month, and Flying Officer Raoul Daddo-Langlois, unsurprisingly known on the squadron as 'Daddy Longlegs',[1] who had arrived in Malta with Grant, Lucas and McNair on the same mid-February Sunderland. The pilots had arrived to find the quiet of Gibraltar, the good food, the twinkling lights, the well-filled shops and the restful nights to be a heaven-sent antidote to the pounding and privations of the past hard weeks on Malta.[2]

On 9 May the combined force of sixty-four Spitfires were flown off *Wasp* and *Eagle*. The first flight of sixteen off *Wasp*, bound for Takali, was led by Stan Grant. The next batch off was led by Flight Lieutenant R H C Sly, an Australian; they were due to land at Hal Far. Ron West led the third group off *Wasp* for Luqa, and two flights were flown off *Eagle* heading for Luqa and Takali.[3]

With the exception of just two aircraft, one of which was lost on take-off and the other developed a fault and had to return to *Wasp*, the remaining Spitfires reached Malta safely. Lessons had been learned from Operation Calendar and this time detailed preparations had been made to receive the reinforcements and to quickly get them airborne again to prevent them from becoming easy targets on the ground. As soon as the Spitfires arrived they were dispersed into protected areas where they were quickly refuelled and rearmed, and within minutes the fighters were airborne again with fresh pilots ready to counter any enemy raids.

Meanwhile, HMS *Welshman*, a fast naval minelayer, had been risked on a high-speed dash through the western Mediterranean. In addition to the normal Malta supplies of food and other stores, she was carrying a hundred spare Merlin aircraft engines and 120 service personnel bound for Malta,

---

1. Beurling and Roberts, *Malta Spitfire*, p.120.
2. Lucas, op. cit., p.95.
3. Shores and Cull with Malizia (*The Spitfire Year*), op. cit., p.244.

most of whom were RAF ground crew to maintain the Spitfires. It was another one of those risky plans involving unescorted ships through the western Med but, in this case, there was no alternative.

Disguised as a French destroyer, *Welshman* made her dash along the North African coastline and was spotted at least twice during her transit but she finally reached Malta during the early hours of 10 May. She unloaded amid the mayhem of air raids and was damaged but she was soon back on her way again later in the day, arriving back in Gibraltar two days later.

The newly arrived Spitfires were spread across the three airfields. Malta had now developed a better form of fighter control, aided by the addition of Group Captain 'Woody' Woodhall, Malta's senior fighter controller. A former pilot in the First World War, Woody had become an expert at interpreting radar plots and then getting Malta's fighters into the right position so that he could then vector them onto the raiders before they reached the island.

The days that followed were crucial. Justifiably dubbed as the Battle of Malta, the period of 9 May to 10 May 1942 was a turning point in the air war over the island, and the two days of hard fighting brought an abrupt end to daytime bombing of Malta. One raid was met by a combined force of fifty Spitfires and Hurricanes. For the first time since the outbreak of hostilities, the RAF countered the raids in equal or superior numbers. Forty-seven enemy aircraft were either destroyed or damaged for the loss of just three RAF fighters.

These two days of fighting not only marked a turning point in the air war but also marked a turning point in the Siege of Malta. Sixty-five Axis aircraft were reported to have been lost or damaged on 10 May, after which the *Times of Malta* enthusiastically reported:

> '*After two days of the fiercest aerial combat that has ever taken place over the island, the Luftwaffe, with its Italian lackeys, has taken the most formidable beating that has been known since the Battle of Britain.*'[4]

Interestingly, though, the German perception of the air war at that time was different. On 10 May, the day that had witnessed the best day of air fighting

4. *Times of Malta*, 11 May 1942.

for Malta's defenders, Kesselring reported to the German High Command that Malta had been neutralized, insisting there was nothing left to bomb.[5]

As a result of this claim, more Luftwaffe combat units were removed from Sicily, with many heading for the Eastern Front. This meant that from now on there would be fewer raids against Malta and in fewer numbers. Furthermore, the next delivery of Spitfires, seventeen aircraft flown off *Eagle*, with *Argus* providing fighter cover, took place on 18 May under Operation LB; the two flights being successfully led to Malta by Laddie Lucas and Buck McNair.

For everyone involved, it was a hard day as captured in the diary of Charles Jacobs on board one of the escorts, HMS *Wishart*. The entry for Monday 18 May reads:

'*Still heading east. 0930 – two torpedoes were fired at Charybdis and passed across our bow about a mile ahead. Partridge dropped two depth charges. Force altered course. We dropped four depth charges. Half an hour later, Ithuriel and Westcott dropped two charges each. Resumed original course. Had two more pings during the day. During forenoon received signal that a Catalina had been shot down 20 miles north of Algiers by fighters. Ithuriel turned back to rescue crew. 1430 – heard heavy explosions well astern. Skipper announced that Ithuriel had signalled for help during a heavy air raid. Two Fulmars went to aid. 1500 – Eagle flew off seventeen Spitfires. 1530 – more heavy explosions astern. 1845 – heard that Ithuriel was ok and was catching up force. One Fulmar had been shot down, the other returned on board Argus. Crew of Catalina were on board Ithuriel. The two pilots badly hurt. Pilot of Fulmar was killed, observer safe. 1930 – Eagle flew off six Albacores. Force turned back for Gib. Enemy aircraft returned. 2015 – two Albacores returned to Eagle. Skipper has told us that it was probable that a force of Italian warships was out looking for us – probably two battleships, six cruisers and twelve destroyers. 2100 – Ithuriel joined force. 2140 – went to action stations. Eight Junkers torpedo-carrying aircraft and three fighters attacked, dropped bombs and torpedoes at Eagle and Argus,*

---

5. Holland, op. cit., p.311.

flying very low. All ships put up heavy barrage. Aircraft continued attack until 2330. Hands to cruising stations.'

The ships came under further attack the following day but returned safely to Gibraltar two days later. After Operation LB, twenty-seven more Spitfires arrived in Malta on 3 June under Operation Style, and then Operation Salient delivered another thirty-two Spitfires just five days later. Malta had been given the lifeline it so desperately needed, although the battle for Malta was far from over.

Back in Britain, Churchill was keen to re-establish Malta as an operating base for offensive operations. There was little point holding on to the island unless it could be used to hit back at the enemy once again. But this would require more than just Spitfires and only a complete replenishment of the island would enable this to happen.

By now, Sir Henry Harwood had arrived in Alexandria to take over as the new commander-in-chief Mediterranean Fleet. Harwood's name had become known back home after the Battle of the River Plate in the South Atlantic, the first naval battle of the Second World War, which ended with the scuttling of the German heavy-cruiser *Admiral Graf Spee* off Montevideo in the river's estuary between Uruguay and Argentina. His early success had seen him promoted and knighted, after which Harwood served as a lord commissioner of the Admiralty and assistant chief of the naval staff before taking up his appointment in the Mediterranean.

Considering all that it had been through in the past two years, the island of Malta was bearing up well. The arrival of Spitfires in large numbers and the successes of 9 May and 10 May had done much to raise the morale of the Maltese. But Malta still faced the very real possibility of starvation. Queuing had become an everyday occurrence as the continuous rationing of food tested resilience and patience; more so, perhaps, than the bombing had done. Even then, having got some food, cooking it was another problem. The shortage of oil and fuel meant there was none to prepare a hot meal. Community kitchens, enthusiastically named Victory Kitchens, were set up as the Maltese continued to weather the storm, but the rather paltry portions were never appetizing.

Not only were the Maltese going hungry but just about every other necessity for day-to-day life was also missing. Even shoes and clothing were a problem. No new materials had reached Malta for some considerable time and so the Maltese had to use whatever materials they could find to make or repair clothing. Unsurprisingly, there was a black market as some sought to profit, and others took to stealing. It was a desperate situation.

But finally there was hope. The promised, but long overdue, convoy was planned for June. However, if Malta was to survive, the convoy had to be a success.

Chapter Fifteen

Operation Harpoon and Operation Vigorous

W ith fewer enemy bombers in Sicily and a far stronger fighter presence in Malta, it was hoped that mounting two large convoys, with a number of supply ships sailing concurrently from both ends of the Med, would successfully get through to the besieged island.

Although running two convoys towards Malta at the same time would divide enemy forces in the central Mediterranean, and so increase the chances of merchant ships getting through, it remained a risky plan; particularly for the ships sailing from the east where the Royal Navy had suffered losses and the Axis still possessed a strong air capability in North Africa.

The forces gathered at both ends of the Med in early June in preparation for Operation Julius. The plan was to break down the operation into two distinct naval operations: Operation Harpoon from Gibraltar in the west and Operation Vigorous from ports in the east.

Harpoon began on 4 June when the convoy WS19z left the Clyde in Scotland. The convoy consisted of five merchantmen: the Blue Funnel liner *Troilus* (7,400 tonnes) with the convoy commodore, Commander J P W Pilditch, aboard; the Hain Steamship Company's *Burdwan* (6,000 tonnes); the *Orari*, a large ship of more than 10,000 tonnes owned by the New Zealand Shipping Company; the American *Chant*, a former Danish vessel (5,600 tonnes); and the Dutch *Tanimbar* (8,000 tonnes), the slowest of the ships and capable of just 13 knots.

The five masters were initially told they were bound for Malta via the lengthy Cape route and were only briefed of the actual plan of sailing through the Med once underway.

The convoy escort, designated Force X, included the anti-aircraft cruiser HMS *Cairo* with the escort's overall commander, Captain Cecil Hardy, aboard. The escort also consisted of: nine destroyers (*Bedouin*, *Marne*, *Matchless*, *Ithuriel*, *Partridge*, *Blankney*, *Badsworth*, *Middleton* and the Polish vessel *Kujawiak*); the fast minelayer *Welshman*; four minesweepers (*Hebe*, *Speedy*, *Rye* and *Hythe*); and six motor launches.

Overall cover for the convoy was to be provided by Force W: the battleship *Malaya*; the aircraft carriers *Argus* and *Eagle* (with Sea Hurricanes, Fulmars and Swordfish embarked); the light cruisers *Kenya*, *Charybdis* and *Liverpool*; and eight destroyers (*Onslow*, *Icarus*, *Escapade*, *Antelope*, *Wishart*, *Westcott*, *Wrestler* and *Vidette*). Also sailing with the ships was the fleet tanker *Brown Ranger* and two corvettes (*Coltsfoot* and *Geranium*) as the replenishment force, designated Force Y, and four submarines (*Safari*, *Unbroken*, *Unison* and *Unruffled*) were positioned ahead of the force to the west of Malta, between Sicily and Sardinia, to provide a screen.

By 11 June the merchant vessels of WS19z, escorted by the cruisers *Kenya* and *Liverpool*, with their own escorting destroyers, were out in the Atlantic to the west of Gibraltar. They were ready to enter the Mediterranean under the cover of darkness, where the convoy was to be joined by the large 9,000-tonne American tanker *Kentucky*, having arrived in the Med after crossing the Atlantic, for the dash to Malta. Between the six merchantmen they carried 43,000 tonnes of supplies, including *Kentucky*'s 14,000 tonnes of oil, fuel and kerosene. The diary entry by Charles Jacobs, on board HMS *Wishart*, for Thursday, 11 June and overnight to 12 June reads:

'*0900 – left Gib with Partridge, Westcott, Ithuriel, Antelope and Vidette. Headed west into Atlantic to pick up convoy of merchantmen loaded with fuel, oil and munitions etc for Malta. We are to relieve escort of two cruisers, Kenya and Liverpool, and destroyers Marne, Middleton, Onslow, Icarus, Escapade and Matchless who will proceed to Gib to oil. We are to escort convoy through Straits into Med, to be joined by Eagle, Argus, Malaya, Charybdis, Cairo, Bedouin, Westcott, Hythe, Speedy, Hebe and a Polish destroyer [Kujawiak], and six motor launches. We are to escort force as far as south of Sardinia. Ships who went to oil will join us and take convoy into Malta. We oil at sea. Brown Ranger has rendezvous with us being escorted by two corvettes. Eagle has special fighter force on board of Hurricanes. 1900 – picked up convoy of five merchantmen, Kenya and Liverpool, Matchless, Middleton, Onslow, Icarus, Escapade and Blankney. Headed back for Straits. 1945 – Wrestler joined convoy. Escapade left for Gib to oil. 12 June, 0400–0800 – other force joined convoy, now consisting of Malaya, Eagle, Argus, Charybdis, Cairo, Kentucky, Liverpool, Marne, Matchless, Onslow, Escapade, Bedouin, Icarus, Middleton, Blankney, Hythe, Speedy, Hebe, Westcott, Wishart, Wrestler, Vidette, Ithuriel, Partridge, Antelope, Polish destroyer [Kujawiak], Welshman, six motor launches and five merchantmen. Headed east at 9 knots.'*

The convoy, now designated GM4, had successfully passed through the Strait of Gibraltar under the cover of darkness during the early hours of 12 June. Then, early the following morning, the large convoy was spotted when the first of several enemy reconnaissance aircraft was sighted overhead the ships.

The ships of Harpoon pressed on, with the destroyers oiling from *Brown Ranger* and *Liverpool* during the rest of the morning. Then, later that afternoon, the crews were called to action stations when an enemy torpedo attack was expected. But there was no attack that day and by dawn the following morning, Sunday, 14 June, the crews were once again at action stations as the ships were now within range of the Italian air bases in Sardinia.

It was mid-morning when the ships came under air attack. The convoy had already set up in two columns with *Kenya* leading one and *Liverpool* the other, and the destroyers and minesweepers formed an outer screen well clear of the merchantmen and carriers. For the rest of the morning the convoy's defences were continuously probed and during one attack by SM.79 torpedo-bombers *Liverpool* suffered extensive damage, although she would be able to return to Gibraltar. Less fortunate, though, was the Dutch freighter *Tanimbar*. She was hit during the attack, catching fire immediately and burning furiously for several minutes before she sank with the loss of four lives. The diary of Charles Jacobs captured the morning attack on the convoy:

'Attack on convoy to Malta. 1022 – went to action stations. Attacked by sixty aircraft, twenty-two of which were torpedo-carriers, the remainder being high and low level bombers, mainly Italian three-engine planes. One transport [Tanimbar] struck by bombs just aft of funnel in third hold. Terrific explosion, sank in five-and-a-half minutes. Motor launch picked

up six survivors. Liverpool damaged by near-miss and turned back for Gib. Later returned to convoy but told by Kenya to go back to Gib. We had five bombs alongside but did not explode and near miss with torpedo astern. Antelope and Westcott escorted Liverpool back at 9 knots. Twelve enemy planes shot down – six were torpedo-carriers and six were bombers. Six were shot down by fighters and six by anti-aircraft fire. We lost one Fulmar. Wishart shot down one torpedo plane. 1215 - 2nd degree of readiness.'

The convoy had suffered its first casualty. Although three Italian aircraft were reportedly shot down, one of the convoy's prized assets was at the bottom, and three of its covering naval ships were no longer there to provide protection. Later in the day the convoy came under further attack but all the ships came through unscathed. The diary of Charles Jacobs continues:

'1815 – action stations. Forty planes attacked convoy, some torpedo-carriers, others high level bombers and dive-bombers – Stukas. Eagle had very near miss at bows, steamed through bomb splashes. No ships hit. One enemy bomber shot down and one Hurricane shot down. 1930 – 2nd degree of readiness.'

Not wishing to hold back the minelayer, *Welshman* was ordered to break away from the convoy to sail on to Malta alone at full speed. The convoy came under further attack that evening, this time by the Italians, but somehow the ships survived intact. By nightfall they were entering the narrow Strait of Sicily to the north of Bizerte, and it was time for the covering Force W to turn back west for Gibraltar, leaving Force X, led by Hardy, to provide the close escort on to Malta. After what had been a long and hard day for the convoy and escorts, Charles Jacobs made his last entry to his diary for the day:

'2015 – action stations. Thirty to forty aircraft attack convoy, similar types of aircraft to last raid. No hits on ships, no planes brought down. 2045 – 2nd degree of readiness. 2130 – turned back for Gib with Malaya, Eagle and Argus, Kenya, Charybdis, Escapade, Icarus, Onslow, Vidette and Wrestler. Convoy was again attacked by sixty aircraft at 2150. We could

see the barrage put up by remaining escort. 2210 – picked up submarine echo, dropped pattern of five depth charges. 2230 – went to action stations, aircraft dropped flares until 0100 to try to find us but failed. 2nd degree of readiness.'

With the heavy warships on their way back to Gibraltar under the cover of darkness, the five remaining merchantmen of Harpoon and their escort continued heading straight for Grand Harbour. The disastrous start to the beginning of the day had been tempered by the fact there had been no further losses.

At dawn on 15 June, the lightly defended convoy came under a co-ordinated surface and air attack near the small island of Pantelleria in the Strait of Sicily. At this point in the Med, the strait is just ninety miles wide and with good visibility, as there was that morning, there was nowhere to hide.

The Italian warships approaching in the distance could now be seen. The convoy was again in two columns with the destroyers either side, and the minesweepers and motor launches covered the stern. Realizing the escorts were outgunned, the destroyers put up a smoke screen to hide the merchant vessels and a change of course was made.

Hardy intended to fight a delaying action in the hope he would soon receive air cover from Malta. Five destroyers – *Bedouin*, *Partridge*, *Ithuriel*, *Marne* and *Matchless* – gathered speed and headed towards the Italian warships in excess of 30 knots.

Every minute that passed brought the two opposing surface forces closer together and bought the convoy's merchantmen valuable time to escape. It was an extremely courageous move by the destroyers. *Bedouin* was out in front and even though she was still out of range her skipper, Commander Bryan Scurfield, gave the order to open fire. Still *Bedouin* pressed gallantly on, followed closely by *Partridge*, but now *Bedouin* was taking hits. Her bridge was hit and her mast shot away, men were killed and wounded. *Partridge*, too, had been hit. In return, an Italian destroyer had been hit and caught fire, but, within minutes, both British destroyers had suffered significant damage and were brought to a halt.

Meanwhile, the three destroyers behind them – *Ithuriel*, *Marne* and *Matchless* – had pressed on at full speed and were firing on the Italian ships as soon as they came within range. With the convoy heading for relative safety, for now at least, four other escorting destroyers – *Blankney*, *Middleton*, *Badsworth* and *Kujawiak* – steamed for the Italians. Shots were exchanged but eventually the Italians broke off to the north and temporarily retired from the battle.[1]

The destroyers fell back towards the convoy but the air attacks by Ju88s had been intense. Without the protection of the destroyers, *Chant* had been hit and was ablaze. She was soon listing badly and it became apparent that she could not be saved and so her crew were taken off by *Rye* and two motor launches. Elsewhere, *Kentucky* had avoided any direct hits but there had been near-misses and she had suffered damage. She soon dropped back, *Rye* dropping back with her to provide protection, but the tanker soon had to be taken under tow by *Ithuriel*.

With the destroyers having returned to station, Pilditch ordered the convoy to head east in search of air cover. The Italian ships were still in the vicinity and it was still not even 8.00 am. There was an awful lot of daylight left in the day.

By mid-morning Malta's Spitfires were providing air cover above the convoy but they were at their maximum operating range and probes by German bombers simply exhausted their fuel to the point they had to return to the island, leaving the convoy exposed once more. It was then that another air attack took place, this time by a mixed force of Ju87s and Ju88s, with *Burdwan* being the enemy's focus of attention. The result was the merchantman suffered serious damage and slowly came to a halt.

With the convoy now down to just two merchant vessels, and with some of his naval escorts tied up dealing with the two stricken vessels, Hardy made one of the most difficult decisions of war – to sink both *Kentucky* and *Burdwan* in order to give every chance for *Troilus* and *Orari* to reach Grand Harbour. Hardy had little time to make such a decision and, in the end, he was faced with little option, but the loss of the *Kentucky*, in particular, would be significant; not only for Malta but also for Anglo-American relations.[2]

---

1. Woodman, op. cit., pp.335–7.
2. Ibid, p.338.

With the crews having been taken off by other ships, *Hebe* and *Badsworth* were left behind to deal with *Kentucky*, *Burdwan*, *Bedouin* and *Partridge*. As things were to turn out, the Italians were already back and in pursuit. As *Hebe* and *Badsworth* both hastily made off, *Kentucky* was finished off by a torpedo from an Italian cruiser, and *Burdwan* was sent to the bottom by a salvo of Italian gunfire. The merchant vessel *Chant* was already on the bottom. As for *Partridge*, she made it back to Gibraltar two days later and even tried to tow *Bedouin* back with her, but when the Italian ships reappeared, the tow had to be cast off to leave *Bedouin* adrift. She was an easy prey for the Italian torpedo-bombers who soon finished her off with the loss of twenty-six lives.

Meanwhile, *Orari* and *Troilus* continued towards Malta at best speed. *Welshman* had made it to Grand Harbour during the day and after quickly unloading, she steamed back to strengthen the convoy's escort. Remarkably, and despite two further air attacks during the day, the surviving ships of the convoy remained intact.

A further attempt by the Axis bombers to reach the merchantmen that evening was successfully driven off by Malta's Spitfires but the surviving ships of the convoy now faced a further problem. The Germans and Italians had laid many minefields in the approaches to Grand Harbour and later that night the convoy found itself in one. Two destroyers, *Badsworth* and *Matchless*, struck mines and were damaged. The freighter *Orari* also struck a mine and was damaged, although she remained afloat, and the Polish escorting destroyer *Kujawiak* hit a mine and sank in the early hours of the following morning.

Just two of the six merchantmen that had set out from Gibraltar a few days before, *Orari* and *Troilus*, reached Malta; one-third of the original convoy. Even then, some 400 tonnes of *Orari*'s cargo had been lost as a result of the damage she had suffered after hitting the mine.

Although it was the middle of the night, people lined the ramparts to welcome the surviving ships into harbour. The naval ships *Cairo* and *Welshman*, plus the four remaining seaworthy destroyers – *Ithuriel*, *Marne*, *Blankney* and *Middleton* – all left Malta on 17 June for another run back through the western Med. All arrived safely in Gibraltar two days later.

The two gallant merchantmen that had reached Grand Harbour, *Orari* and *Troilus*, were emptied. They had brought 13,500 tonnes of precious supplies to Malta and they would now have to wait until there were more ships made available for their journey home. Although two cargo ships were certainly better than none, it was a poor return for so much effort.

Meanwhile, as Operation Harpoon had set sail from Gibraltar, so did Operation Vigorous from the eastern end of the Med. Designated MW11, it was, of course, a vital convoy. But more than that, it would hopefully demonstrate, to the British at least, that the Allies possessed enough firepower – surface, sub-surface and air – to get a convoy through the eastern Mediterranean.

On 12 June, eleven merchant ships with their naval escorts sailed from two ports: Haifa in Palestine and Port Said in Egypt. The transport ships formed three separate groups. MW11a comprised five vessels: Alfred Holt's *Ajax* (7,500 tonnes), Ellerman's liners *City of Edinburgh*, *City of Lincoln* and *City of Pretoria* (each up to 9,000 tonnes), and the Norwegian vessel *Elizabeth Bakke* (5,500 tonnes). MW11b consisted of two tankers, the 8,000-tonne Anglo-American Oil Company's *Bulkoil*, with the convoy's commodore, Rear Admiral Hugh England on board, and the Royal Mail Line's *Potaro* (5,400 tonnes). The third group, designated MW11c, comprised the Dutch cargo vessel *Aagtekirk* (6,800 tonnes), the Hain Company's *Bhutan* (6,100 tonnes), Ellerman's *City of Calcutta* (8,000 tonnes) and the Bolton Steamship *Rembrandt* (5,500 tonnes).[3]

Most of the Mediterranean Fleet was involved, designated as Force A, with Vian flying his flag in *Cleopatra*. Without either a capital ship or a carrier, the convoy was augmented by warships from the Indian Ocean and Kenya to bring the total covering and escort force to seven light cruisers, from the 4th and 15th Cruiser Squadrons: *Newcastle*, *Birmingham*, *Cleopatra*, *Dido*, *Hermione*, *Euryalus* and *Arethusa*. There was also the anti-aircraft cruiser, HMS *Coventry*, and twenty-six destroyers.[4] This main force was supported

---

3. Ibid, pp.350–3.
4. The escorting destroyers were: three from the 2nd Destroyer Flotilla (*Fortune*, *Griffin* and *Hotspur*); nine Hunt-class escorts of the 5th Destroyer Flotilla (*Dulverton*, *Exmoor*, *Croome*, *Eridge*, *Airedale*, *Beaufort*, *Hurworth*, *Tetcott* and *Aldenham*); four Australian N-class escorts of the 7th Destroyer Flotilla (HMAS *Norman*, *Napier*, *Nestor* and *Nizam*); three of the 12th Destroyer Flotilla (*Pakenham*, *Paladin* and *Inconstant*); three of the 14th Destroyer Flotilla (*Jervis*, *Javelin* and *Kelvin*); and four of the 22nd Destroyer Flotilla (*Hero*, *Hasty*, *Sikh* and *Zulu*).

by four Flower-class corvettes (*Delphinium*, *Erica*, *Primula* and *Snapdragon*), two Bangor-class minesweepers (*Boston* and *Seaham*), four motor torpedo boats and two rescue ships, both former cross-Channel ferries (*Antwerp* and *Malines*), as well as the old battleship HMS *Centurion*, now serving as an auxiliary and loaded with supplies bound for Malta. In addition to these vessels, nine submarines would provide a covering screen ahead of the force.[5]

The timing of Vigorous, a more complex convoy than most, was not great for several reasons. Firstly, Harwood had only just arrived in Egypt and so the fleet had lost the experience of Cunningham. Secondly, mid-June provided very long hours of daylight and clear weather in the eastern Med. Thirdly, there was, perhaps, a misconception within the convoy's planners that the RAF enjoyed air superiority over the region. With Malta's recent influx of Spitfires, the naval planners may have felt that all the convoy needed to do was to get within reasonable range of the island, after which sufficient fighter cover would be provided until the ships sailed into Grand Harbour; this would not be the case.

There was a further problem, too. Rommel renewed his offensive in the desert the day before the convoy was due to sail. This may have been coincidental or, equally, it may have been deliberately timed in the knowledge that Vigorous was about to take place. Either way, it meant the RAF would be preoccupied in the region and many Allied airfields that would have provided air cover for the convoy were instead overrun.

The air plan to cover Vigorous was becoming more complex. Many different types of aircraft were to be involved and from several different locations in the region, including a number based in Malta. These included Beaufighters, to be used as long-range fighters, and a detachment of Beauforts from 217 Squadron, which had been on their way to Ceylon but were held over in Malta to support Vigorous and specifically to attack the Italian fleet if necessary.[6]

Although it is easy to say with hindsight that the timing of the Vigorous convoy was not ideal, those planning it, and certainly those responsible for

---

5. The nine submarines were *Proteus*, *Thorn*, *Taku*, *Thrasher*, *Porpoise*, *Una*, *Uproar*, *Ultimatum* and *Umbra*.

6. The Beauforts of 217 Squadron would, in fact, end up remaining on the island for a couple of months to attack Axis shipping heading for North Africa.

its execution, were faced with little choice. Malta could hardly wait until Harwood had been in post longer, or until the hours of daylight reduced later in the year, or, indeed, to see whether the RAF could actually achieve air superiority over the region. And so Vigorous had to run.

The four merchant vessels of MW11c were the first to move. They sailed from Port Said, escorted by *Coventry* and eight of the Hunt-class destroyers.[7] This 'small' convoy, known internally as Operation Rembrandt, headed west along the coast to give the impression this was the only force heading for Malta. Then, early on 12 June, the five merchantmen of MW11a left Haifa, escorted by the 7th Destroyer Flotilla and the two minesweepers.

That evening, the lead ships of Operation Rembrandt came under attack by fifteen Ju88s based in Crete. With bombs falling within feet of her, *City of Calcutta* suffered damage to her engine room, reducing her speed to just 11 knots; she was ordered to make for Tobruk, escorted by *Exmoor* and *Croome*.

MW11c now turned back to rendezvous with the other ships of Vigorous, by which time MW11b had sailed from Alexandria with *Centurion*, the two rescue ships and an escort of five destroyers[8] plus the four corvettes. But the combination of overloading and a badly maintained hull meant that *Elizabeth Bakke* was unable to maintain the convoy speed of 13 knots, and so she was duly ordered into Alexandria escorted by *Zulu*.

The three surviving components of Vigorous met to the north of Mersa Matruh on the afternoon of 13 June. That evening the convoy came under a number of air attacks, and more engine problems among the ships further depleted the convoy. Three ships – *Aagtekirk*, *Erica* and *Primula* – were unable to maintain convoy speed and so were cast off; *Erica* headed for Mersa Matruh and the others made for Tobruk, escorted by *Tetcott* to provide some anti-aircraft protection. Sadly, though, the destroyer could only provide minimal protection when the ships came under air attack just a few miles from Tobruk, with *Aagtekirk* so badly damaged that she caught fire and burnt out before running aground near the port.

---

7. *Tetcott* being the only one of the nine Hunt-class destroyers not part of this smaller convoy.
8. The five destroyers were *Pakenham*, *Fortune*, *Paladin*, *Kelvin* and *Zulu*.

Despite a number of air attacks during 14 June, largely driven off by RAF fighters from the surviving Allied airfields in North Africa, the main convoy pressed on towards Malta. The merchantmen and *Centurion* were formed up in four shallow columns, with the two rescue ships in the centre, and the cruisers formed an outer screen with the destroyers and minesweepers a mile behind the cruisers.[9]

Despite a number of near misses, the convoy remained intact until the early evening when *Bhutan* received a direct hit from a Ju87 Stuka and sank in just minutes. Fortunately for the men on board, the close presence of the rescue ships meant that only sixteen of the ship's complement of 169 remained unaccounted for. With the wounded and other survivors on board, the two rescue ships made for Tobruk before returning to Alexandria.

As night fell, Vian ordered the escorting destroyers into an anti-submarine screen ahead of the convoy. Vian was then informed that a Wellington had spotted a strong Italian naval force, including two battleships, four cruisers and a number of destroyers, steaming south in the Gulf of Taranto towards the convoy.

It was estimated the Italian warships would be in a position to mount an attack during the course of the following morning. Vian informed Harwood back in Egypt. The convoy had already suffered losses and with its protective force depleted, plus the fact that good weather was forecast for the following day, Vian explained that it would be impossible to hold off an attack by the Italian fleet and so he asked Harwood if he should retire.

The decision was reluctantly made to abandon the convoy's attempt to get through to Malta and for the surviving ships to return east. There then followed an exchange of messages between the two commanders as to when the convoy should turn back. Turning a large convoy round would not be easy, particularly at night, but Vian decided to make best use of the hours of darkness to do this rather than to further delay.

The order to turn back was sent from *Cleopatra* at 01.45 am on 15 June.[10] During the hours that followed, the ships made a number of changes in

9. Woodman, op. cit., pp.355–6.
10. Ibid, pp.358–9.

course in an attempt to deceive the Italian ships. The convoy also came under attack from fast torpedo-armed German E-boats, which damaged the light cruiser *Newcastle* and the destroyer *Hasty*; the latter having suffered such serious damage and the loss of twelve lives that she had to be scuttled after the survivors had been taken on board *Hotspur*.

With the Italian warships in range of Malta's strike aircraft, nine Beauforts took off in darkness to carry out an attack at first light. As the last to get airborne, 21-year-old Flying Officer Arthur Aldridge had become separated from the others but he was the first to find the Italian fleet. When he came across four Italian cruisers protected by eight destroyers, he was all alone and it was early dawn.

Aldridge and his crew took in the magnificent sight of so many ships in front of them; they had never seen anything like it. With a calm sea and the ships so serene, the whole scene barely looked real. But, as Aldridge later explained in his book *The Last Torpedo Flyers*, there was no time to lose:

> '*No time, no feeling. This was war, my life was on the line; they were trying to destroy our convoy and starve Malta. There was a job to be done, these Italians were my enemy.*'[11]

Although it was still only dawn, visibility was more than sufficient for Aldridge to see the ships from his height but he knew that down at sea level, it would still seem dark. There was no time to wait for the others; besides, they may not even find the ships. Taking up a position so that he could attack out of the dark half of the sky, Aldridge decided to attack from the front sector at an angle of forty-five degrees to take advantage of the converging speeds and so increase his chances of success.

Aldridge started his run-in towards the ships, focusing on the leading Italian cruiser, the biggest ship, as he had been trained to do. Of all torpedo-carrying aircraft, the Beaufort was a particularly vulnerable type when running in against a ship. The aircraft had to be kept perfectly steady, with wings level and the speed maintained at a painfully slow 140 knots if the

11. Aldridge with Ryan, *The Last Torpedo Flyers*, pp.194–206.

torpedo was to have the best chance of running true. Aldridge later described his attack:

> '*I opened my throttles to get my speed up to 140 knots, the right speed for dropping a torpedo from a height of 60 to 80 feet. Now it was all about timing my release. My finger was on the button. The cruiser was lined up. A thousand yards, nine hundred yards …. I was going to aim off but not by much, because my target wasn't moving very fast. Eight hundred yards. I pressed! It felt right.*'[12]

Aldridge had in his sights the 10,000-tonne heavy cruiser *Trento*, and it was only after he had released his torpedo that his aircraft was spotted and a fusillade of gunfire opened up. But, by then, he was skilfully jinking his Beaufort away to safety. Then came the buffeting from the explosion just as the Beaufort passed the cruiser. The torpedo had struck *Trento* with a devastating blow. Smoke poured from her and the mighty cruiser came to a halt. Destroyers rushed to her aid and soon had her covered by a smoke screen.

The other Beauforts soon arrived but they were met by a barrage of anti-aircraft fire. They split into two sections but with so much anti-aircraft fire, all torpedoes missed their targets.[13] The *Trento* had been disabled and was later finished off by the submarine *Umbra*, and for his solo attack Arthur Aldridge would later be awarded a Bar to the DFC he had been awarded earlier in the war.

Meanwhile, the ships of Vigorous were making their way back to port. All afternoon they suffered further air attacks as they entered Bomb Alley between Crete and Libya. The cruiser *Birmingham* and her escorting destroyer, *Airedale*, were both severely damaged by Stukas, with *Airedale* left a smouldering wreck to be scuttled the following day. It was also during the afternoon that Vian received news that the Italian fleet had given up the chase and had turned to hold off to the west of Greece, ready to head south again should the convoy turn back towards Malta.

---

12. Ibid.
13. Spooner (*Faith Hope and Malta GC*), op. cit., pp.74–5.

News that the Italians had given up the chase led Harwood to signal Vian once more, suggesting it was a golden opportunity to get the convoy through to Malta, assuming that the escorting ships had enough fuel to reach the island. There was also the suggestion that only the four fastest merchantmen, escorted by the cruiser *Arethusa* and two destroyers, should make the dash to Malta.[14]

But Vigorous was in a desperate situation. The surviving ships and their escorts still faced further air attacks from Axis-held airfields in Libya and the Italian fleet was still in a position to mount an attack. Furthermore, the constant zig-zag of the diversionary tactics and the hard defensive manoeuvring against several air attacks had run the ships short of fuel; they were also short of ammunition. With everything seemingly against the convoy, that evening Harwood made the decision to give up on the idea of resurrecting an attempt to get any of the ships through to Malta and for Vian to return the remaining force to Egypt.

By now, Vigorous was to the south-west of Crete. As the ships withdrew back towards Alexandria under the cover of darkness, the cruiser *Hermione* was torpedoed and sunk during the early hours of 16 June by a German U-boat lying in wait to the south of Crete. Furthermore, one of the Australian destroyers, HMAS *Nestor*, was out of action having been struck by bombs. She was taken in tow by HMS *Javelin* but she had become so nose-down in the water that she had to be scuttled after her crew were transferred to the towing destroyer.

That evening Vian entered Alexandria with his ships. Five of the merchantmen – *Potaro*, *City of Lincoln*, *City of Edinburgh*, *City of Pretoria* and *Rembrandt* – were still there with him. *Bulkoil* and her escort sailed into Port Said and *City of Calcutta* was on her way to Alexandria from Tobruk. Despite the obvious fact they were not in Grand Harbour where they should have been, it had been a remarkable display of seamanship on the part of the merchant crews to have stayed with the convoy throughout such a difficult passage. Nonetheless, it was a depressing and low moment for all those involved.

---

14. Woodman, op. cit., p.365.

Within four days of Vigorous' miserable return to Alexandria, Rommel had taken Tobruk, and by the end of the month British forces had fallen back to El Alamein, just sixty miles from Alexandria.

Operation Vigorous was yet another disaster, despite the courage and gallantry of those who had fought so bravely to get the convoy through. No ships had reached Malta and many had been lost or damaged in the attempt. Although there had been a number of enemy aircraft claimed as shot down, that was hardly the point. The central Mediterranean had proved impassable to the British. Even though the Italian ships had not engaged the convoy, they had provided enough of a threat to prevent the convoy from getting through. Also, for various reasons, the submarine screen had not proved much of a success with only one Italian cruiser sunk, and that was only after it had first been crippled by Arthur Aldridge's Beaufort.

Fortunately for all those involved with the Malta convoys, the Regia Marina would be unable to repeat this success. Oil had always been Germany's Achilles heel and the Italians were to become starved of oil and fuel by the Germans who believed the Regia Marina, in particular, had been far too generous with the use of its warships. It now meant the largest of the ships in the Italian fleet would be unable to make further major forays into the Mediterranean.

But all that was unknown to the British at the time. The fact was that the combined efforts of Operation Harpoon and Operation Vigorous had resulted in just two merchantmen reaching Malta. All that planning and all that effort for such little return, which effectively mounted to no more than just a few days of supplies.

That evening, 16 June, Gort broadcast to the island, frankly relaying the situation. The convoys had largely failed but he still offered the islanders hope, explaining that every effort would be made to replenish the stocks when a favourable opportunity presented itself.[15]

With such heavy losses suffered during the two convoys, it was difficult to see how another attempt to re-supply Malta could be made. The island was truly besieged and her isolation complete. The next convoy, assuming that one could be mounted, would be the most critical of all and would ultimately decide the fate of Malta.

---

15. *Times of Malta*, 17 June 1942.

Chapter Sixteen

'Screwball'

With Rommel only sixty miles or so from Alexandria, it made an Axis invasion of Malta unnecessary. For now, the German High Command decided to continue with the siege and to maintain their campaign to bomb or starve the island into submission.

With so many Spitfires having arrived in Malta, it was time to get a man in at the top who better understood fighter operations. Hugh Pughe Lloyd had been on the island for what had been a very difficult year. Not only had he had to deal with the Axis air raids but he also had to deal with the Axis re-supply routes to North Africa. The fighter ace, Laddie Lucas, later said of Lloyd:

> '*Under pressure – real pressure – Lloyd was, without doubt, the most accomplished field commander I personally saw in the Royal Air Force in wartime. He was fearless but he had judgment. He also understood the wider, strategic issues. He didn't say a lot, but when he spoke the sentences bit. He was firm and hard, but humanity was always close at hand.*'[1]

Lloyd had also done his bit in getting Spitfires to Malta but it was now time to make that change. With Lloyd assigned to RAF Headquarters in the Middle East as its senior air staff officer, his replacement, Air Vice-Marshal Keith Park, arrived by flying boat on 14 July to run the air war over Malta.

Aged 50, Park was a former First World War flying ace and had become a household name after commanding Fighter Command's 11 Group during the Battle of Britain. Few commanders knew the Luftwaffe better. His group had taken the brunt of the aerial fighting during Britain's darkest

1. Lucas, op. cit., p.89.

days of 1940 and now, as Malta's AOC, he was again to face his old adversary, Albert Kesselring, who had commanded one of the opposing Luftwaffe air fleets during the Battle of Britain.

Park had brought to Malta with him the experienced Wing Commander John Thompson, another veteran of the battles of France and Britain, with a DFC for at least six victories, to take over the Takali Wing. Park soon had some of the RAF's most experienced fighter pilots around him and was quick to introduce a change in fighter tactics.

Unlike Lloyd before him, who had to work within the limitations of numbers and performance of the Hurricane, Park was fortunate to have so many Spitfires available and so he could use his tactics to best effect. Working with greater numbers and improved fighter performance, combined with an improvement in radar performance to give earlier warning and quicker reaction times on the ground, the Spitfires got at the raiders before they were over the island.

The plan essentially involved three formations of fighters. While two took care of any fighter escort, the third formation of Spitfires would fly straight at the bombers to get them to break up before they reached the island. Even if the bombers were not shot down, many would ditch their bombs and turn for home in an attempt to escape. Park also instructed his pilots not to go above 20,000 feet. Although this meant the Axis fighters would approach the island with a height advantage, they were forced to come down to an altitude where the Spitfire V performed at its best.[2]

Although the Spitfires were regaining control of the sky over Malta, Park was only too aware of the shortage of fuel and how quickly the situation could change. The arrival of more than a hundred Spitfires during the past couple of months had done wonders for the air war but he was still losing more than a dozen of them every week, although a vast improvement in the island's search and rescue capability had meant that many pilots had been saved to re-join the battle. However, should his fighters be unable to get into the air, because the island had run out of fuel, then the Axis would quickly dominate the sky once more.

---

2. Holland, op. cit., pp.338–9.

The fact that the desert war had reached a critical stage did not help when it came to the allocation and prioritization of fuel in Malta. On one hand it was important to stop the Axis convoys from re-supplying Rommel's forces in the desert, but to do so required fuel for the submarines and offensive aircraft, and on the other hand it was vital to defend Malta, and that required fuel for the fighters.

At that time in the campaign it was estimated that Malta had enough fuel to keep its forces going for at least another five or six weeks, but it was an extremely delicate situation and required careful balancing by men such as Gort, Park and Leatham. The only real solution was another convoy, but that would not happen until at least August. And so all the fighter pilots could do for now was to do their bit, and to keep the Axis bombers from creating further death and destruction on the island.

One of Park's young sergeant pilots serving with 249 Squadron at Takali was a 20-year-old Canadian called George Beurling. A smiling but untidy individual, with a shock of fair, tousled hair above penetrating blue eyes, Beurling was described by Laddie Lucas as highly strung, brash and outspoken.[3] But Beurling would go on to become by far the RAF's highest-scoring fighter pilot over Malta.

Beurling had only recently arrived on the island, having flown off *Eagle* during Operation Salient amid the chaos of June. Born in Quebec, Beurling had been something of a loner as a child, and having performed badly at school, he lacked the qualifications to join the RCAF. But he had taken flying lessons and had been granted a pilot's licence by the age of 18. Keen for action, Beurling had tried to join the Finnish Air Force during the Russo-Finnish war but was too young and so had worked his passage to Britain on a merchant ship to join the RAF, only to be turned away after failing to produce his birth certificate. After briefly returning to Canada before trying again, Beurling was eventually accepted into the RAF in September 1940. After pilot training he was posted to Spitfires and initially to 403 Squadron RCAF before he took part in fighter sweeps across the Channel with 41 Squadron.

---

3. Lucas, op. cit., p.104.

Beurling dedicated himself to learning the art of air combat, but he was still much a loner and often angered his commanders with his disdain for teamwork. He did not enjoy the disciplined missions over northern France and whenever the opportunity arose, he would break off to engage Luftwaffe fighters. He scored his first two victories in this manner during May 1942, both Focke-Wulf FW190s over the English Channel, but his methods made him unpopular with his superiors. Granted his wish for a transfer, Beurling was posted to Malta, which he viewed as 'The Fighter Pilot's Paradise'.[4]

Like Adrian Warburton before him, George Beurling had arrived in Malta as something of a misfit. He did not drink, nor did he smoke, and he also tried not to swear; his prime expletive to everything or anyone that he did not like was 'screwball'. And so he simply became known as 'Screwball Beurling', although he was also known to some as 'Buzz'.

Beurling's arrival in Malta coincided with Laddie Lucas taking command of 249 Squadron from Stan Grant. Lucas took an early opportunity to have a chat with Beurling and immediately warmed to him. Lucas was confident that he could get the best out of the young Canadian and so he placed Beurling under the watchful eye of Raoul Daddo-Langlois, now one of his flight commanders, and later said of Beurling:

'There were plenty of rough edges, but as with a fine games player the abilities were instantly apparent. He was something of a rebel, yes; but I suspected that his rebelliousness came from some mistaken feeling of inferiority. I judged that what Beurling most needed was not to be smacked down but to be encouraged.'[5]

Beurling settled to flying in combat over Malta like a duck to water. His baptism of fire was on the morning of 12 June when, flying with three other squadron pilots, his formation intercepted eight Bf109s. He did not claim a victory that day, although he may have damaged one of the 109s, but after that he claimed a series of successes that had no equal.

---

4. Shores and Williams, op. cit., p.126.
5. Lucas, op. cit., pp.104–5.

His first success occurred during the morning of 6 July. Beurling was flying one of the squadron's eight Spitfires, led by Flight Lieutenant Norman Lee, scrambled to intercept a raid of three Cant Z.1007 bombers, escorted by fourteen Regianne Re.2001s and twenty-four Macchi MC.202s, heading for Luqa. Four of the Spitfires, including that of Beurling, tore into the bombers. In his book *Malta Spitfire*, Beurling describes what happened next:

> '*The first job was to turn back those Cants, no matter what else happened, so we promptly crashed through the fighter screen to get the bombers. We met them head on before they reached the island and by the grace of God and eight Spitfires stopped them in their tracks and made them unload in the sea…. I got a two-second angle shot in on another and could see cannon shells and machine gun bullets pepper his fuselage.*'[6]

Beurling claimed one of the Cant bombers as damaged before he sent one of the escorting 202s into the sea. Spotting another Macchi on the tail of a Spitfire, he then quickly sent the second fighter into the ground near Zeitun.

After two more patrols he was flying his fourth sortie of that day during the early evening. He and Daddo-Langlois had been scrambled to intercept three Ju88s escorted by Bf109s heading for Takali. While his flight commander attacked the bombers, Beurling took on the escort, sending one of the 109s into the sea. He later reported:

> '*Two 109s dropped on me, but I did a quick wing-over and got onto one's tail. He saw me coming and tried to climb away. I figured he must be about 800 yards away from me when I got him in the sights and let go at him. It was a full deflection shot, and I had to make plenty of allowance for cannon-drop. I gave him a three-second burst, smack on his starboard flank, and got him in the glycol tank. He started to stream the stuff, leaving a long white trail of smoke …… I followed my man down to sea level, where he burst into flames and went into the drink.*'[7]

---

6. Beurling and Roberts, op. cit., p.137.
7. Shores and Cull with Malizia (*The Spitfire Year*), op. cit., pp.392–5.

It had been a remarkable start to his combat career over Malta and two days later Beurling added a further 109 to his total, sending it into the sea to the south of Gozo; he also claimed another and a Ju88 as damaged. Then, on 10 July, he was credited with another 109 during the morning, which he hit in its belly, causing the German to dive straight into the sea, and, later that morning, he shot down another MC.202. His combat report stated:

'*The [Macchi] went into a steep dive, pulled out and twisted away, rolled and pulled into a climb. Finally he went into a loop at the end of this climb and I nabbed him just at its top. A two-second burst blew his cockpit apart. The pilot baled out in a hell of a hurry. I circled over him as his parachute opened. He seemed to be healthy, so I gave "May Day" on the RT, specifying that the gent was an Italian, not one of our boys.*'[8]

With his overall score on eight, six of which had been shot down in the past five days, Beurling was awarded the Distinguished Flying Medal. His citation reads:

'*Sergeant Beurling has displayed great skill and courage in the face of the enemy. One day in July 1942, he engaged a number of enemy fighters which were escorting a formation of Junkers Ju88s and destroyed one fighter. Later during the same day he engaged ten enemy fighters and shot two of them down into the sea, bringing his total victories to eight.*'[9]

Beurling was already an ace over Malta and then two days later he claimed a further three Italian fighters in a day. Having returned from an earlier sortie, Beurling was one of two pilots to volunteer to get airborne again to search for a missing squadron colleague. The weather was unusually poor that day and they came across two Italians at low level that they could see popping in and out of the cloud. With his colleague providing cover, Beurling wasted no time in getting at the enemy fighters. He reported:

8. Ibid, p.406.
9. Supplement to the *London Gazette*, 28 July 1942, p.3303.

'I simply sneaked up behind the tail-ender and gave him a one-second squirt. He burst into flames and went down. Without further ado I whipped round on the other lad ….. I came right underneath his tail. I was going faster than he was; about fifty yards behind. I closed to about thirty yards and I was on his port side coming in at about 15 degrees angle. I could see all the details on his face because he turned and looked at me just as I had a bead on him. He dived in beside his mate. From the firing of the first shot until both Macchis went down no more than six or seven seconds had elapsed. Things happen fast in this racket.'[10]

But Beurling did not have it all his own way and two days later he was fortunate to get away with his own life when his Spitfire was riddled through the fuselage and wings by more than twenty rounds. Then, after a lull in the fighting lasting a few days, he suffered a personal loss when his best friend, 25-year-old Pilot Officer Joseph Paradis, a French-Canadian, was killed on 22 July. Also killed during the action was Flight Sergeant Don 'Shorty' Reid of 185 Squadron. Reid was circling where Paradis had gone into the sea but he was then bounced by 109s. Reid, another Canadian, and with five victories to his name, had only just celebrated his twentieth birthday; six days after Reid's death came the announcement of his DFM.

The loss of Paradis was a blow to Beurling but he was not the only squadron pilot killed during July 1942. It was a month that was proving hard and bloody on both sides, and Paradis had been the squadron's seventh pilot killed in action in just four weeks.

It was an extremely tough period of air fighting. Malta's squadrons had lost thirty-six Spitfires, either destroyed or badly damaged since the start of the month. It was a high rate of attrition but Park dug his heels in for more reinforcements. Not only did he need more Spitfires but he also needed more pilots with combat experience, and would not accept those still wet behind the ears like some that had been sent to Malta before. This was yet another critical phase in the defence of Malta and Park got his way. Thirty-

---

10. Shores and Cull with Malizia (The Spitfire Year), op. cit., pp.408–9.

one more Spitfires duly arrived, having flown off *Eagle* as part of Operation Pinpoint on 15 July.

The Spitfires had been delivered as part of the same operation that had seen *Welshman* complete another heroic run through the Med. After Harpoon, she had returned to the Clyde for dry-docking and a brief tidy up before being laden with stores once again. Then, having taken on more stores in Gibraltar, mainly ammunition, *Welshman* had sailed with *Eagle*, the cruisers *Charybdis* and *Cairo*, and five destroyers. With *Eagle* having flown off her Spitfires, *Welshman* detached at full speed to run along the North African coast under the welcome cover of a heat haze. She then survived a number of air attacks, an attempted pursuit by three Italian destroyers and a torpedo attack by an Italian submarine, but with *Welshman* running at full speed of up to 40 knots she survived unscathed and made it to Grand Harbour during the early hours of 18 July. Then, after quickly offloading her cargo, which also included foodstuffs and mail, she was on her way again under the cover of darkness to arrive safely back in Gibraltar three days later.

It had been a remarkable effort by *Welshman*'s skipper, Captain William Friedberger, and his crew, and her homeward passage to Gibraltar coincided with the delivery of more Spitfires to Malta, this time under Operation Insect. Having returned to Gibraltar from Pinpoint, *Eagle* set sail on 20 July, again accompanied by *Charybdis* and *Cairo* with five destroyers. Twenty-eight Spitfires were flown off the carrier early the following morning, all of which arrived safely in Malta.

There had also been successful Magic Carpet runs during the month by the submarines *Parthian* and *Clyde*. Malta had also been boosted by the arrival of more Beauforts with experienced torpedo-bombing crews from Gibraltar and Egypt to enable the RAF to resume its offensive operations against the Axis convoys. Typically, a formation of up to a dozen torpedo-carrying Beauforts would go off in search of a worthwhile target while protected by a similar number of Beaufighters tasked to deal with any enemy fighters that might be accompanying the ships.

It was soon realized just how valuable the Beauforts were. When used properly, they proved to be a prime means of stopping supplies reaching Rommel's forces in North Africa. The aircraft, previously from various detachments passing through Malta, were now formed into a composite unit, which underwent many administrative permutations, ranging from 39 Squadron to 217 Squadron, to 86 Squadron, and then back to 39 Squadron, and so on.

The unit was led by Squadron Leader Jimmy Hyde, a newly arrived pilot on the island, who took over command from the very capable Patrick Gibbs. Until that point Gibbs had unofficially masterminded Beaufort operations from Malta, for which he had just received a Bar to his DFC. Although Hyde was given command of the Beauforts, Gibbs remained with the unit, but, on 24 July, Hyde was killed while leading six Beauforts attacking an Axis convoy heading down the Greek coast. With the loss of Hyde, Gibbs was officially given command of the Beauforts.

Malta's Beaufighters were also integrated into the same unit and Gibbs was soon leading a unique and comprehensive Luqa-based strike-force, consisting of Beauforts and crews from three different squadrons to carry out torpedo attacks, and a mixed force of Beaufighters acting as fighter-bombers. Towards the end of August, Gibbs scored two main successes. First he crippled the 7,800-tonne tanker *Pozarica*, which later beached off Corfu, and he was then responsible for massively disrupting Rommel's oil supplies when he found the 5,000-tonne tanker *San Andrea*. Escorted by Beaufighters, Gibbs ran at the tanker from the Italian coast. The ship's crew would have considered an attack from that direction to have been least likely and despite Macchi fighters in the area, Gibbs put his torpedo into the side of the tanker from just 500 yards. Moments later it exploded, earning Gibbs the DSO.[11]

As much as any one individual, Patrick Gibbs had helped put paid to Rommel's plans in North Africa. Gibbs even had the use of a photo-reconnaissance aircraft from 69 Squadron, either a Maryland, Spitfire or Baltimore, to fly with his formations and to provide an instant post-raid assessment of damage caused during their attacks. It had almost become Gibbs' private air force.[12]

---

11. Spooner (*Faith Hope and Malta GC*), op. cit., p.77.
12. Spooner (*Supreme Gallantry*), op. cit., pp.173–4.

George Beurling, meanwhile, was after revenge for the loss of his best friend, Joseph Paradis. A day after Paradis had been killed, Beurling was involved in a long duel with a Re.2001 before he eventually blew the left wing off the Italian fighter. But Beurling's best day over Malta was on 27 July when he shot down two Italian MC.202s and two Luftwaffe Bf109s. His first successes occurred early in the morning when he was one of a number of Spitfires that intercepted a raid of nine Ju88s heading for Takali. The Spitfires were too late to stop the attack on the airfield but they spotted several Macchis. Beurling first brought down one, forcing it to crash-land on Gozo, before latching on to the second and opening fire with devastating accuracy. Beurling later recorded:

'I spotted four Macchis running in line astern and took Number Four. They saw me coming and pulled into a climbing turn to the right. As they did I came up on my man's starboard quarter and let him have a burst. It was a straight deflection shot which went into his engine and radiator. He flicked into a spin, but managed to pull out and crash-landed on Gozo….A second or so later I got Number Three exactly the same way. The poor devil simply blew to pieces in the air.'[13]

His successes against the 109s occurred later on, about midday, when he was flying one of six Spitfires that attacked the fighter escort for five Ju88s to the north of Grand Harbour.

With fourteen victories, all achieved during July, Beurling had become Malta's top-scoring fighter ace of the war. But he was far from finished. Two days later, he shot down another Bf109 to the north-east of the island, bringing his total while flying from Malta to at least fifteen (seventeen overall) and earning him a Bar to his DFM. His citation reads:

'Since being awarded the Distinguished Flying Medal in July 1942, Sergeant Beurling has destroyed a further 9 enemy aircraft, bringing his victories to 17. One of his exploits was the destruction of four enemy fighters

---

13. Beurling and Roberts, op. cit., pp.165–6.

in one day; during these brief combats he also damaged a further two hostile aircraft. His courage and determination are a source of inspiration to all.'[14]

It was a staggering performance. His relentless concentration on aerial fighting led him to become a master at deflection shooting, which combined with his remarkable awareness in the air had enabled him to become the most lethal of fighter pilots. Although he was particularly deadly at range, which he put down to his remarkably good eyesight, he was also prepared to press in to his target closer than most to achieve success. He had also mastered the Spitfire better than many others. Such was his confidence in the aircraft to recover from unusual positions, that he was prepared to use violent manoeuvres, or even get the aircraft to flick stall, to get an opponent off his tail.

Unsurprisingly, the Luftwaffe, too, had its aces during this hectic period of air fighting. Oberleutnant Gerhard Michalski, the 25-year-old *Gruppenkommandeur* of II./JG 53, shot down seven Spitfires during July alone. He was the Luftwaffe's most successful pilot over Malta at the time. Credited with twenty-six victories over the island, bringing his overall total to forty-eight, Michalski was awarded the Knight's Cross before his unit moved to North Africa in October. Another successful Luftwaffe ace was 22-year-old Oberleutnant Siegfried Freytag, the *Staffelkapitän* of 1./ JG 77. Known as the 'Malta Lion', Freytag was credited with twenty-five victories during the summer of 1942, all but two being Spitfires. He would bring his overall total to seventy-eight during November to make him the Luftwaffe's highest-scoring ace to have operated over Malta. There was also Oberfeldwebel Herbert Rollwage of II./JG 53 with twenty victories over Malta during the year. And so it went on.

These figures provide firm evidence of just how hard the air battle was being fought over Malta during the summer of 1942. As for George Beurling, he was reluctant to become an officer but such were his leadership qualities in the air that he was overruled and so he was commissioned with the rank of pilot officer with effect from 30 July.[15]

---

14. Second Supplement to the *London Gazette*, 4 September 1942, p.3861.
15. Supplement to the *London Gazette*, 22 September 1942, p.4116.

After gaining his eighteenth victory on 8 August, a Bf109 near Zonqor Point, Beurling was jumped by more 109s and his aircraft was hit in the engine, forcing him to belly-land in a stonewalled field. Apart from a superficial cut to his arm, he walked away unhurt. The following week he shared in the destruction of a Ju88 to the north-east of Linosa, but the enervation of daily combat, combined with the poor rations and a touch of Malta Dog, meant that Beurling was then bedridden for the rest of August.

Despite Beurling's many successes, and those of others, Malta was still on its knees. It was a particularly hot summer and conditions were, at times, unbearable. The island was in ruins and the population was growing hungrier by the day. Farmers handed over all their crops, there was a shortage of potatoes, the bread ration had been cut again and the milk allocation was restricted to hospitals and children under the age of 9.[16] The situation for the island of Malta remained critical.

16. Holland, op. cit., p.341.

Chapter Seventeen

Pedestal – The Biggest Convoy of Them All

For many, the lasting image of the siege of Malta is that of the tanker SS *Ohio*, barely afloat and surrounded by supporting vessels, limping into Grand Harbour at the end of Operation Pedestal to deliver her precious cargo of oil.

Pedestal, the biggest and most famous Malta convoy of them all, has rightly taken its place in history as one of Britain's most important strategic victories of the Second World War. However, only five of the fourteen merchantmen allocated to the convoy reached Grand Harbour, at a cost of many lives. The *Ohio* was the last of the five to arrive in Grand Harbour and the date – 15 August – coincided with the celebration of the Feast of the Assumption (the Assumption of the Virgin Mary into Heaven). And so the name *Konvaj ta' Santa Marija*, or Santa Maria Convoy, still gets used to this day in Malta, with the island's public holiday and celebrations still, in part, celebrating the arrival of the convoy.

Following the disasters of Harpoon and Vigorous, it was vital that Pedestal got through. British planners knew that this was probably the last chance. Desperately short of food, fuel and ammunition, the outcome should the ships of Pedestal not get through would surely have resulted in the surrender of Malta. Indeed, the end of September had already been discussed as a likely date of surrender, and it was only as late as that because of the arrival of the two ships from Harpoon and because the Magic Carpet runs had still taken place; albeit, only ever bringing a limited amount of supplies.[1]

The Pedestal convoy was planned to sail from Britain on the earliest possible date in August 1942. Planning had been underway since the disappointment of Operation Harpoon and the failure of Operation Vigorous. The outcome

---

1. Ibid, p.343.

of Vigorous, in particular, ruled out another attempt through the eastern and central Mediterranean, and so the decision was made to assemble the largest force to date in one single convoy from the west, in another attempt to relieve Malta.

Pedestal was essentially to be a re-run of Harpoon and recognized the need for adequate carrier-borne forces to provide the convoy with air protection, as well as the need for sufficient tanker capacity. But finding a number of suitable ships would not be easy, whether they be merchant vessels to carry the cargo or naval warships to protect them. Besides, speed was of vital importance and so ships capable of meeting the minimum convoy speed of about 15 knots were required if they were to have any chance of getting through.

The suspension of Arctic convoys until the shortening of days in autumn released a number of warships from the Royal Navy's Home Fleet. But the key to the convoy's success would be fuel and oil, and there was no British oil tanker left that was either big enough or fast enough. Only the Americans had such tankers and during a visit to Washington by the British Prime Minister, Winston Churchill, in June, which took place in the immediate aftermath of Harpoon and Vigorous, Churchill requested the loan of the American-built oil tanker SS *Ohio*.

Also requested were two American freighters: *Santa Elisa*, an 8,379-tonne vessel owned by the Grace Line of New York, and *Almeria Lykes*, owned by Lykes Brothers Steamship Company of New Orleans and registering 7,773 tonnes. Understandably, there was some opposition to the request, not helped by the recent loss of *Kentucky* during Harpoon, but just a matter of days later the *Ohio* crossed the Atlantic and steamed into the Clyde.

Built for the Texas Oil Company and launched in 1940, *Ohio* was 9,514 tonnes and capable of reaching 19 knots. After much debate, the American tanker was handed over to a British crew and overnight she became transferred from American to British registry with the Eagle Oil and Shipping Company.

Ohio had already been fitted with one 5-inch (130mm) gun on its stern, and a 3-inch (76mm) anti-aircraft gun in the bows before leaving America, but she was now moved to King George V Dock in Glasgow to be fitted with Oerlikon and Bofors anti-aircraft guns. She was also specially strengthened to protect the tanker against the shock of bombs exploding nearby. Her engines were mounted on rubber bearings, to reduce shock, and all steam-pipes were supported with steel springs and baulks of timber.

Finally, under the command of 40-year-old Captain Dudley Mason, and with twenty-four naval ratings and soldiers to serve the guns, bringing her total company to seventy-seven, *Ohio* was ready. She then sailed down to the Clyde where she was loaded with 11,500 tonnes of kerosene and diesel fuel oils. *Ohio* would be the only ship carrying this precious cargo but should anything happen to her, the convoy's other merchantmen were to carry fuel supplies in drums as they had no method of storing oil or fuel in their holds.

While the merchant ships were gathering in the Clyde Estuary, the naval forces had already arrived at Scapa Flow. Under the overarching codename of Operation Pedestal, there were to be a number of smaller operations taking place: Op Berserk, the co-ordination of aircraft carriers; Op Bellows, the further reinforcement of Malta's Spitfires, which were to be flown off the flat-topped modified battle-cruiser HMS *Furious*; and Op Ascendant, which would see the return of Harpoon's two surviving merchantmen, *Troilus* and *Orari*.

Malta's supplies – including fuel, ammunition, food, medical and equipment – were to be spread relatively evenly among the fourteen merchantmen allocated to the convoy. This would ensure a proportion of each would get through to Malta in the case of losses among the convoy.

In addition to the three American ships – *Ohio*, *Almeria Lykes* (commanded by Captain W Henderson) and *Santa Elisa* (Captain T Thompson) – the other eleven merchantmen making up the convoy were all British, some of which had already completed Malta runs, and all were fitted with defensive anti-aircraft guns.

With the exception of *Empire Hope* (commanded by Captain G Williams), a war-built standard refrigerated ship of 12,688 tonnes, the rest were all fast cargo-passenger liners: *Brisbane Star* (Captain F Riley) and *Melbourne Star* (Captain D MacFarlane) were both Blue Star liners at 12,791 tonnes and 12,806 tonnes respectively; two of the ships were Alfred Holt's vessels, the 7,516-tonne Blue Funnel liner *Deucalion* (Captain Ramsay Brown) and Glen Line's 8,982-tonne *Glenorchy* (Captain George Leslie); the Scottish Steamship Company provided the 7,347-tonne *Clan Ferguson* (Captain A Cossar); the Federal Steam Navigation Company had made available the

A scene typical of most days in early April 1942 during another devastating air attack on Malta's dockyards. (*Author's collection*)

With the dockyard in ruins, the resilient light-cruiser HMS *Penelope*, a stalwart of Force K, had been hit so many times that she earned herself the now legendary name of HMS '*Pepperpot*'. Her many holes were patched up enough for her to slip out of Grand Harbour on 8 April 1942. Although she suffered a further air attack the following day, *Penelope* eventually made it to Gibraltar to undergo extensive repairs. So iconic was this image at the time that it was turned into a postcard. (*Author's collection*)

The reverse of the George Cross awarded to 'The Island of Malta' dated 15 April 1942. (*GCIA*)

With a shortage of British aircraft carriers to re-supply Malta with more fighters, the British Prime Minister, Winston Churchill, turned to the United States for help. The result of Churchill's plea was Operation Calendar in April 1942, involving the American carrier USS *Wasp*, to fly off forty-eight Spitfires to Malta. (*Author's collection*)

A Spitfire V of 603 Squadron at Takali after flying off the *Wasp* on 20 April 1942. This image was obviously staged for the camera to highlight the soldier, sailor and airman maintaining the aircraft in its pen. (*AHB*)

Lord Gort, a highly decorated and greatly respected army officer, arriving in Malta on 7 May 1942 to replace Sir William Dobbie as the new governor and commander-in-chief of Malta. Ahead of Gort is flag officer Malta, Vice Admiral Sir Ralph Leatham. (*IWM*)

HMS *Welshman*, a fast naval minelayer, arrived in Grand Harbour on 10 May 1942 after her daring solo dash through the western Mediterranean, having sailed from Gibraltar and along the North African coast posing as a French destroyer. In addition to the normal supplies of food and other stores, *Welshman* was carrying a hundred spare Merlin aircraft engines and 120 service personnel, most of whom were RAF ground crew to maintain the Spitfires. (*GCIA*)

An RAF Beaufighter, the most versatile of all aircraft in Malta, pictured at Luqa during 1942. (*AHB*)

Laddie Lucas arrived in Malta as a relatively inexperienced fighter pilot but took over command of 249 Squadron during June 1942. Shortly afterwards he was awarded the DFC for three victories. (*AHB*)

Fast-tracked to flag rank, Rear Admiral Philip Vian (centre) commanded the 15th Cruiser Squadron in the Mediterranean and was a key naval figure in Malta's survival. Based in Alexandria, his ships provided protection for a number of convoys through the hazardous eastern Med. (*IWM*)

The Dido-class cruiser HMS *Charybdis* pictured at the start of Operation Harpoon in June 1942. To the right of her is HMS *Argus*. Both ships formed part of the convoy's covering force, designated Force W. (*Author's collection*)

The Crown Colony-class cruiser HMS *Kenya*, taken from *Wishart* during the early stages of Harpoon. (*Author's collection*)

Ships of the Harpoon convoy in the western Mediterranean on 12 June, taken from *Wishart*. Tragedy was to strike soon after and only two merchantmen would eventually reach Malta. (*Author's collection*)

Oiling at sea from the auxiliary RFA *Brown Ranger* during Operation Harpoon. The picture was taken from *Wishart* on 13 June 1942, and looking across the auxiliary can be seen the destroyers *Antelope* (also alongside the RFA), *Ithuriel* (furthest forward) and in the distance is *Wrestler*. (*Author's collection*)

Not wishing to hold back the fast minelayer, HMS *Welshman* was ordered to break away from the Harpoon convoy to sail on to Malta alone at full speed. She arrived in Grand Harbour on 15 June 1942. (*GCIA*)

Air Vice-Marshal Keith Park (right), the former commander of RAF Fighter Command's 11 Group during the Battle of Britain, took over as the air officer commanding Malta from Hugh Pughe Lloyd (left) in July 1942. (*AHB*)

The Blue Funnel liner *Troilus* was just one of Harpoon's two merchant vessels to make it to Malta. After unloading she would have to remain in harbour for two months until another convoy could be put together to provide protection for her return. (*IWM*)

The carrier HMS *Eagle* surrounded by her naval screen during Operation Pinpoint, when thirty-one more Spitfires were delivered to Malta on 15 July 1942. (*Author's collection*)

With twenty-six victories while serving with 249 Squadron in Malta, fifteen of them during July 1942, George 'Screwball' Beurling, a 20-year-old Canadian, was by far the RAF's highest-scoring fighter pilot over the island and became a legend among the Maltese. He is pictured here with the rudder of one of the two Macchi MC.202s he shot down on 27 July, this aircraft coming down on the small island of Gozo. (*IWM*)

The destroyer HMS *Ithuriel* pictured at the start of Operation Pedestal. Two days later she attacked an Italian submarine, forcing it to surface after which it was rammed by the destroyer. The submarine was crippled in the attack, although *Ithuriel* suffered bow damage during the ramming but managed to return to Gibraltar to undergo repairs. (*Author's collection*)

Oiling from *Brown Ranger* during the early stages of Pedestal, the largest and most famous Malta convoy of them all. The photo was taken from *Wishart* on 10 August 1942, and also pictured alongside the auxiliary is HMS *Antelope*, another destroyer of Force Z. (*Author's collection*)

A classic and well-published photograph of ships of Pedestal taken from the carrier HMS *Victorious* during the early part of the convoy. The two carriers astern are *Indomitable* (nearest) and *Eagle*, and the three escorting cruisers on the left are (L-R) *Charybdis, Sirius and Phoebe. (IWM)*

Another classic photo of Pedestal's three carriers (L-R) *Victorious, Indomitable* and *Eagle.* Pedestal's first disaster occurred during the early afternoon of 11 August when *Eagle* was torpedoed by the German submarine *U-73* and sank within minutes, taking with her to the bottom sixteen Sea Hurricanes and more than 200 officers and men. (*IWM*)

The Blue Star liner *Brisbane Star* was left to make her own way to Malta after being torpedoed during the evening of 12 August. Remarkably, she arrived in Grand Harbour during the afternoon of 14 August to become the fourth merchantman of the Pedestal convoy to reach Malta. (*IWM*)

The last of the five surviving merchantmen of Pedestal to arrive in Malta was the tanker *Ohio*. To many, this classic image of the American tanker limping into Grand Harbour on 15 August, surrounded by supporting vessels keeping her afloat, provides the lasting memory of the Malta convoys. The *Times of Malta* later wrote: 'If ever there was an example of dogged perseverance against all odds, this was it.' No one could have put it better. (*GCIA*)

Malta's outstanding but quite unorthodox reconnaissance pilot, Adrian Warburton. While operating from the island, Warby was decorated with the DSO and Bar, and a DFC and two Bars, for his 360 operational sorties; a truly remarkable achievement. Sadly, though, he was killed flying over Europe in 1944. (*Via Tony Spooner*)

The chief justice, Sir George Borg, receiving the George Cross on behalf of the people of Malta from the island's governor, Lord Gort, at a ceremony held at Palace Square on 13 September 1942. (*GCIA*)

King George VI arrives in Grand Harbour on 20 June 1943 aboard HMS *Aurora* to be greeted by thousands lining the bastions and revetments of Valletta and the Three Cities. (*GCIA*)

The George Cross Island Association was founded in 1987 to honour the peoples of Malta and those who fought to defend and supply the island during the siege. Here members of the GCIA gather after a service held at St Paul's Cathedral, Mdina, in 1990. The two gents chatting (3rd and 4th from left) are Tony Spooner (on the right of the two), who led the Wellingtons of the Special Duties Flight at Luqa, and Charles Jacobs, the author's father, who served in the destroyer HMS *Wishart* during the Malta convoys. (*Author's collection*)

On 29 May 1992, fifty years after the award of the George Cross to the island of Malta, the 10-tonne bronze Siege Bell Memorial at Valletta was inaugurated by Queen Elizabeth II and the President of Malta. The Queen is seen mixing with veterans and locals in front of the bell. (*Author's collection*)

A service held by members of the GCIA at the Siege Bell Memorial in 1996. The memorial is located next to the Lower Barrakka Gardens in Valletta and commands a spectacular position overlooking Grand Harbour. (*Author's collection*)

10,624-tonne *Dorset* (Captain J Tuckett); the Union Castle Line provided the 7,795-tonne *Rochester Castle* (Captain R Wren); Port Line the 8,535-tonne *Port Chalmers* (Captain H G Pinkney); and Shaw, Savill & Albion provided two ships, *Waimarama* (Captain R Pearce) and *Wairangi* (Captain H Gordon), at 12,843 tonnes and 12,400 tonnes respectively.[2]

Under the convoy commodore, Commodore A G Venables, sailing in *Port Chalmers*, the merchant ships of Pedestal were to receive protection from two large forces: one, Force X, commanded by Rear Admiral Harold Burrough, would provide close escort for the merchantmen all the way to Malta, and Vice Admiral Neville Syfret's Force Z was to provide overall cover in the western Med.[3] Between these two large forces there were four aircraft carriers, two battleships, seven cruisers and thirty-two destroyers.

The plan was that once the convoy reached the Skerki Channel, an area of relatively shallow open sea in the narrow Strait of Sicily between Sicily and Tunisia, Force Z would return to Gibraltar to refuel. These were the main fighting units of three carriers – *Eagle*, *Victorious* and *Indomitable* – under the command of Rear Admiral Sir Lumley Lyster, flying his flag in *Victorious*, and the battleships *Rodney* and *Nelson*. Three of the cruisers were to provide anti-aircraft fire for the carriers (*Charybdis* for *Eagle*, *Sirius* for *Victorious* and *Phoebe* for *Indomitable*) in addition to the fifteen destroyers.[4] This would leave Force X, comprising the four remaining cruisers (*Nigeria*, *Kenya*, *Manchester* and *Cairo*) and the destroyer flotilla,[5] to proceed to Malta with the merchantmen.

Also involved in Pedestal was Force R, the refuelling detachment to operate in the western Mediterranean, and Force Y, consisting of two destroyers, *Matchless* and *Badsworth*, to carry out Op Ascendant. Finally,

---

2. Smith, *Pedestal*, p.252 (compiled from Lloyd's Register of Shipping 1941–42; General Register of Shipping and Seamen, Cardiff; United States Maritime Commission, Washington D.C.).

3. Smith, op. cit., pp.253–4.

4. The fifteen destroyers of Force Z were: *Antelope*, *Eskimo*, *Ithuriel*, *Laforey*, *Lightning*, *Lookout*, *Quentin*, *Somali*, *Tartar*, *Vansittart*, *Westcott*, *Wilton*, *Wishart*, *Wrestler* and *Zetland*.

5. The destroyer flotilla of Force X were: *Ashanti*, *Bramham*, *Bicester*, *Derwent*, *Foresight*, *Fury*, *Intrepid*, *Icarus*, *Ledbury*, *Pathfinder* and *Penn*.

two of Malta's submarines, *Safari* and *Unbroken*, were to mount patrols to the north of Sicily, and six other subs – *Utmost*, *United*, *Uproar*, *Ultimatum*, *Unruffled* and *P.222* – were to patrol between Malta and Tunisia.[6]

With overall operational command, Syfret transferred to the battleship HMS *Nelson* at the end of July after the ship had returned to Scapa Flow. It was at Scapa that Syfret held a conference to discuss the operation. Then, on 31 July, *Nelson*, accompanied by her sister-ship *Rodney*, the carriers *Victorious* and *Argus*, accompanied by *Sirius* and a number of destroyers, sailed from Scapa Flow to rendezvous out in the Atlantic to the west of the Strait of Gibraltar with *Eagle* and *Charybdis* from Gibraltar, and *Indomitable* and *Phoebe* from Freetown.

The rendezvous went well, after which the three main carriers and their escorts carried out Op Berserk. The carriers' aircraft carried out dummy attacks against the fleet to give training for the gunners and to test communications between the ships in preparation for the main convoy. With training complete, *Argus* left for Gibraltar and would play no further part in the main operation. Also joining the force were *Furious*, tasked with flying off the thirty-eight Spitfires to Malta under Op Bellows, and her escort of *Manchester* plus two destroyers.

The start of the main convoy was less than two days away and there followed a series of refuels for the destroyer flotilla, with all the associated problems that tended to bring. Refuelling was often slow, not helped by the poor weather out in the Atlantic, and there were invariably problems with leaking connections, and so some of the destroyers were sent on ahead to Gibraltar to refuel before re-joining Force Z.

Meanwhile, the main convoy, designated WS21s, had sailed from the Clyde during the evening of 2 August. The fourteen merchantmen, led by the cruiser HMS *Nigeria*, formed up and were joined the following morning by the rest of their escort. On board *Nigeria*, Burrough met with Venables and the masters of the merchant vessels for the final briefing. Then, during their passage south, the convoy practiced manoeuvres and changing formation in preparation for their run through the Med.

---

6. Woodman, op. cit., p.379.

Having completed Op Berserk, the carriers joined up with the rest of the fleet while some of the escorting ships shuttled in and out of Gibraltar to complete refuelling. By Sunday, 9 August the entire convoy had assembled. There was time for just one final exercise, with all the ships involved, before the convoy sailed through the Strait of Gibraltar during the night, allowing time for some of the warships to call in quickly at Gibraltar to take on more fuel.

Conditions were favourable for the ships that night. It was moonless and offered varying degrees of visibility. It was even foggy at times, meaning the convoy could pass through the Strait unobserved from the shore. There were, however, still many watchful eyes on board the numerous fishing vessels and other merchant ships out in the Strait, even under the cover of darkness, with plenty of lookouts only too keen to report to their Axis contacts. Besides, sailing such a large number of ships towards the Med would never have gone unnoticed; either from aerial reconnaissance or from the interception of radio transmissions between the ships during Op Berserk.

Regardless of how much the enemy knew of the Pedestal convoy before the ships entered the Med, once daylight broke there was nowhere to hide. The weather was gloriously hot with nothing but clear skies during the day. Fortunately, though, the shortage of fuel meant the large Italian warships would not venture out to intercept the convoy. This meant the Axis commanders would instead have to rely on aircraft, submarines, E-boats and other torpedo boats to mount an attack. Their plan, therefore, was to attack the convoy as it passed through the Strait of Sicily, coinciding with the Royal Navy's carriers and heavy warships turning back to Gibraltar, after which Italian cruisers would attack what was left of the convoy having passed through the Strait.

While Pedestal was making its way eastwards towards Malta, another convoy, using the remnants of MW11, and re-designated MW12, was heading west from Port Said and Haifa. The idea was to deceive the enemy into thinking that the Allies were once again sailing convoys from both ends of the Med at the same time; a repeat of Harpoon and Vigorous.

Under Operation MG3, three merchantmen – *City of Pretoria*, *City of Lincoln* and *City of Edinburgh* – constituting convoy MW12a, set sail from

Port Said during the evening of 10 August with their escort of three cruisers (*Arethusa*, *Euryalus* and *Coventry*) and ten destroyers. Then, early the following morning, convoy MW12b, consisting of the transport *Ajax*, with her escort led by Vian in *Cleopatra* and consisting of another cruiser *Dido* plus five destroyers, left Haifa.

The two forces joined up and carried out manoeuvres during daylight. Then, as the convoy was passing to the north of Alexandria, Vian took most of the warships off to bombard Rhodes under the cover of darkness, and the merchantmen and their escorts returned to port. By using false radio transmission, the illusion of the 'convoy' was continued for some time. MG3 had passed without incident and, ironically, created no reaction from the enemy. It is, therefore, something of an irony that MW12 might well have made Malta, but that was not to have been known at the time.[7]

While MG3 was underway in the eastern Med, the two surviving merchantmen of Harpoon, *Troilus* and *Orari*, slipped away from Malta under the cover of darkness for their run west back to Gibraltar. They had been in Grand Harbour for seven weeks and were now running empty apart from carrying some sick and wounded, as well as a number of captured Axis aircrew heading for prisoner of war camps elsewhere. Their two escorting destroyers, *Badsworth* and *Matchless*, had already arrived to escort them. Following the pattern of an Axis convoy, the formation set off towards Cape Bon, after which they followed the North African coastline westwards. With the enemy subsequently occupied by the large convoy of Pedestal, all four ships arrived safely back in Gibraltar, after which the two merchantmen returned to Britain.

Back in the western Med, Pedestal was steaming in four columns at a convoy speed of just over 13 knots. The first day passed without incident and those destroyers that had been in to Gibraltar to refuel had all re-joined the ships. During the course of the night and into the following morning, three cruisers and twenty-four destroyers took on fuel from the fleet auxiliaries *Dingledale* and *Brown Ranger*; a hazardous operation knowing that U-boats were around.

---

7. Ibid, p.385.

Daybreak on 11 August brought a fine and sunny day. Sunshine and clear skies would have been the last thing those on board the ships would have wanted. As the convoy zig-zagged along a mean eastwards line of advance, the fleet's surveillance radars picked up Axis reconnaissance aircraft shadowing the ships. Air patrols were mounted by the carriers and a number of interceptions took place but it was now only a matter of time before the convoy came under air attack.

Pedestal's first disaster occurred during the early afternoon when the convoy was about seventy miles to the south of Cape Salinas, the southernmost point of the island of Majorca. Seemingly undetected by the covering force and escorts, Kapitänleutnant Helmut Rosenbaum had been watching the mighty *Eagle* closely through the periscope of the *U-73*. A pre-war officer, Rosenbaum was an experienced U-boat commander and was a week into his eighth patrol. He had patiently worked his submarine through the carrier's destroyer screen and had now closed to a position to mount his attack.

With Rosenbaum satisfied he was in the right place, the *U-73* fired a salvo of torpedoes at *Eagle*. Four struck with devastating accuracy, causing the carrier to sink in just eight minutes and taking with her to the bottom sixteen Sea Hurricanes and more than 200 officers and men. Although the carrier had sunk quickly, 927 men from the ship's company of 1,160 officers and men[8] were rescued by the destroyers *Laforey* and *Lookout* and the tug *Jaunty*. For more than an hour the U-boat was hunted but without success. Rosenbaum and his *U-73* had got away; his reward on returning to port would be the Knight's Cross and command of a U-boat flotilla.

The sinking of *Eagle* was a devastating blow for Pedestal. The loss of a carrier was disastrous at any time but the convoy was early into its passage and there was still a long way to go. Furthermore, many had witnessed the end of *Eagle* and word travelled fast among the rest of the convoy, but there was no time to dwell.

Meanwhile, *Furious* had pressed on and soon reached her flying-off position some 550 miles to the west of Malta. With more U-boats likely to be in the area, there would have been a certain amount of eagerness to get

---

8. Figures taken from the *Times of Malta* dated 26 August 2012.

the Spitfires away so that *Furious* could head back towards Gibraltar and avoid suffering the same fate as *Eagle*.

The thirty-eight Spitfires were flown off in three flights of eight and two of seven. Among those flying off *Furious* were some notable pilots heading for key posts in Malta. The first flight was led by Group Captain Walter Churchill. Aged thirty-four with a DSO and DFC, he was one of the RAF's older fighter pilots and was now on his way to take command of Takali. The second flight was led by Wing Commander Arthur Donaldson, another experienced fighter pilot with a DFC, who was to take over the Takali Wing from John Thompson who, in turn, would take over command of the Hal Far Wing. The third flight off *Eagle* was led by Flight Lieutenant Eric Woods, another fighter ace with a DFC, who was to take command of 249 Squadron. And so it went on.

By mid-afternoon all the Spitfires had gone, with all but one arriving safely in Malta; one had suffered a technical problem after take-off and returned to land on *Indomitable*.

That evening there were two air attacks on the convoy. The first took place just after sunset with enemy bombers attacking at heights of about 10,000 feet, but the barrage of anti-aircraft fire put up by the fleet prevented the bombers obtaining any real accuracy. The second, by torpedo-bombers, took place soon after but was carried out at long range and also resulted in no losses among the ships.

As the convoy continued eastwards, daybreak on 12 August produced the start of another beautiful sunny day with calm seas and visibility up to fifteen miles. The ships were now sandwiched between Sardinia and Tunisia. Radar reports warned of Italian reconnaissance aircraft in the area as the convoy came within easy reach of enemy air bases in Sardinia, Sicily and Pantelleria, where the Axis had assembled some 600 aircraft.[9]

Soon after 6.00 am the first of the fleet's fighters were flown off the carriers to provide a protective umbrella above the convoy. Three hours later,

---

9. The Axis air assets available to attack the convoy comprised: 146 German bombers, mainly Ju88s; seventy-two German fighters, nearly all Bf 109s; 232 Italian fighters; sixteen Ju87 dive-bombers; and 139 Italian bombers, many of which were the highly effective SM.79 torpedo-bombers.

nineteen Ju88s were reported to be approaching the convoy at high level from the east. It was to be the first of four major raids during the day. Once again, the anti-aircraft barrage put up by so many ships was formidable but the fleet's fighters proved most effective and there were no losses among the ships.

Then, at midday, the destroyer *Ashanti* reported at least nine enemy raiders ahead. It was the first of what turned out to be three waves of attack. This time the raiders were Italian bombers, which laid mines ahead of the convoy while CR.42s carried out a diversionary attack against the ships to draw anti-aircraft fire. The convoy turned hard to port to avoid the mines but it was the third wave of Italian bombers approaching the convoy, a mixed force of more than forty SM.79s and SM.84s that caused the biggest threat. The fleet held the Italians off but then the Luftwaffe's Ju88s were back, approaching the ships in small groups above 10,000 feet.

As the fleet's fighters did all they could to intercept the raid the Ju88s carried out dive-bombing attacks against the convoy. Somehow, all the ships escaped any direct hits but there were several near misses. One merchant vessel to suffer damage was *Deucalion*. She was on her second Malta run and had been acting as the convoy's port column guide, but a stick of bombs fell around her. The explosions resulted in damage to the ship, flooding one of her holds and half-flooding another, and so reducing her speed until she came to a halt.

The two other merchantmen of the port outer column, *Clan Ferguson* and *Rochester Castle*, steamed past. They had to keep going and could not stop to help. With *Deucalion* unable to keep going, the Hunt-class destroyer *Bramham* was sent to her aid and to provide the damaged merchantman with protection. Ramsay Brown and his crew eventually got *Deucalion* going again to the point that she could make some speed, at best up to 12 knots, and so she turned to the south-east to try to reach Malta along the coastal route.

With *Bramham* gone, Syfret ordered *Wilton*, another Hunt, to reinforce Force X. The rest of the afternoon was spent driving off enemy submarines as they continued to probe. One attack by *Ithuriel*, commanded by 31-year-old Lieutenant Commander David Maitland-Makgill-Chrichton, forced the Italian submarine *Cobalto* to surface after which it was rammed by the destroyer just abaft the conning tower, crippling the submarine, although *Ithuriel* also suffered bow damage during the ramming.

Later that afternoon, at about 6.30 pm, a large enemy formation, estimated to be a hundred aircraft, was sighted heading towards the convoy. Against them were twenty-two of the fleet's fighters but within minutes the first attack was underway. The mixed raiding force of torpedo-bombers, other bombers at higher level, minelayers and dive-bombers carried out their attacks.

The fleet's fighters did all they could to harass and break up the raid as the convoy turned hard to avoid the torpedoes and mines. Having dropped back from the main convoy to pick up *Cobalto*'s survivors, *Ithuriel* came under attack by Ju87s but despite her condition, the destroyer made good speed and avoided the falling bombs to catch up with the rest of the convoy.

A further forty enemy bombers were now straight ahead, followed by a dozen Ju87s. Picking on *Indomitable* in a clear attempt to take out the carrier and its fighters, one bomb hit the forward anti-aircraft gun, killing a number of marines, and another landed near the forward lift, penetrating the upper deck and exploding above the main hangar. The wardroom, where many of the off-duty aircrew were sheltering, was wrecked by a bomb and killing all those inside. In all, fifty of the carrier's company were killed and as many again wounded, leaving *Victorious* as Pedestal's only carrier with a useable flight deck.[10]

Indomitable was a floating liability and so her recovering aircraft were transferred to *Victorious*, although the latter's flight deck had become congested. Syfret detached *Charybdis*, *Lightning*, *Somali* and *Lookout* to assist. Meanwhile, Italian SM.79s torpedoed the destroyer *Foresight* in the stern, breaking her back and bringing her to a halt. She was then taken under tow by *Tartar* but would be scuttled the following morning.

With the ships about to enter the Strait of Sicily, and with *Indomitable* on fire and severely damaged, Syfret gave the order for Force Z to detach from the convoy. He would take his ships back to Gibraltar along the North African coast to provide cover while his damaged ships – *Indomitable*, *Rodney*

---

10. *Malta War Diary*, 12 August 1942.

and *Ithuriel* – were left to sail direct for Gibraltar under the escort of the destroyers *Amazon*, *Antelope*, *Westcott*, *Wishart* and *Zetland*.

It was just before 7.00 pm and not yet dark. The convoy was still too far from Malta for the island's Spitfires to provide any worthwhile air cover, and so the merchantmen and their escort were now at their most vulnerable. But although the order to detach Force Z had been given slightly earlier than planned, the large enemy air attack had subsided and it was hoped there would be no further air attacks that evening. It was also hoped that the enemy submarine threat had subsided for the night. And so when the cruisers *Nigeria* and *Cairo*, and the tanker *Ohio* were all torpedoed by the Italian submarine *Axum* to the north of Bizerte just before 8.00 pm, it came as something of a surprise.

With just four torpedoes, Tenente di Vascello Ferrini's *Axum* had caused chaos and disruption. *Nigeria* had been hit on the port side, below her bridge, causing a fire as well as flooding her and making her list to port; fifty-two lives were lost. Two torpedoes had hit *Cairo*, destroying her stern and disabling her engines, with a further loss of twenty-three lives, and *Ohio* was hit in the pump room, disabling its main steering and causing a fire.

There is never a good time for a convoy to be hit but this particular attack happened at a critical time, just as the convoy was changing its formation from four columns to two and when the cruisers were particularly crucial to the formation change as column leaders. Furthermore, *Nigeria* was the flagship of the close escort, with Burrough on board, and so she was crucial to the defence of the convoy.

Dealing with the cruisers first, *Cairo* was sunk having been finished off by gunfire from *Derwent*, after her crew were taken off by other ships. *Nigeria* was badly damaged but the fire was soon brought under control and so she was not about to sink. Nonetheless, she could not continue and so the destroyers *Bicester* and *Wilton* were detached to mount guard for her. As for the rest of the situation, Force X was denied its commander until he could be taken aboard another ship, and the convoy would have to continue without any fighter control capability. With *Nigeria* out of the battle, Captain Richard Onslow succeeded in running *Ashanti* alongside the circling flagship to ensure Burrough and some of his staff could transfer aboard; it was a great piece of seamanship in such difficult conditions.

Elsewhere, *Ohio* had been hit amidships, ripping open a large section. With a hole some 25 feet square in her port side, and another hole in the starboard side causing flooding, the great tanker seemed to be out of control. Her deck had been broken open and was buckled from beam to beam. But, somehow, the ship held together. Mason ordered the engines to be shut down as all available on board fought the fire. The crew eventually brought the fire under control and soon the tanker resumed a speed of 13 knots. The blast had, however, destroyed the ship's gyro and knocked the magnetic compass off its bearings, and the crew were left to steer *Ohio* using the aft emergency gear.

In a matter of just a few minutes, the convoy had become scattered and was now in disarray. While Syfret and Burrough tried to sort Pedestal out, more disaster was about to follow when the convoy came under a further heavy air attack about 8.30 pm, nearly half an hour after sunset. The Axis were going for the jugular. Nearly forty torpedo-bombers, mainly Heinkel He111s and Ju88s, escorted by Messerschmitt Bf110s, attacked from the north-west without warning.

The main targets were the merchantmen. First to be hit was *Brisbane Star*. She was hit by a torpedo in both sides, causing her to take on water. Unable to keep up with the convoy, she withdrew inshore under the cover of a smoke screen, hoping to survive the night under the cover of darkness.

Next to be hit was *Empire Hope*. She suffered two direct hits in one of her holds, causing her cargo of fuel and ammunition to explode and setting her stern on fire. With no power to her engines, the order was given to abandon ship. Her survivors were picked up by *Penn* before the blazing *Empire Hope* was sent to the bottom later that night by the torpedoes of an Italian submarine.

There was more tragedy as *Clan Ferguson* was hit by a torpedo, causing her cargo of aviation fuel and explosives to blow up the ship. The fading light suddenly became illuminated by flames before *Clan Ferguson* slipped beneath the waves. Minutes later she was gone. It seemed impossible that anyone could have survived the inferno but, remarkably, sixty men were to survive.

It was now just after 9.00 pm but there was still more to come. First, the Italian submarine *Alagi* hit *Kenya* with a torpedo but the cruiser was not damaged badly enough to withdraw and she maintained convoy speed. Meanwhile, away to the south-west near the Cani Rocks, the poor *Deucalion*, which had been making her way separately from the main convoy with her escort *Bramham*, was attacked by two torpedo-carrying bombers. *Bramham*'s gunners put up the best defensive anti-aircraft fire they could but they could not prevent the merchantman from being hit. She burst into flames and with no chance of saving her, the order was given to abandon ship. Moments later an explosion took *Deucalion* and her cargo to the bottom, the survivors safely aboard the escort.

It had been a chaotic end to what had been a terrible day. The past hour, in particular, had been a disaster. With *Deucalion*, *Clan Ferguson* and *Empire Hope* all gone, eleven merchantmen were left, and the only two to have kept up with the lead elements of the convoy were *Glenorchy* and *Wairangi*. Behind them, but now making good speed to catch up, were *Waimarama* and *Santa Elisa*, and then stretched out were *Melbourne Star*, *Dorset*, *Almeria Lykes* and *Rochester Castle*, all of which had survived the onslaught of the bombers. *Brisbane Star* was making her own way to the south-west and *Ohio* was slowly passing through the area where *Clan Ferguson* and *Empire Hope* had been hit, the latter still burning as the tanker passed through. Meanwhile, the destroyer *Bramham*, with *Deucalion*'s survivors on board, had come across *Port Chalmers* and escorted her east towards Malta. They soon came across the destroyer *Penn* and so the three ships proceeded in line towards Cape Bon.

Despite the largest Italian warships being prevented from putting to sea because of the shortage of fuel, a cruiser squadron, consisting of three heavy cruisers and three light cruisers, plus seventeen destroyers, were on their way to meet the convoy. During the course of the night, Malta-based Wellingtons located and attacked the enemy naval force heading to intercept the convoy. Eight bombs were dropped but no hits were claimed, although the cruiser force was seen to alter course immediately, after which the Wellingtons made further runs over the cruisers, dropping flares each time, and causing the ships to split up and break formation.

As the leading destroyers of Force X were passing Cape Bon during the early hours of 13 August, they were ambushed by a mixed force of German E-boats and Italian MAS torpedo boats. Detecting small and mainly wooden fast torpedo boats at night was all but impossible and so when the first attack came in against *Intrepid*, *Icarus* and *Fury* at about 1.00 am, it came as a surprise. The situation was made worse by the fact that the ships had little in the way of protection against such attacks. Furthermore, the rising sea state, which had now become choppy with a strengthening breeze, made aiming and gun control for the defenders exceedingly hard.

It was another devastating attack against the convoy. With the ships and their escorts stretched out, it was relatively easy for the fast torpedo boats to cause havoc. For several hours enemy boats attacked the convoy and then disappeared again into the darkness. During the melee, the cruiser *Manchester* was torpedoed at point-blank range with the loss of thirteen lives. Listing badly and no longer of any use to the convoy, she was scuttled shortly before the night was out. More than 150 of her crew were taken off by the destroyer *Pathfinder* and most had taken to lifeboats and were left to make for the Tunisian coast and internment. The *Manchester* was the largest warship to be sunk by motor torpedo boats during the war, with the loss of eleven lives.[11]

The attacks continued throughout the hours of darkness with four of the merchantmen hit. *Glenorchy* was torpedoed in the port side, the explosion killing six of those inside the engine room and wrecking the area where the lifeboats were located. With so much water pouring in, the situation soon became hopeless and so the ship's master, Captain George Leslie, gave the order to abandon ship. Taking to what lifeboats were left, all but Leslie abandoned ship. But *Glenorchy*'s master would not leave the stricken vessel. With oil spread across the water and the air filled with its pungent and flammable stench, it was impossible for the crew to make it back to the ship to rescue their skipper.

Although there had been a brief lull after the loss of *Manchester* and *Glenorchy*, a second wave of torpedo boats attacked just after 3.00 am and it was then that the next merchantman was lost. This time it was *Wairangi*'s turn to run out of luck. Just as those on board could make out the shapes of two Italian torpedo boats, the torpedo struck. *Wairangi* was hit in the

---

11. Figure taken from the Malta Roll of Honour, 1940–1943.

port side, striking in the area of one of her holds and sending a column of water high into the air. The adjacent areas of the ship quickly flooded and the merchantman was soon listing to port. With her crew desperately fighting off the circling torpedo-boats, the master, Captain Gordon, made the decision to scuttle the vessel rather than let it fall into enemy hands. The lifeboats were lowered and the charges set.

Meanwhile, the American *Almeria Lykes* had been attacked by two German *Schnellboote* and had been hit in one of her forward holds. She could no longer continue and so her skipper, Captain Henderson, gave the order to abandon ship. Her crew of 105 all made it safely aboard the lifeboats before Henderson and four volunteers went back on board to set the scuttling charges, although these did not sink the ship.

Not far from *Wairangi* and *Almeria Lykes*, the second American freighter, *Santa Elisa*, also met her end. Her master, Captain Thompson, had seen the attacks on the other ships in front of them and so he brought his ship to a halt. For some time *Santa Elisa* sat there in the water before Thompson decided to make a run for it. But they had been seen and were soon under attack from two Italian torpedo-boats. While one ran alongside strafing the merchantman, the second torpedoed her in the starboard bow from point-blank range. There was a terrific explosion in the forward part of the ship, setting her on fire, and with the danger of her cargo of fuel and ammunition blowing up, Thompson gave the order to abandon ship. The survivors were picked up by the destroyer *Penn* and other survivors from *Manchester*, *Wairangi* and *Almeria Lykes* were picked up by *Eskimo* and *Somali*.

When daylight came, all four inert merchantmen – *Glenorchy*, *Wairangi*, *Almeria Lykes* and *Santa Elisa* – were still afloat, but enemy aircraft were soon overhead and determined to finish off the ships. From the shore, the survivors of *Glenorchy* could still see their ship some three miles off the coast. Ten men had volunteered to make it back to the ship to rescue their master, George Leslie, but as they were launching back out to sea a sudden blast rocked their lifeboat as the stricken merchantman came under attack. Nonetheless, they pressed on but were eventually beaten back by the sight of the sinking ship, still with their gallant skipper aboard, and with a circling Italian torpedo-boat and enemy aircraft overhead. With no other option, the would-be rescuers returned to shore to be taken prisoners along with the other survivors by the Vichy French.[12]

The *Wairangi*, *Almeria Lykes* and *Santa Elisa* were also quickly finished off by Ju87s and He111s. But the decision by the Luftwaffe to concentrate on the four derelict merchantmen, and not to relocate and attack the ships still underway, had given the surviving ships of the Pedestal convoy valuable time to regroup.

Five of the seven remaining merchantmen – *Port Chalmers*, *Rochester Castle*, *Waimarama*, *Melbourne Star* and *Dorset* – were already reassembling, *Ohio* was lagging several miles behind and *Brisbane Star* was making her own way to Malta. The two remaining cruisers, *Charybdis* and *Kenya*, screened by the destroyers that were left – *Bramham*, *Fury*, *Icarus*, *Intrepid*, *Ledbury*, *Pathfinder* and *Penn* – provided protection for the surviving merchantmen but the convoy had now been depleted.

As daylight broke, those aboard the surviving ships surveyed the scene. Just two days before there had been a mighty armada of ships as far as the eye could see, but now there were just seven merchantmen left, and not all of those were visible, and what seemed like a handful of destroyers. And there was still more than eighty miles to go.

Perhaps the only good news that day was that the Italian naval ships had hauled off, still well away from the convoy, and would not attack. Rather than allocate any fighter cover for the Italian ships, Kesselring had decided instead to use his combat aircraft directly against the convoy. Without air cover, and with the convoy getting closer to Malta, the Italian warships headed for port at Messina.

But the enemy bombers were soon back. By now, three of the transports – *Rochester Castle*, *Waimarama* and *Melbourne Star* – had joined up and were steaming full speed astern of *Charybdis*, but the convoy was still stretched and so there were easy pickings to be had.

It was just after 8.00 am when the Ju88s attacked and this time it was the poor *Waimarama* that got the full force of the attack. Four bombs struck the ship towards the rear, detonating her cargo of fuel and ammunition.

---

12. Woodman, op. cit., pp.424–6 (taken from Roskill, *A Merchant Fleet at War*, pp.199 *et seq*).

Those nearby could only watch the end of *Waimarama* with sickening horror. Her bow was seen to rear upwards and then the ship crashed down to starboard. So intense had the explosion been that *Melbourne Star*, some 400 yards astern, was caught in the blast and showered by debris just as another Ju88 attacked. There was little time for *Melbourne Star*'s master, Captain MacFarlane, to react but somehow the merchantman ploughed on through the burning sea, although thirty-three men of the defensive gun crews jumped over the stern, fearing for their lives as flames swept aft along the ship.[13]

Further behind, Dudley Mason had to manoeuvre *Ohio* around *Waimarama*'s burning grave as her few survivors, just eighteen of the original complement of 112 men, were picked out of the flaming sea by *Ledbury*. It was a remarkable piece of seamanship by *Ledbury*'s skipper, Commander Roger Hill, who skilfully manoeuvred his ship and braved the hazardous scene to pick up the survivors, including those who had leapt from *Melbourne Star*.

With *Ledbury* back up to full speed to catch the rest of the convoy, the survivors of Pedestal steamed on. By mid-morning, *Port Chalmers*, *Dorset* and *Ohio* had finally joined station. The surviving convoy was now in two columns. The port was led by *Kenya*, with *Rochester Castle* astern and followed by *Dorset*, and the starboard column, led by *Charybdis*, consisted of *Melbourne Star*, *Ohio* and *Port Chalmers*.

Then it was the turn of *Ohio* to suffer again. Nearing Pantelleria at about 9.30 am, she was singled out by a large force of about sixty Ju87 Stukas. The ships were now close enough to Malta for the island's Beaufighters and Spitfires to help break up the enemy formations but still a number got through. Every anti-aircraft gun on the merchantmen and escorting ships opened up but still many of the Stukas penetrated the dense barrage.

Near to *Ohio*, *Ashanti*'s gunners defiantly did all they could to protect the tanker but near misses buckled *Ohio*'s hull plates and her forward tank filled with water. The tanker also had the misfortune to be hit by a Stuka, shot down by the combined barrage of *Ohio*'s and *Ashanti*'s gunners,

---

13. Ibid, pp.434–6.

with the aircraft coming down on the tanker's deck but, luckily, it did not explode.

German Ju88s and Italian torpedo-bombers had also joined the attack. The Axis commanders knew the convoy was nearing Malta and was now in range of RAF fighters, and so there would be few opportunities left to attack the ships.

While the air battle raged above, the attacks on the convoy continued. One Ju88 was hit and skidded across the water into the starboard side of *Ohio*, forward of the upper bridge, in a ball of flames and with wreckage and debris falling on the tanker from stem to stern. The crew performed magnificently to avoid the countless number of mines and torpedoes but the stricken tanker was eventually straddled by two sticks of bombs, lifting her from the water before she came crashing down again. For a while the tanker kept on steaming until another explosion on her starboard side sent her reeling to port, rupturing her boilers and sending the ship into darkness, and finally leaving *Ohio* dead in the water.

The other merchantmen were also in trouble. *Dorset* had been brought to a halt after her engine room flooded following near misses by a number of bombs exploding within feet of her. *Port Chalmers* had been attacked by a dozen Italian torpedo-bombers but had somehow come through unscathed, as had *Melbourne Star*. *Rochester Castle* had also suffered near misses under her bows and had been lifted from the water. Her engines were out of action and a number of small fires had started across the ship.

In the operations room at Lascaris, those on watch had followed the convoy's progress nervously. All they could do now was to pray as three of the merchantmen – *Melbourne Star*, *Port Chalmers* and *Rochester Castle* – started their final dash for Malta with their escorts. With Malta now in sight and the ships getting closer to the island by the hour, Spitfires provided air cover overhead and by later that afternoon they had been joined by Malta's local escort, the minesweepers *Hebe*, *Hythe*, *Rye* and *Speedy*, to take them safely through the swept channel.

By early evening their voyage was complete. The three merchantmen had successfully run the gauntlet all the way from Gibraltar and completed the final dash to Malta. At about 6.30 pm, *Rochester Castle* became the first merchant vessel of Pedestal to enter Grand Harbour. She had a gaping hole in her side and so there was no time to waste to get her unloaded. She was followed soon after by *Port Chalmers* and then *Melbourne Star*. Those on board the ships were up on deck to witness their arrival. It was a sight they would never forget. They had arrived to cheering crowds and the sound of the Royal Malta Artillery band playing from the ramparts of Fort Saint Elmo to welcome the ships into harbour.

But for the rest of the convoy the battle for survival went on. Having seen the three merchantmen to safety, Burrough ordered *Bramham* and *Penn* to stay with *Ohio* and *Dorset* while *Ledbury* was sent to the Gulf of Hammamet to look for any more survivors from *Manchester*, unaware they had already made dry land to become prisoners of war. Burrough then headed back to Gibraltar in *Ashanti*, accompanied by other surviving ships of Force X: *Charybdis*, *Kenya*, *Fury*, *Icarus*, *Intrepid* and *Pathfinder*. As they passed the labouring *Ohio*, Burrough signalled his valediction: 'I am proud to have known you.'[14] Despite enduring a number of attacks during their passage back, all arrived safely in Gibraltar, as did *Eskimo* and *Somali*.

Even though three of the merchantmen had made it to Malta, three more still remained out at sea. *Brisbane Star* was still making her way independently but the two ships left behind by the convoy, *Ohio* and *Dorset*, were still in trouble and miles away from Grand Harbour.

Sadly for the *Dorset* it was a case of so near yet so far. She was just over seventy miles from Malta but having lost all power, she was in a critical state. She had suffered severe flooding, one of her holds was ablaze and there was no means of fighting the fire. It was about 11.00 am when Captain Tuckett finally gave the order to abandon ship. *Bramham* had arrived to provide assistance and there was talk of towing *Dorset* in to Grand Harbour but further air attacks by Ju88s put paid to the idea. By early evening the majestic-looking *Dorset* had sunk lower and lower into the water until she was no longer there.

The poor *Ohio* was also in a desperate state. She had come under further air attacks, too, as the Axis pilots tried to finish off the tanker. The destroyer *Penn*, commanded by Commander James Swain, tried to take her in tow

---

14. Ibid, p.440.

using a heavy ten-inch Manila hemp rope, but the tanker was listing so badly to port that the two ships were not making any headway; the sea and easterly wind was even causing them to drift backwards.

Both ships were now sitting ducks. It was still only mid-afternoon and with another air attack developing, Swain ordered the destroyer to full speed in an attempt to start the tow. A German bomber dived down on *Ohio* but was shot down by the tanker's gunners, but not before releasing its bombs, one of which hit the tanker in the same area that the earlier torpedo had struck, causing *Ohio* to effectively break her back.

With the tanker a sitting duck in the water, it was decided to take the crew off until after darkness. The arrival of Malta's minesweeper *Rye* later that afternoon prompted another attempt to get the tanker under tow and with the crew having returned on board *Ohio*, the combined efforts of *Penn* and *Rye* got the tanker moving. But then the Luftwaffe returned.

The tow was immediately halted to allow *Penn* and *Rye* to get away and provide some defensive fire, just as eight Ju88s attacked. As bombs fell once more, a near-miss destroyed *Ohio*'s rudder. Another bomb penetrated the deck, starting a fire below in the engine room and with water flooding in, Mason again gave the order to abandon ship.

Although the tanker was derelict and dead in the water, *Ohio* was not about to sink. There was still time in the day for two more bombing attacks, causing further structural damage to the tanker, before darkness finally brought a period of calm.

The two destroyers *Bramham* and *Ledbury* now arrived alongside and assisted. No one gave up on *Ohio* and as ideas about what to do next were exchanged, a working party was put back on board. Under the direction of *Penn*'s skipper, James Swain, the combined resources were pooled throughout the night in an attempt to resume the tow.

By daylight on 14 August, the tanker was still stationary in the water as all attempts to get her moving again had failed. With the gunners back on board the tanker in preparation for the inevitable air attacks, a further attempt was made to get *Ohio* under tow. With *Rye* and *Ledbury* ahead in a tandem-tow, and with *Penn* adding her power to the starboard side, progress was made but then the Stukas were back, although Malta's Spitfires drove them off.

The attack had temporarily disrupted the tow and so, once again, the surrounding ships took position; *Penn* still on the starboard side with *Bramham* now securing the port. Ahead, *Rye* and *Ledbury* again took up the tow. Slowly the formation moved and was soon maintaining a remarkable and respectable 6 knots.

Meanwhile, *Brisbane Star* was making her final approach to Malta. She had proceeded independently of the main convoy, sailing around Cape Bon and keeping inshore before making direct for Malta under the umbrella of the island's Spitfires. Although Captain Riley had faced challenges while passing through neutral waters, mainly from Italian reconnaissance aircraft and by the Vichy French authorities, all trying to identify the ship and work out her intentions, *Brisbane Star*'s lone detour had worked. She finally entered Grand Harbour during the afternoon of 14 August to another cheering crowd, and became Pedestal's fourth merchantman to reach Malta.

Back out at sea, *Ohio*, with her decks awash, was slowly sinking but by the evening Malta was in sight. With Spitfires overhead, and the threat of any further air attacks all but gone, *Ohio* limped towards the island, surrounded by a flotilla of ships, all intent on getting the stricken tanker into harbour.

But *Ohio*'s epic journey was still not complete. It was difficult to control her direction and there were still some difficult turns to make. But no one was going to give up. Not now. With *Bramham* on the port side and *Penn* on the starboard, and with *Rye* now acting as a stabilizer at her stern, *Ohio* crept towards Grand Harbour inch by inch. The last part of her journey was torturously slow for everyone involved.

As the formation reached Delimara and Zonqor Points, *Ledbury* leant a hand to shove the tanker's bow to make the turns. After edging her way round a minefield as daylight broke, Malta's tugs arrived. Finally, the broken-backed and almost derelict hull of *Ohio* made the tight turn inside the mole, rounded Ricasoli Point and, barely afloat, limped into the entrance of Grand Harbour soon after 8.00 am on 15 August.

Ohio, the last of the five surviving merchant ships of Pedestal to have made it to Malta, arrived to cheering crowds lining the ramparts and bastions while bands played rousing and patriotic pieces – *Rule Britannia*, *God Save the King* and the *Star Spangled Banner* – before people spontaneously fell silent as a mark of respect for the crew who had lost their lives. Tears were stinging red–rimmed eyes as *Ohio* edged towards Parlatorio Wharf in French Creek.[15] The *Times of Malta* later wrote:

'If ever there was an example of dogged perseverance against all odds, this was it.'[16]

As Pedestal drew to a close, the unloading of the merchant ships reached its final phase. The cargoes of *Port Chalmers*, *Rochester Castle* and *Melbourne Star* had already been unloaded, and *Brisbane Star* was almost done. Of the five merchant ships to have arrived in Malta, *Port Chalmers* was the only one not to have sustained any significant damage. The *Rochester Castle* was in a terrible state. Berthed in French Creek, she would need months of repairs before she had any chance of returning to duty. She eventually left Malta in November, and *Melbourne Star* would not leave until December.

With no time to waste, pipes were hauled aboard and emergency salvage pumps discharged *Ohio*'s kerosene while a fleet auxiliary, the *Boxall*, pumped the fuel oil into her own tanks. As the fuel and oil flowed out, *Ohio* sank lower and lower in the water. With the last of her precious oil discharged, *Ohio* settled on the bottom.

The cargoes unloaded from Pedestal's five surviving merchantmen would provide enough fuel and supplies to keep Malta in the war; 32,000 tonnes of general cargo had reached the island, together with petrol, diesel oil, oil fuel and kerosene. It was enough, it was thought, to keep Malta going for about ten weeks longer than the island's existing stock, which had been down to just a handful of weeks.

But it had been a very high price to pay with the loss of more than 350 lives and many fine ships, including nine of the fourteen merchantmen: *Clan Ferguson*, *Deucalion*, *Dorset*, *Empire Hope*, *Glenorchy*, *Waimarama*, *Wairangi*, and the American vessels *Almeria Lykes* and *Santa Elisa*. Also sunk was an aircraft carrier (*Eagle*), two cruisers (*Cairo* and *Manchester*) and a destroyer (*Foresight*). Furthermore, 53,000 tonnes of supplies had not reached Malta at all, but had gone to the bottom of the Mediterranean instead.

---

15. *Times of Malta*, 26 August 2012.
16. *Times of Malta*, 24 August 1942.

During the period of Pedestal, Malta had not remained entirely raid-free, although only the occasional enemy aircraft had over-flown the island. Malta's fighters had flown 414 sorties in support of Pedestal, the Spitfires flying all but the twenty-five flown by Beaufighters. At least fourteen enemy aircraft had been shot down for the loss of four Spitfires and one Beaufighter.[17]

But although Pedestal might, to some, be considered a tactical failure, it was certainly a strategic victory. It had also given an immeasurable boost to the morale of the Maltese people at a time when the island had been at its lowest ebb.

There were many awards made for Pedestal, including knighthoods for Syfret (KCB) and Burrough (KBE) for their 'bravery and dauntless resolution in fighting an important convoy through to Malta in the face of relentless attacks by day and night from enemy submarines, aircraft, and surface forces.'[18]

But to many, it was the ever-lasting image of *Ohio*, being kept afloat by supporting vessels and limping into Grand Harbour, that best captures the courage of those who took part in Pedestal. The oil tanker is still fondly remembered in Malta, where to this day she is considered the saviour of the beleaguered island. With the heroic tanker effectively broken in two, there were insufficient facilities in the dockyard to repair *Ohio* and so the two halves were used for storage. After the war they were towed offshore and scuttled by naval gunfire.

For his outstanding courage and leadership, the master of *Ohio*, Captain Dudley Mason, was awarded the George Cross, the highest gallantry award for civilians. Mason's citation reads:

'*During the passage to Malta of an important convoy Captain Mason's ship suffered most violent onslaught. She was a focus of attack throughout and was torpedoed early one night. Although gravely damaged, her engines were kept going and the Master made a magnificent passage by hand-steering and without a compass. The ship's gunners helped to bring down one of the*

17. Shores and Cull with Malizia (The Spitfire Year), op. cit., p.515.
18. Supplement to the *London Gazette* no.35695, 8 September 1942, pp.3911–2.

attacking aircraft. The vessel was hit again before morning, but though she did not sink, her engine room was wrecked. She was then towed. The unwieldy condition of the vessel and persistent enemy attacks made progress slow, and it was uncertain whether she would remain afloat. All next day progress somehow continued and the ship reached Malta after a further night at sea. The violence of the enemy could not deter the Master from his purpose. Throughout he showed skill and courage of the highest order and it was due to his determination that, in spite of the most persistent enemy opposition, the vessel, with her valuable cargo, eventually reached Malta and was safely berthed.'[19]

In addition to Mason's George Cross, there was one Distinguished Service Order, six Distinguished Service Crosses and eight Distinguished Service Medals awarded to members of *Ohio*'s crew. Several other commanders, officers and crew, both Royal Navy and Merchant Navy, also received gallantry awards for their part in Pedestal, including a DSO to each of the four other masters of the surviving merchantmen: Captains MacFarlane, Pinkney, Riley and Wren.

In the same way that it might be said the RAF had saved Britain during the summer of 1940, the Royal Navy and Merchant Navy had saved Malta in the summer of 1942. However, it did not mean it was the end of the island's struggle, far from it, but Pedestal had at least kept Malta in the war.

---

19. Supplement to the *London Gazette* no.35695, 8 September 1942, p.3911.

Chapter Eighteen

The Siege Ends

In the aftermath of Pedestal, the unloading of the merchantmen had passed without interference from Axis bombers and the survivors of the convoy, nearly 600 men, soon left the island; more than 200 of them left for Gibraltar on 18 August in *Penn*, *Ledbury* and *Bramham* with the rest gradually evacuated from Malta by submarine or aircraft.

Malta would still depend on essential supplies being delivered by fast minelayers and submarines and, brutal as it may sound, there was still not enough food or medical supplies to go round.

As far as the air war being mounted from Axis airfields in Sicily was concerned, Pedestal seemed to have knocked the stuffing out of the enemy. Furthermore, twenty-nine more Spitfires arrived in Malta during August, having flown off *Furious* under Operation Baritone, and then twenty-seven more arrived at the end of October under Operation Train.

There were now plenty of aircraft on the island and the success of Pedestal meant that fuel was available in sufficient quantities to take the fight back to the enemy. The first offensive sweep over Sicily by Malta's Spitfires, led by Walter Churchill, took place just days after *Ohio* had arrived. Sadly, though, Churchill was to be killed soon after, while leading a major sweep over Sicily on 26 August. His Spitfire was seen to receive a direct hit by flak and blew up, crashing in flames.[1] He had been in Malta just two weeks.

These fighter sweeps across Sicily were, in reality, producing little and so they were soon abandoned. In fact, September proved to be a rather quiet month. The war in the desert had become dormant, which favoured the British as it was easier to re-supply Allied forces through Egypt than it now was for Rommel across the Mediterranean. September was also a quiet

---

1. Shores and Williams, op. cit., p.177.

month as far as the air war was concerned, with fewer raids than previous months.

Although there might have been a lull in some quarters, Malta's submarines and aircraft had been busy on the offensive. Patrick Gibbs returned home during the month but the Beaufort Wing he had created on the island was having a devastating impact on the changing war in the Mediterranean, with little fuel getting through to Axis forces in the desert.

It was a great all-round effort from Malta's units and demonstrates the great co-operation and co-ordination that existed between the Royal Navy, Fleet Air Arm and RAF strike forces, all acting as one. For example, in a few days in September, the torpedo-bombers of the Fleet Air Arm sank the 4,300-tonne Italian merchantman, *Monti*, a Wellington sank the tanker *Picci Fasio*, Beauforts sank the 7,000-tonne *Menara*, and the submarine HMS *United* sank an Italian salvage vessel *Rostro* and a schooner *Giovanna*. *Unruffled* opened her account by sinking the Vichy-French *Liberia* (3,900 tonnes) and a petrol-carrying schooner *Aquila* in the same day. In all, the Allies sank nearly 34,000 tonnes at sea during the month.[2]

September also saw the arrival of torpedo-carrying Wellingtons of 38 Squadron, known in Malta as Fishingtons (as opposed to the ASV-equipped Wellingtons known as Goofingtons), which now gave Malta a true night offensive capability for the first time. Using radar to find enemy shipping at night, the Wellingtons then had the ability to attack any targets using their torpedoes. Four aircraft that had been on their way to the Middle East were detained in Malta and, in no time at all, the Fishingtons were scoring successes against enemy ships, with one of the pilots, Flying Officer 'Hank' Donkersley, a Canadian, being particularly successful; he would soon be awarded a DFC and Bar.

Screwball Beurling was now back in action after his unfortunate experience of Malta Dog, although the lack of air raids against the island gave him little or no opportunity to add to his score. He had to wait until the end of September before his next success, when he claimed the destruction of two 109s and a further one damaged to the north-east of Zonqor Point. This

---

2. Spooner (*Supreme Gallantry*), op. cit., pp.213–7.

brought his overall number of victories to twenty, for which he was awarded the Distinguished Flying Cross. His citation reads:

> '*Since being awarded a Bar to the Distinguished Flying Medal, this officer has shot down a further three hostile aircraft, bringing his total victories to twenty. One day in September 1942, he and another pilot engaged four enemy fighters. In the ensuing combat, Pilot Officer Beurling destroyed two of them. As a relentless fighter, whose determination and will to win has won the admiration of his colleagues, this officer has set an example in keeping with the highest traditions of the Royal Air Force.*'[3]

Beurling added eight more victories during October. On 10 October he was testing his recently serviced Spitfire when he was vectored to intercept two Bf109Fs flying at low level over Filfla. He found the 109s flying in line abreast and attacked the starboard first, hitting it in the forward part of the aircraft and sending it down onto the island where it belly flopped before flicking over onto its back. The second tried to make its escape but Beurling hit its fuel tank causing it to blow up.

This period marked the start of another few days of intense air activity over Malta, a period later to become known as the 'October Blitz'. It was Kesselring's last roll of the dice. The relative calm of previous weeks was well and truly shattered on 11 October when the first of many air raids took place. It was, however, a relatively modest raid compared to raids earlier in the war, with just seven Ju88s escorted by twenty-five MC.202s and four Bf109Fs. But with more than a hundred Spitfires in Malta, now serving with five squadrons, the defenders intercepted the raid in numbers before the attackers had even reached the island. A few of the bombers got through but they had become scattered and were rushed into making their attacks, and so caused little damage. There were, however, five more raids during that opening day of the new air offensive, followed by two at night.

This renewed period of air activity provided Beurling with the ideal opportunity to add to his score. On 13 October he attacked a formation of

---

3. Supplement to the *London Gazette*, 16 October 1942, p.4487.

Ju88s and Bf109s to the north of Saint Paul's Bay. During the following few minutes he shot down one Ju88 and damaged another, before sending two 109s into the sea. He was involved in further heavy fighting over Malta during the following day, claiming a Ju88 plus two escorting Bf109s destroyed. But soon after, his own aircraft was hit. Beurling was forced to bale out and came down in the sea, fortunately to be picked up just twenty minutes later.[4]

Although the October Blitz would last for two weeks, and cost the defenders more than forty Spitfires,[5] the air battle was, in reality, over as a contest after just three days.[6] The Luftwaffe's losses were simply too high. During the first week alone, fifty-three Ju88s were claimed as shot down plus half as many again claimed as probable, and a dozen Bf109s were confirmed lost.

On 15 October, the *Times of Malta* was already claiming success after reporting the headline '82 IN FOUR DAYS – Malta's Answer to Luftwaffe's New Bid'. In the report that followed, it stated that the Axis had lost its 1,000th aircraft over or near the island, with the landmark victim falling to the guns of none other than Beurling.[7]

It was to be Beurling's last flight over Malta. He was due for a rest. At the end of October came the announcement of his award of the Distinguished Service Order:

'*Since being awarded the Distinguished Flying Cross, Pilot Officer Beurling has destroyed a further six (sic) enemy aircraft, bringing his total victories to 28. During one sortie on 13 October 1942, he shot down a Junkers 88 and two Messerschmitt 109s. The following day, in a head-on attack on enemy bombers, he destroyed one of them before he observed his leader being attacked by an enemy fighter. Although wounded, Pilot Officer Beurling destroyed the fighter. Then climbing again, although his aircraft was hit by enemy fire, he shot down another fighter before his own aircraft was so*

---

4. Shores and Williams, op. cit., p.126.
5. Shores and Cull with Malizia (The Spitfire Year), op. cit., pp.648–9.
6. Holland, op. cit., p.395.
7. *Times of Malta*, 15 October 1942.

damaged that he was forced to abandon it. He descended safely on to the sea and was rescued. This officer's skill and daring are unexcelled.'[8]

George 'Screwball' Beurling was by far the RAF's highest-scoring fighter pilot over Malta and became a legend among the Maltese. At the end of October he flew off the island with other personnel who had come to the end of their tour of duty, but tragedy struck as their B-24 Liberator crashed into the sea while making its approach to land in Gibraltar. Many on board were drowned but Beurling, despite having his leg in plaster, got out of the aircraft and swam to safety; he was one of only three survivors. Beurling then returned to Canada where he was used to promote the country's war effort; such was his prowess as a fighter pilot. He later returned to operational flying and added two more victories to his total during 1943. But Beurling struggled with authority when given non-flying appointments and was allowed to retire from service shortly before the end of the war. He also struggled to adjust to peacetime life away from military operations and his life came to an end in 1948 when he was killed in a flying incident while on his way to volunteer for service with the air force of the new state of Israel.

A replenished and revived Malta soon led to a shift in the balance of the desert war. The Royal Navy and RAF were regaining their dominance of the central Mediterranean as the Italian fleet, starved of fuel and hurt by its losses, was long finished as a fighting force. Royal Navy submarines returned to the island and with the RAF's striking force building up again, it was not long before one-third of Axis supplies destined for Rommel's forces in North Africa were not getting through. Aided by Ultra intercepts of convoy movements received from Bletchley Park, Malta's submarines and torpedo-carrying Beauforts, escorted by Beaufighters, frequently attacked Axis convoys passing through the Med.

In just a few weeks, more than 100,000 tonnes of enemy supplies were sent to the bottom, and all this at a time when Rommel was building up his forces for his assault at El Alamein. Then, during the battle itself, which began on 23 October 1942, seven of eleven Axis ships that had tried to reach

8. Supplement to the *London Gazette*, 30 October 1942, p.4753.

Tobruk were sunk and three more badly damaged. The battle of El Alamein would end in defeat for Rommel after less than three weeks.

After suffering such high losses at sea, the Axis took to transporting more troops and supplies from Sicily to Tunisia by air and so Takali's long-range Beaufighters of 227 Squadron went out to hunt for them. One young Beaufighter pilot to achieve much success during this period was Flight Lieutenant Dallas Schmidt, a 22-year-old Canadian and known to everyone as 'Smithy'. Schmidt had arrived on the island during August and was awarded a DFC in October. Tasked with attacking the enemy transports operating between Sicily and Tunisia during November, he claimed two Junkers Ju52s and shared in the destruction of a Dornier Do24 in one day. This was followed a few days after by another Ju52 and later in the month he also claimed an Italian CR.42 destroyed to the south of Sfax while attacking enemy shipping. Then, the following month, Schmidt claimed at least five more enemy aircraft shot down plus several more damaged, earning him a Bar to his DFC.

Attacking enemy transports was not easy as they were usually escorted by Ju88s or Bf109s, but another Malta-based Beaufighter pilot to achieve success during these operations was 24-year-old Wing Commander John Buchanan. A dynamic and outstanding pilot and leader, Buchanan had flown as a bomber pilot earlier in the war, earning a DFC and Bar during his 230 operational sorties over thirteen different countries. After a rest from operations, he had been posted to Malta to command 272 Squadron and despite having only ten hours previous experience of flying fighters, Buchanan quickly took to his new role. His first two victories in November were, in fact, seaplanes but these were followed by two Junkers Ju52s in the space of three days, to which he added a Messerschmitt Bf110 and two Axis bombers in a further two days of activity. By the end of the month, Buchanan had shot down seven enemy aircraft in his first two weeks in command.[9] News soon came of the award of a DSO to Buchanan, his citation including:

_____

9. Shores and Williams, op. cit., p.156.

'He arrived in Malta in November 1942, and, within the next 14 days, led his squadron in 6 bombing attacks on enemy shipping. During these operations, Wing Commander Buchanan destroyed 6 enemy aircraft in combat. He is a magnificent leader whose great skill and fine fighting qualities have been of incalculable value.'

The Beaufighter proved to be the most versatile aircraft in Malta, operating in many different roles. As a night fighter its crews were credited with sixty bombers destroyed,[10] which had done much to curtail the number of night raids and their successes had boosted the island's morale.

Since the start of the siege in June 1940, Malta had become a breeding ground for fighter pilots with many mounting up impressive personal scores. Over a thousand air victories had been claimed by Malta's fighter pilots, plus a further 200 or so claimed by the anti-aircraft gunners. The air campaign had produced about seventy Malta aces, each having claimed at least five enemy aircraft shot down; eleven were credited with ten victories or more, and many other pilots who had flown from the island went on to achieve further success elsewhere.[11]

There had also been some outstanding reconnaissance pilots. They had become Malta's watchful eyes and included the man who was arguably the best of them all – the fearless and unorthodox Adrian Warburton. He had arrived back in Malta during August 1942 for his third operational tour, during which he was promoted to squadron leader and received a second Bar to his DFC. In February 1943 he was given command of the newly formed 683 Squadron, equipped with photo-reconnaissance Spitfires and Mosquitos. Warburton was then involved in the vital pre-invasion reconnaissance of the landing beaches in Sicily, his work being successfully co-ordinated with American forces for which he was awarded a Bar to his DSO and an American DFC. By the time his second DSO was announced, Warburton had flown a total of 375 operational sorties, all but fifteen of them being from Malta, involving 1,300 hours of flying.[12]

10. Spooner (*Faith Hope and Malta GC*), op. cit., p.98.
11. Shores and Cull with Malizia (*The Spitfire Year*), op. cit., pp.650–1.
12. Supplement to the *London Gazette*, dated 6 August 1943.

At any other time and, perhaps, in any other theatre, Warby would not have been allowed to become the character that he was and to do what he did. His achievements have been described to be as remarkable as those of two of the RAF's most illustrious pilots: Douglas Bader and Guy Gibson. But Adrian Warburton rarely gets recognition and there is no mention of him in the official RAF history of the Second World War.[13]

But no book about Malta during the Second World War would be complete without mentioning him. Besides, Air Marshal Sir Arthur Tedder, then the C-in-C Mediterranean Air Command, is reported to have described Warburton as 'the most valuable pilot in the RAF'.[14] There can be no higher compliment than that. Sadly, though, like so many legendary characters of the Second World War, Warburton did not live to see the peace that he had fought so gallantly for. In April 1944 he was flying an American aircraft on an unusual mission over Europe when both aircraft and pilot disappeared without trace. Years of rumours and speculation about his fate came to an end in 2002 when his remains were found in the cockpit of the aircraft wreckage buried deep in a Bavarian field, and Adrian Warburton was buried in the Durnbach War Cemetery in Germany.

As for Malta's submarines, one to achieve notable success during the latter weeks of 1942 was HMS *Safari*, commanded by 37-year-old Commander Ben Bryant. *Safari* had spent the early part of her time in the Mediterranean operating from Gibraltar, but after Pedestal had been transferred to Malta to join the Tenth Flotilla.

Safari conducted her first patrol from the island at the end of September. It lasted two weeks, during which she torpedoed two Italian merchant vessels, causing both to run aground to be written off, and two other small vessels believed to be carrying Axis troops bound for Greece and Crete. On her second patrol from Malta, during October, *Safari* sank an Italian merchant vessel, the 5,400-tonne *Titania*, part of an Axis convoy bound for Tripoli, and while supporting the Allied landings of Vichy French North Africa, under Operation Torch, in November, she sank an Italian motor

---

13. Spooner (*Warburton's War*), op. cit., p.111 (taken from *Evidence in Camera* by Constance Babington-Smith).
14. Spooner (*Faith Hope and Malta GC*), op. cit., p.122.

vessel to the east of Tunisia. Three days later she sank a German transport vessel, the 2,600-tonne *Hans Arp*, in the Gulf of Sirte, and five days later she sent a smaller unidentified Axis vessel to the bottom.

By the end of 1942 *Safari* had sunk at least four more Italian vessels, earning Bryant a DSO to add to his DSC awarded earlier in the war. But instead of returning to Malta at the end of this patrol, *Safari* was moved to Algiers to join the Eighth Flotilla, after which many more successes followed before Bryant handed over command at the end of April 1943. By then he had completed ten Mediterranean patrols in command, had sunk at least twenty-nine vessels of various kinds, totalling 40,000 tonnes, and had been awarded a Bar to his DSO. Then came the announcement of a second Bar to his DSO, making Ben Bryant one of the Royal Navy's most decorated submarine aces.

But despite its great military successes in the immediate aftermath of Pedestal, Malta had remained an island facing starvation. The convoy had kept Malta in the war but the island's livestock had long gone, as had most of Malta's other animals. Furthermore, the people were also suffering from disease. There had been outbreaks of polio and meningitis during the siege, and scabies and other skin complaints were rampant; even the bugs and fleas seemed to realize that all they had to feed on were humans.[15]

After such a long period of being underfed and living in appalling sanitary conditions, it is no surprise that resistance to disease had diminished. Many were suffering from tuberculosis and dysentery, with the main hospital at Imtarfa having long been overflowing with patients.[16]

By November 1942 the living conditions in Malta were as difficult as they had been at any time during the long siege. The islanders were once again on the brink of starvation, and starvation meant surrender.[17] The only way the situation was ever going to improve was for more convoys to arrive, and at regular intervals.

But the Royal Navy's support to the Eighth Army in defeating Rommel in North Africa had meant that another convoy to Malta during either

---

15. Spooner (*Supreme Gallantry*), op. cit., pp.207–9.
16. Holland, op. cit., pp.408–9.
17. Spooner (*Supreme Gallantry*), op. cit., p.225.

September or October had been out of the question. At the beginning of November there was an attempt to run *Empire Patrol* through the eastern Med from Alexandria. Being a refrigerated ship she was carrying much-needed food in addition to petrol and other supplies but she suffered mechanical problems and ended up in Cyprus instead. A similar attempt, under Operation Crupper, was mounted from the other end of the Mediterranean but ended in failure when the two merchantmen, *Ardeola* and *Tadorna*, both carrying precious foodstuffs for Malta's civilian population, were shelled and then boarded by Vichy French naval officers from torpedo-boats; both vessels were taken into Bizerte where their cargoes were seized.[18]

To partly compensate for these failures, *Manxman* sailed from Alexandria on 10 November loaded with powdered milk for babies and young children, as well as dry cereals and preserved meat. She was escorted part of the way by six destroyers and arrived alone in Grand Harbour two days later. As soon as she had unloaded her supplies, *Manxman* was off again, this time to Gibraltar.

At least it was something but it was never going to be enough. Six days later, as part of Operation Stoneage, *Welshman* arrived in Grand Harbour with a further consignment of essential supplies. Again it helped but Malta needed at least one convoy soon if the relief of the island was to be fully achieved.

It was only after the Allied victory at El Alamein that enough naval ships could be spared to put together another Malta convoy. Leaving Port Said on the evening of 16 November, four merchantmen – the Glen and Shire Line's *Denbighshire* (9,000 tonnes), the Dutch *Bantam* (9,300 tonnes), and two American vessels, *Robin Locksley* (7,000 tonnes) and *Mormacmoon* (8,000 tonnes) – set sail for the island. Designated MW13, the four vessels sailed under the escort of the 15th Cruiser Squadron,[19] now commanded by Rear Admiral Arthur Power (Philip Vian's replacement), flying his flag in

---

18. Woodman, op. cit., pp.457–8.
19. The 15th Cruiser Squadron comprised: HMS *Cleopatra*, HMS *Arethusa*, HMS *Dido*, HMS *Euryalus* and HMS *Orion*.

Cleopatra, and seven destroyers of the 14th Destroyer Flotilla.[20] The convoy was then joined by ten Hunts of the 12th Flotilla.[21]

Having refuelled in Alexandria, Power's cruisers and destroyers caught up with the convoy at daybreak on 18 November, just as the weather was deteriorating. By early evening the ships were off Derna when they came under air attack. The cruiser *Arethusa* was hit by a torpedo in the forward part of the ship, causing serious fires on board and the loss of 155 lives. As darkness fell the fires were brought under control and, escorted by the destroyer *Petard*, *Arethusa* eventually made it back to Alexandria; she was the last of the Royal Navy's ships involved with Malta escort duties to be damaged by the enemy.[22]

The rest of the convoy continued until they were within range of Malta's Spitfires, after which all four merchantmen arrived safely in Grand Harbour during the early hours of 20 November to deliver 35,000 tonnes of food and other essential supplies.

It was clear that the Axis aircraft were fully occupied in the desert war and elsewhere, and could only offer a token effort to stop the convoy getting through. The Luftwaffe, in particular, had become overstretched across too many fronts. Each time the Germans had come close to neutralizing Malta, greater demands had been placed on the Luftwaffe's resources from elsewhere.

The quantities of supplies delivered by MW13 eased the situation in Malta considerably and meant the Magic Carpet runs could be brought to an end. It also meant that Force K could be resurrected in Malta, with two cruisers, *Dido* and *Euryalus*, plus four destroyers of the 14th Flotilla: *Jervis*, *Javelin*, *Kelvin* and *Nubian*.

Just ten days later, on 1 December, four more merchant ships left Port Said as part of Operation Portcullis. The convoy, MW14, consisted of the

---

20. The 14th Destroyer Flotilla comprised: HMS *Jervis*, HMS *Javelin*, HMS *Kelvin*, HMS *Nubian*, HMS *Pakenham*, HMS *Paladin* and HMS *Petard*.
21. The Hunt-class destroyers of the 12th Flotilla were: HMS *Aldenham*, HMS *Beaufort*, HMS *Belvoir*, HMS *Croome*, HMS *Dulverton*, HMS *Exmoor*, HMS *Hursley*, HMS *Hurworth*, HMS *Tetcott* and the Greek Navy's *Pindos* (ex *Bolebroke*).
22. Woodman, op. cit., pp.459–60.

British Federal liner *Suffolk* (13,900 tonnes), the 9,800-tonne Glen Liner *Glenartney*, and two American cargo vessels, *Agwimonte* (6,700 tonnes) and *Alcoa Prospector* (6,800 tonnes). The four merchantmen were soon joined by the *Yorba Linda*, a 7,000-tonne American-owned tanker sailing under a Panamanian flag, from the recently Allied-occupied Libyan port of Benghazi, escorted by two Hunts. This brought the convoy's escort strength up to seven destroyers and the following day the cruiser *Orion* and three more destroyers joined the ships, having sailed from Alexandria. Then, on 4 December, *Cleopatra* and the ships of Force K from Malta arrived on station.

Maintaining a healthy 16 knots, the convoy proceeded safely to Malta with only the occasional disturbance by enemy torpedo-carrying aircraft here and there. All the ships entered Grand Harbour during the morning of 5 December to a rousing reception from the Maltese. From now on convoys would come and go from Malta relatively unscathed. The siege of Malta was over.

Air-minded historians might claim that it was during October 1942, when the RAF defeated the Luftwaffe's final attempt to blitz Malta that the siege ended, whereas history seems to have ended the siege of Malta on 20 November 1942 – the date when convoy MW13 entered Grand Harbour: two years, five months, one week and two days after the first day, and making the siege of Malta the longest in British history.

But for those in Malta at the time, it took the arrival of the following convoy, MW14, in early December, and then the safe arrival of more ships during the following weeks, for those on the island to realize, and believe, that the siege had truly ended.

The war, of course, was still far from over but Rommel's defeat at El Alamein and the Allied landings of Operation Torch, both occurring during November 1942, marked the beginning of the end of the desert war, although it would take another six months to finally kick the Axis out of North Africa. The last battles of the desert war were fought in Tunisia, less than 200 miles from Malta, and so the island was well placed to continue severing the enemy's supply lines. But unlike earlier offensive operations conducted from Malta, there would be no let-up this time. The island had enough of everything to sustain its effort against Axis forces in the region.

The war in North Africa finally ended on 13 May 1943 with the Axis surrender. During the final six months, about 230 Axis ships had been sunk in the Mediterranean, mostly by Malta-based submarines and aircraft.[23]

Then, on 20 June, Malta welcomed King George VI. It was just over a year after he had awarded the George Cross to the island and its people. The King arrived aboard the cruiser HMS *Aurora* and was greeted by thousands lining the bastions and revetments of Valletta and the Three Cities. He was to be the first of a number of high-profile visitors to Malta in the aftermath of the siege, including the British Prime Minster, Winston Churchill, who visited the island in November, and others included the Allied supreme commander, General Eisenhower, and General Bernard Montgomery, who had commanded the British Eighth Army to victory in North Africa.

More ships, aircraft, men and provisions poured into Malta in preparation for the Allied landings in Sicily, called Operation Husky, which began during the night of 9/10 July 1943. Ten days later, the final air raid against Malta took place; it was the 3,340th alert since the opening day of the siege.[24] Then, on 3 September, Italy surrendered. However, the convoy system would remain in place in the Mediterranean until the summer of 1944, with the occasional losses, as the Luftwaffe still occupied airfields in south-east France and German U-boats continued to operate in the western Med.

Malta had done what no one before the war had thought was possible. The island had been defensible after all. Furthermore, Malta had played a vital role in the Allied victory in North Africa. But strategic success had come at a huge cost. To sustain Malta between June 1940 and December 1943 it had taken well over a hundred passages by merchant ships, of which seventy-nine had arrived, although many of these had been damaged and many lives lost. Of the seven independent supply runs by merchant vessels, all but one had failed. The Merchant Navy and other marine units had lost 200 men, and in supporting the convoys the Royal Navy's losses were huge: one battleship (*Barham*); two aircraft carriers (*Ark Royal* and *Eagle*); five cruisers (*Cairo*, *Hermione*, *Manchester*, *Neptune* and *Southampton*);

23. Holland, op. cit., p.415.
24. Ibid, p.425.

nineteen destroyers; several minesweepers; and about forty submarines had all been sunk. Many other vessels had suffered severe damage. The Royal Navy had also lost nearly 4,000 personnel (2,200 on surface ships and 1,700 submariners). The siege had also cost the lives of about 1,600 Maltese civilians and the same number of servicemen (approximately 700 soldiers and 900 airmen). The RAF had lost 547 aircraft in combat and a further 160 on the ground.[25] More than 170 fighter pilots were lost during the defence of Malta and a further ten were lost while ferrying fighters to the island off carriers. A further thirty-five members of Beaufighter crews perished and nineteen members of the Fleet Air Arm were killed in the defence of Malta-bound convoys during 1942 alone.[26]

Malta now lay in ruins and there was much clearing up to do. Grand Harbour was a complete mess and among the sunken ships there were destroyers, submarines and harbour craft, as well as the wrecks of several merchantmen, including the legendary *Ohio*. It would take years to recover.

Malta's population had endured everything during the long siege – bombing, death, starvation and disease. But, although the fortress island had repeatedly been brought to its knees, Malta had never fallen.

---

25. Woodman, op. cit., p.470.
26. Shores and Cull with Malizia (The Spitfire Year), op. cit., p.664.

Bibliography and References

Published Sources

Aldridge, Arthur with Ryan, Mark, *The Last Torpedo Flyers: The True Story of Arthur Aldridge – Hero of the Skies* (Simon & Schuster UK Ltd, London, 2013)

Allaway, Jim, *Hero of the Upholder* (Airlife, Shrewsbury, 1991)

Attard, Joseph, *The Battle of Malta: An Epic Story of Suffering and Bravery* (William Kimber, London, 1980)

Austin, Douglas, Churchill and Malta (Spellmount Publishers Ltd, Stroud, 2014)

Bailey, E A S (Ed) *Malta Defiant & Triumphant: Rolls of Honour 1940–1943* (Private Publication, 1992)

Barnham, Denis, *Malta Spitfire Pilot: Ten Weeks of Terror April–June 1942* (Grub Street, London, 2013, first published by William Kimber, London, 1956)

Beurling, George & Roberts, Leslie, *Malta Spitfire: The Diary of an Ace Fighter Pilot* (Grub Street London, 2011, first published by Oxford University Press, Toronto, 1943)

Boffa, Charles J, *The Illustrious Blitz: Malta in Wartime, 1940–41* (Progress Press, Malta, 1995)

Bradford, Ernie, *Siege: Malta 1940–1943* (Penguin Books, London, 1987, first published by Hamish Hamilton, 1985)

Coldman, Alfred, *Malta: An Aviation History* (Publishers Enterprises Group, 2001)

Cull, Brian, *249 At War* (Grub Street, London, 1997)

Cull, Brian & Galea, Frederick, *Gladiators over Malta: The Story of Faith, Hope and Charity* (Wise Owl Publications, Malta, 2008)

Cull, Brian & Galea, Frederick, *Hurricanes over Malta June 1940–April 1942* (Grub Street, London, 2002)

Cunningham of Hyndhope, *A Sailor's Odyssey: The Autobiography of Admiral of the Fleet Viscount Cunningham of Hyndhope* (Hutchinson, London, 1951)

De la Billière, General Sir Peter, *Supreme Courage* (Little, Brown, London, 2004)

Douglas-Hamilton, The Lord James, *The Air Battle for Malta: The Diaries of a Spitfire Pilot* (Pen & Sword, Barnsley, 2006, first published by Mainstream Publications, 1991)

Galea, Michael, *Malta Diary of a War 1940–1945* (Publishers Enterprise Group, 1992)

Gibbs, Patrick, *Torpedo Leader* (Grub Street, London, 1992)

Halley, James J, *The Squadrons of the Royal Air Force & Commonwealth 1918–1988* (Air Britain, Tonbridge, 1988)

Hogan, G, *Malta: The Triumphant Years, 1940–43* (Hale, London, 1978)

Holland, James, *Fortress Malta: An Island Under Siege 1940–43* (Phoenix, London, 2004)

Howard, M, *The Mediterranean Strategy in the Second World War* (Greenhill Books, London, 1993)

Ireland, B, *The War in the Mediterranean 1940–43* (Arms and Armour Press, London, 1993)

Jacobs, Peter, *Aces of the Luftwaffe: The Jagdflieger in the Second World War* (Frontline Books, London, 2014)

Johnson, AVM J E & Lucas, Wg Cdr P B, *Winged Victory* (Stanley Paul, London, 1995)

Kappes, Irwin J, *Mers-el-Kebir: A Battle Between Friends* (MilitaryHistoryOnline. com)

Lucas, Laddie, *Five Up* (Wingham Press, Canterbury, 1978)

Lucas, Laddie, *Malta: The Thorn in Rommel's Side* (Stanley Paul, London, 1992)

McKay, Sinclair, *The Secret Life of Bletchley Park: The WWII Codebreaking Centre and the Men and Women Who Worked There* (Aurum Press Ltd, London, 2010)

Micallef, Joseph, *When Malta Stood Alone 1940–43* (Private Publication, Malta, 1981)

Neil, Tom, *Onward to Malta* (Transworld Paperbacks, 1994, first published by Airlife, Shrewsbury, 1992)

Orange, Vincent, *Park: The Biography of Air Chief Marshal Sir Keith Park GCB KBE MC DFC DCL* (Grub Street, London, 2000)

Poolman, Kenneth, *Faith, Hope and Charity: The Defence of Malta* (Crécy Publishing, Manchester, 2009, first published by William Kimber, London, 1954)

Rogers, Anthony, *Battle over Malta* (Sutton Publishing Limited, Gloucestershire, 2000)

Rossiter, Mike, *Ark Royal: The Life, Death and Rediscovery of the Legendary Second World War Aircraft Carrier* (Corgi Books, London, 2007)

Scott, Stuart R, *Battle-Axe Blenheims: No 105 Squadron RAF At War 1940–1* (Alan Sutton Publishing Ltd, Stroud, 1996)

Shankland, Peter & Hunter, Anthony, *Malta Convoy* (Fontana Press, London, 1961)

Shores, Christopher, *Aces High Volume 2* (Grub Street, London, 1999)

Shores, Christopher & Cull, Brian with Malizia, Nicola, *Malta: The Hurricane Years 1940–41* (Grub Street, London, 1987)

Shores, Christopher & Cull, Brian with Malizia, Nicola, *Malta: The Spitfire Year 1942* (Grub Street, London, 1991)

Shores, Christopher & Williams, Clive, *Aces High* (Grub Street, London, 1994)

Simpson, Michael, *Life of Admiral of the Fleet Andrew Cunningham: A Twentieth Century Naval Leader* (Frank Cass Publishers, London, 2004)

Slader, J, *The Fourth Service: Merchantmen at War 1939–45* (Brick Tower Press, London, 1994, first published by Hale, London, 1994)

Smith, Peter C, *Pedestal: The Convoy That Saved Malta* (Crécy Publishing Ltd, Manchester, 2002, first published by William Kimber, London, 1970)

Smith, Peter C, *Eagle's War: The War Diary of an Aircraft Carrier* (Crécy Publishing Ltd, Manchester, 1995)

Smith, Peter C, and Walker, Edwin, The Battles of the Malta Striking Forces (Ian Allan, London, 1974)

Spooner, Tony, *Clean Sweep: The Life of Air Marshal Sir Ivor Broom KCB CBE DSO DFC**AFC* (Crécy Books Ltd, Manchester, 1994)

Faith Hope and Malta GC (Newton Publishers, Swindon, 1992)

In Full Flight (Macdonald, London, 1965)

Supreme Gallantry: Malta's Role in the Allied Victory 1939–1945 (John Murray, London, 1996)

Warburton's War (William Kimber, London, 1987)

Stones, Donald, *Dimsie* (Wingham Press Ltd, Wingham, 1991)

Terraine, John, *The Right of the Line* (Wordsworth Military Library, Ware, 1997)

Wingate, John, *The Fighting Tenth: The Tenth Submarine Flotilla and the Siege of Malta* (Leo Cooper, London, 1991)

Woodman, Richard, *Malta Convoys* (John Murray Ltd, London, 2000)

The National Archives, Kew – File & Document References

ADM 199/75   Enemy Air Attacks on RN and Merchant Shipping, 1940–41

ADM 199/373   Vice-Admiral Submarines: War Diaries, 1939–40

ADM 199/414   Mediterranean Command: War Diaries, 1941

ADM 199/424   Vice-Admiral Malta and Admiral (Submarines) War Diaries, 1942

ADM 199/681   Naval Operations in Mediterranean, 1941–43

ADM 199/830   Operation Substance Reports, 1941

ADM 199/831   Operation Halberd Reports, 1941

ADM 199/835   Operation Harpoon Convoy Reports, 1942

ADM 199/1030   Various Convoys: Reports, 1943

ADM 199/1110   Operation Harpoon: Reports of Proceedings of HM Ships, 1942

ADM 199/1242   Operation Pedestal (Malta Convoy) Reports, 1942

ADM 199/1243   Operation Pedestal (Malta Convoy) Reports, 1942

ADM 199/1244   Operation Vigorous (Convoys from Eastern Med to Malta) Reports, 1942

ADM 199/1316   Enemy Air Attacks on HM Ships: Reports, 1943–44

ADM 199/1922   Admiral Submarines: Patrol Reports of HMS Utmost, 1941–45

ADM 199/2406   Food Rationing and Economy in Expenditure of Victualling Stores at Malta, 1941–42

ADM 223/82   Admiralty Operational Intelligence Daily Reports, 1940

ADM 236/48   HMS Upholder, 1 January 1941–31 August 1942

AIR 23/5708   Use of Takali Aerodrome by Fleet Air Arm, 1940

AIR 27/498	No 249 Squadron Operations Record Book, 1 May 1940–31 Dec 1943
AIR 27/606	No 69 Squadron Operations Record Book, 1 Sept 1940–31 Dec 1941
AIR 27/607	No 69 Squadron Operations Record Book, 1942
AIR 27/610	No 69 Squadron Operations Record Book, 1 Sept 1940–31 Dec 1941
AIR 27/926	No 126 Squadron Operations Record Book, 1 June 1941–31 Dec 1943
AIR 27/1140	No 185 Squadron Operations Record Book, 1942–43
AIR 27/1419	No 229 Squadron Operations Record Book, 1942–43
AIR 27/1471	No 242 Squadron Operations Record Book, 1 Oct 1939–31 Dec 1942
AIR 27/1540	No 261 Squadron Operations Record Book, 1941–42
AIR 27/2070	No 601 Squadron Operations Record Book, 1942
AIR 27/2079	No 603 Squadron Operations Record Book, 1925–43
AIR 27/2342	No 1435 Squadron Operations Record Book, 1 July 1942–31 Dec 1943
AIR 28/334	RAF Station Hal Far Operations Record Book, 1929–46
AIR 28/502	RAF Station Luqa Operations Record Book, 1 June 1940–31 Dec 1941
AIR 28/503	RAF Station Luqa Operations Record Book, 1942
AIR 29/29	Malta Night Fighter Unit Operations Record Book, 1 Sept–30 Nov 1941
AIR 29/860	HQ Flight Hal Far Operations Record Book, 1 Jan 1939–31 Mar 1940
AIR 50/49	Air Ministry Combat Reports: No 126 Squadron, 1 July 1941–30 Apr 1945
AIR 50/77	Air Ministry Combat Reports: No 185 Squadron, 1 July 1941–31 Aug 1942
AIR 50/86	Air Ministry Combat Reports, No 229 Squadron, 1 May 1940–31 Aug 1944
AIR 50/92	Air Ministry Combat Reports: No 242 Squadron, 1 May 1940–30 June 1942
AIR 50/96	Air Ministry Combat Reports: No 249 Squadron, 1 July 1940–31 Dec 1943
AIR 50/504	Takali Station Flight: Malta Wing (185, 242 & 1435 Sqns), 1 Dec 41–31 Mar 42

Index

The index includes Allied ships, units and personnel included in this book. Where more than one rank is used for an individual throughout the book, the most senior is shown.